IDEOLOGY AND REVOLUTION IN MODERN EUROPE
An Essay on the Role of Ideas in History

TRYGVE R. THOLFSEN

IDEOLOGY AND REVOLUTION
IN MODERN EUROPE
An Essay on the Role of

Ideas in History

COLUMBIA UNIVERSITY PRESS
NEW YORK   1984

Library of Congress Cataloging in Publication Data

Tholfsen, Trygve R.
Ideology and revolution in modern Europe.

Includes bibliographical references and index.
1. Europe—History—1789–1900—Philosophy. 2. Europe
—History—20th century—Philosophy. 3. Revolutions—
Europe—Philosophy. 4. Ideology—Political aspects—
Europe. 5. Europe—Intellectual life. I. Title.
D299.T49 1984   940'.01   84-3178
ISBN 0-231-05886-1 (alk. paper)

Columbia University Press
New York   Guildford, Surrey
Copyright © 1984 Columbia University Press
All rights reserved

Printed in the United States of America

Clothbound editions of Columbia University Press Books are
Smyth-sewn and printed on permanent and durable acid-free paper

Book design by Ken Venezio

For Ann

Contents

Preface

This book deals with two interlocking topics: the influence of intellectual forces on the development of radical and revolutionary politics in modern Europe; analytical and conceptual problems that arise in an inquiry into the role of ideas in historical processes. Part 1 describes the centrality of ideas and beliefs, themselves the product of a history in which intellectual forces were actively involved, in modern political history. Part 2 outlines the substantive and methodological assumptions underlying that interpretation, in relation to countervaling assumptions which, it is argued, inhibit an adequate assessment of the evidence.

Since the problem of the role of ideas is intrinsic to historical inquiry, it has received a good deal of attention from historians in the course of their research on particular events such as the French Revolution. After a period of declining interest during the middle decades of this century, the problem is once again moving into the foreground. The question has also figured prominently in theoretical discussion of the historical process, notably in Marxist writings and in responses to them. On the whole, historians prefer to deal with such questions concretely, as they arise in the study of specific events and developments. This book reflects that preference. Recently, however, as a result of changes in the intellectual and historiographical landscape since the Second World War, the historian encounters the problem of the role of ideas in a form that requires closer attention to theoretical issues. On the one hand, there is a widespread tendency, most visible in the new social history, to privilege social phenomena at the expense of ideas and to assign a *de facto* primacy to the former. On the other hand, even historians who do not share that inclination have been dissatisfied with received interpretations of the role of intellectual forces.

There is general agreement that the notion of ideas as "causes" of events is problematical at best; the nature of their influence or role has to be specified more precisely. Partly as a result of work in critical philosophy of history, difficulties of conceptualization are widely recognized. Moreover, there is a consensus that it is necessary to attend closely to the social and institutional matrix in which ideas develop and exercise an influence. Idealist interpretations have been found wanting. As Felix Gilbert has said, "Whatever view one might have about the relation of the material to the ideal world, it is no longer possible to see ideas as determining events or floating freely above them."[1] That in turn underlines the analytical problem posed by the interpenetration of cultural and social phenomena: merely to describe the role of ideas in a particular process is extremely difficult, apart from the question of assessing their relative importance. That difficulty is reflected in the comment that "slogans cast in the archaic shorthand of 'ideas' versus 'social forces' " are not helpful.[2] Similarly, Keith Baker, who is actively engaged in reconstructing our understanding of the ideological origins of the French Revolution, has suggested that we "set aside the untenable distinction between ideas and events—and the artificial and sterile problems about the relationship and priority between them—that has so often introduced confusion and absurdity into discussion of intellectual history."[3] At the very least, then, it is clear that an account of the role of ideas in the genesis of particular events confronts manifold problems of conceptualization.

At the same time, moreover, an awareness of the strength and pervasiveness of social and institutional structures has led many historians to tilt the balance of interpretation in that direction. This tendency is not the result of the application of a monocausal theory, but rests on a pluralistic basis. The manner in which the role of ideas is minimized or denied has changed a great deal since 1905, when Max Weber characterized *The Protestant ethic and the spirit of capitalism* as, in part, a refutation of the doctrine of "the more naive historical materialism" that ideas originate as a "reflection or superstructure of economic situations."[4] Even within Marxism economistic and mechanistic theories of causation were under attack as early as the 1890s. In fact, economic determinism and reductive materialism have persisted chiefly as a pseudoproblem, diverting attention from genuine issues. The new social history—whether neo-Marxist, quasi-Marxist, or non-Marxist—depreciates the role of ideas in subtle and interesting ways that deserve careful attention. Its analysis of the social matrix in which ideas develop and function is exemplary. Practitioners of the new social history have produced some of the best work of the 1960s and 1970s. Partly because of their success, however, they have tended to exaggerate the explanatory power of a social interpretation of history.

In this historiographical situation a historian looking into the role of ideas in the genesis of a particular event not only has to examine the pertinent evidence but also has to consider the heuristic assumptions that enter into his analysis. A brief summary of the interpretation to be developed in part 1 will indicate the presence of a range of assumptions to be discussed in part 2.

The thesis of chapters 2–4 is that various patterns of radical and revolutionary politics so prevalent in Europe since 1789 have been profoundly affected by intellectual forces. While social and institutional factors were of obvious importance, they were in no sense sufficient causes. In the case of the French Revolution, the Enlightenment was an essential ingredient in the process that brought it about and was a constituent of the event itself. Thus, it was a prerequisite not only to the occurrence but also to the very existence of the Revolution. Marxism, a very different *idée-force*, imparted a distinctive character to the socialist movements that emerged in the wake of the French Revolution and the Industrial Revolution, and was an important element in the two great revolutions of the twentieth century. Finally, the genesis of fascism has to be understood, in part, in terms of the interplay between various ideological traditions—each the product of a long history—in the distinctive cultural milieu of pre-1914 Europe. The three phenomena—the French Revolution, socialist movements, and fascism—were closely connected historically. In each case, however, disparate intellectual forces played rather different roles. We can nevertheless make two claims concerning the influence of ideas in this segment of the political history of modern Europe: (1) intellectual forces were deeply involved in the processes that brought these phenomena into being and shaped their character; (2) these forces were themselves the product of a long history, in which ideas, beliefs, and traditions were actively implicated.

Chapter 5 discusses some of the substantive and methodological assumptions underlying that interpretation. The first section considers the problem of conceptualizing the "role" of ideas in processes and situations in which cultural and social phenomena are inextricably intertwined.[5] That, in turn, raises the question of the extent to which such an "influence" or "impact" corresponds to the causal relations of the world of nature and also the question of the utility of causal language in describing it. This discussion is intended to clarify the meaning of the thesis that the Enlightenment was both an ingredient in the process that brought about the Revolution and a constituent of the event itself. Thus, the historian has to make explicit not only his views of causation but also his conception of the nature of the object of inquiry, since both affect his assessment of the role of ideas in the origins of a particular event or development. The interpretation presented in part 1 also presupposes a conception of specifically *historical* processes in which ideas play their part, involving relationships of continuity and change through time between phenomena characterized by a significant degree of "uniqueness." A cluster of assumptions concerning the historicity of the human world is outlined in chapter 5, section 2. The concluding section of the chapter makes explicit the view of historical understanding and explanation presupposed by the interpretation. This triad of assumptions is intended to provide a conceptual base that makes possible the empirical examination of the role of ideas in particular events and developments. They may be counterposed to somewhat different assumptions discussed in chapters 6 and 7.

Although historians and social scientists are committed to pluralistic views of causation, there is nevertheless a widespread tendency in practice to assign a significant degree of causal primacy to social and institutional phenomena. The kinds of substantive assumptions that tend to slant interpretation in that direction are discussed in chapters 6 (section 1) and 7. Marxist theories receive the most extensive discussion, first because they represent the most systematic and coherent statement of a position that is widely held; secondly, because both in their theory and practice, Marxist historians have provided a valuable body of work on the role of ideas in history. The questions at issue do not involve reductionist or materialist theories, but rather the formulation of working assumptions that are conducive to empirical inquiry into the nature of the interplay between the "forces" or "factors" at work in particular processes.

A more elusive problem concerns the manner in which methodological and epistemological assumptions affect substantive conclusions. We can take as our point of departure the familiar observation that an epistemology presupposes an ontology; a logic of explanation is not necessarily ontologically neutral. In the new social history the tendency to depreciate the role of ideas is reinforced by the methodological and epistemological assumptions of mainstream social science. As historians make increasingly effective use of the concepts and methods of the social sciences, such assumptions require careful scrutiny. I shall argue, in chapter 6, section 2, that a theory of explanation which assumes that particular events must be explained by reference to general knowledge of the behavior of types of phenomena is unsatisfactory, because it excludes the specific content of ideas and tends to assign greater explanatory weight to social and institutional structures that conform more readily to its logical requirements. Moreover, such a theory of explanation requires a conception of causation that is too rigid to encompass historical processes and the role of ideas in them.

Finally, I shall also argue, in chapter 6, section 3, that the nomological and synchronic orientation of social science interposes obstacles to an understanding of specifically historical processes involving the interplay between unique phenomena in relationships of continuity and change through time. Since ideas, beliefs, and traditions are central to such processes, they are vulnerable to a nomological approach that concentrates on regularities in types of phenomena and to a synchronic approach that concentrates on a given segment of the human world without reference to its past or to the role of the past in shaping it. Moreover, these difficulties arise even in kinds of social science that give full weight to cultural phenomena.

There is an obvious danger in a preoccupation with a critique of putatively inadequate assumptions and theories. In every aspect of the problem we are dealing with polarities that require careful handling; they do not lend themselves to dichotomous, either/or formulations. The past cannot be understood in exclusively idiographic and diachronic terms; nomological and synchronic modes of analysis are also necessary. History and social science stand in an ambivalent relationship of tension and complementarity. If the generalizing orientation of the social sciences is at odds with certain essential aspects of the historical mode of understanding, it is also indispensable. History cannot operate effectively without the knowledge that the social sciences provide of the generic characteristics of human behavior. Techniques and concepts drawn from the social sciences have been put to good use by historians. Similarly, the historian requires the synchronic analysis that is linked to the nomological epistemology of social science. The social sciences have developed concepts and techniques adapted to the study of a society at one point in time, so as to yield an account of the interrelations between elements within a sociocultural whole. Methods that work for the study of Bali are clearly applicable to fifth-century Greece. On the other hand, the very virtues of the social sciences pose a threat to the historical enterprise if they become dominant. The raison d'être of the social sciences lies in their transhistorical approach. If that generalizing impulse is not kept within bounds and bent to specifically historical purposes, it can undermine the historian's distinctive function. While synchronic modes of analysis are essential to historical understanding, they yield only a partial picture. These methodological and epistemological problems become even more pertinent as the social sciences take a greater interest in language and meaning.

Similarly, there is no point in defining the problem in terms of competing claims for primacy for social or cultural forces or in terms of a clash between "idealist" and "materialist" theories. On the contrary, it is necessary to establish the nature and significance of the interplay between disparate elements in processes that vary a great deal. Precisely because of the obvious strength and pervasiveness of social and institutional structures, however, it is necessary to make a special effort to examine the role of ideas in particular events and developments. In the academic world we are especially aware of the manner in which ideals tend to be instrumentalized and the extent to which practical interests determine the course of events. We are also familiar with the way in which historians like Leopold Ranke and Friedrich Meinecke invested the German *Machtstaat* with a moral gloss. Social history has shown the ambiguous connection between German idealism and the class structure. If we wish to draw on the insights of idealist historicism, we have to give a good deal of weight to *Gewaltver-hältnisse*. Having said all this, however, the fact remains that there is an area of human freedom, spontaneity, and creativity—to use the idiom of idealism—within which have developed cultural and symbolic forms that have been rather important, not only in the history of science but in politics as well.

From this perspective, it is argued in part I that the revolutionary movements so prominent in Europe since the end of the eighteenth century cannot be explained by reference to transhistorical models of revolution; nor can they be accounted for primarily in terms of industrialization, urbanization, and the development of capitalism. On the contrary, the French Revolution—along with the new ideology and practice to which it contributed—has to be understood in relation to the unique history of Western culture. Over the *longue durée*, ideas and beliefs whose creation and development manifested a significant degree of freedom and spontaneity were actively involved in that history. What was decisive for the emergence of the modern revolutionary phenomenon was the adventitious conjuncture in the late eighteenth century of cultural and social developments stretching into the remote past.

Acknowledgments

I am deeply grateful to Michael Ermarth, who generously found time to write a searching critique of the penultimate draft of the book. James Sloan Allen, Douglas Sloan, and Jonas Soltis made a number of helpful suggestions. Edward Malefakis read the chapter on fascism. Thanks are owed to John Higham, Isabel Knight, and Leonard Krieger, who commented tactfully on an early draft. I also had the benefit of thoughtful criticism from the reader commissioned by the Press. Bernard Gronert, of the Columbia University Press, welcomed the project from the very outset and has offered continuing support and counsel. In addition to such intellectual resources, the necessary material base was provided by sabbatical leave from Teachers College.

I owe a more remote but no less substantial debt to two teachers: Hajo Holborn, a master of historical theory and practice, and Ralph E. Turner, an exponent of the new social history *avant la lettre*.

IDEOLOGY AND REVOLUTION IN MODERN EUROPE
An Essay on the Role of Ideas in History

CHAPTER ONE

Conceptual Problems

Before turning to the role of ideas in the political history of modern Europe, we shall consider briefly some of the theoretical and conceptual problems involved in such an inquiry. Although working assumptions are discussed more fully in chapter 5, certain of them, concerning the nature of that role and of historical processes, need to be made explicit at the outset. This is necessary not only because these assumptions underlie the interpretation that follows, but also because the historical material in part I is intended to illustrate and support the position outlined in chapter 5 and to indicate the limitations of the theories examined in chapters 6 and 7. Thus, there is a circular relationship, in the hermeneutic sense, between the two parts of the book. The rest of this introductory chapter discusses other aspects of the relationship between historians' assumptions, usually only implicit, and their conclusions concerning the role of ideas in particular events. We shall consider first the essays of Otto Hintze, written in the context of a critique of idealist historicism in early-twentieth-century Germany, because they bring into focus a number of theoretical issues in a somewhat different form from that in which they have been posed in the 1960s and 1970s. We shall also examine a few manifestations of the tendency, among historians of diverse methodological and ideological orientations, to privilege social factors in history. Finally, turning to the topics to be dealt with in part 1, we shall examine two aspects of the problem of defining assumptions that are conducive to an empirical inquiry into the role of ideas in political history. First, taking as a point of departure Hintze's formulation of the relationship between ideas and interests, a carefully defined position that corresponds to the views of many historians today, I shall argue that this model narrows the range of inquiry and needs to be broadened if we are to understand the processes that shaped the character of radical and revolutionary politics in modern Europe. Secondly, turning to recent theoretical discussion of culture as a source of critical and utopian impulses that transcend socially determined interests, I shall suggest that such presumably universal characteristics are in fact specific to Western culture, a unique entity produced by a history in which cultural forces were actively involved.

The interpretation to be developed in the next chapter comprises two interconnected claims: first, that the Enlightenment was important in the genesis of the French Revolution of 1789 both as a primary ingredient in the process that produced it and as a constituent essential to its existence; and second, that the Enlightenment was itself the end product of historical processes in which intellectual forces played a significant part. Those claims, in turn, presuppose interlocking conceptions about the ways in which ideas exercise an influence and the "historical" character of the processes in which ideas are involved.

The claim that ideas played an important part in the origins of an event asserts what in ordinary language is referred to as a cause-and-effect relationship. Yet the connection between ideas and their consequences is significantly different in many ways from the causal relations characteristic of the natural world. While penicillin may be said to cause the destruction of certain bacteria, the Enlightenment cannot be said to have "caused" the French Revolution. The nature of the relationship between ideas and an event is problematical and poses considerable difficulties in conceptualization. We are not dealing with a separate "cause" and "effect," but rather with two interconnected entities, one of which not only influenced the other, but also became an essential component of it; moreover, the connection between them is logical and conceptual in character, an intrinsic relation different from the extrinsic relations of the world of nature. Finally, the cultural forms that played a part in the occurrence of an event were themselves the product of processes, unknown to the world of nature, in which antecedent traditions and beliefs were involved. In order to avoid any tendency to assimilate historical processes to the causality of nature, I have found it convenient to use noncausal terminology.

The primary difficulty with the word "cause" is that it has come to be associated so closely with the causal relations characteristic of the physical world. A billiard ball strikes another and causes it to move; a geological shift on the San Andreas fault causes an earthquake. David Hume's classic account of causation depicted a relationship of constant conjuncture between types of events or phenomena. Cause and effect are separate and distinct; there is no more than a contingent connection between them. In the human world, however, we are not dealing with external and contingent relations between separate entities. The connection between the Enlightenment and the French Revolution, like that between an intention and an action, is noncontingent; that is, it is logical and conceptual in character. It is an intrinsic connection, unlike the extrinsic relations of the natural world: a connection between premises—broadly defined to include values, beliefs, ideas, attitudes, concepts—and actions based on them. Moreover, the relationship between the Enlightenment and the French Revolution is not one between a separate "cause" and "effect," but rather between two interconnected entities, one of which not only influenced the other but also became an essential component of it. The Enlightenment was constitutive of the event whose occurrence it affected.

When we turn to a second aspect of the role of ideas in history, the manner in which they have influenced cultural development and contributed to the emergence of the intellectual and ideological matrix of events, the constitutive relationship is more pronounced. Christianity was an active ingredient in the cultural development of medieval and modern Europe in a double sense: as an influence and as a component. The scientific and intellectual revolution of the seventeenth century was not an external "cause" of the Enlightenment. Rather, it brought into being new ideas, which were ingredients in the process out of which emerged the Enlightenment. The intellectual revolution of the seventeenth century, embracing the new science as well as the legacy of the Renaissance and Reformation, contributed to the components of Enlightenment thought. And the Enlightenment, in turn, took shape as a result of a conscious response to the events and developments of the seventeenth century. We are not dealing with separate causes and effects, but rather with a dialectical collaboration between the *philosophes* and the legacy of the past.

Yet there is much to be said for Paul Conkin's briskly pragmatic advice that historians continue their long-standing practice of talking about ideas as causes: "The 'role of' anything suggests causality. If meanings do condition behavior, then in some sense of that loaded word, they are 'causes.' . . . In this sense of cause as necessary precondition, or the most common use of causal language by historians, ideas do have a causal role. Why back away from that fact?"[1] Beginning with Thucydides, historians have produced excellent studies of the "causes" of events. Lawrence Stone has been notably successful in the analysis of the interaction between disparate causes, with particular attention to cultural phenomena. There is no reason why historians should not continue to follow Max Weber's example and use the word cause in a non-Humean sense. John Searle's account of causation lends itself to historical application.[2] Moreover, it is well to be reminded that whether we use the word cause or role or influence, we are talking about some sort of making-things-happen relationship. Thus, characterizing ideas as playing an important part in history implies a good deal more than a symbolic-expressive relationship between language and various aspects of the human world of which it is a part. Such a historical role cannot be conceptualized adequately by a descriptive semiotics of power or action or by describing the symbolic-constitutive relationship between language and politics, for it comprises the further claim that ideas were significant factors in the processes underlying both the occurrence of events and the development of the components of such events and the context in which they occurred.

Without subscribing to the idealist thesis that the word cause be banished from the historian's vocabulary on ontological and epistemological grounds, I am suggesting, however, that the use of noncausal language facilitates a more precise description of the role of ideas in history, without the intrusion of inappropriate models of causation or explanation. The concept of "necessary cause" is a case in point. On the one hand, its utility is plain enough. Characterizing the Enlightenment as a necessary cause of the French Revolution is a succinct and unequivocal way of saying that in the absence of the former the latter could not have occurred, and that social forces and circumstances were insufficient to have brought about the event. But such a formulation does not carry us very far. It does no more than open the way to more important questions. Moreover, it structures the inquiry in such a way as to narrow the range of answers. For one thing, it appears to invite a quest for a multitude of "necessary causes" that can lead to an infinite regress. Operating in terms of necessary causes makes it difficult to distinguish between the roles played by different "causes." While the financial crisis was a necessary prerequisite to the Revolution of 1789, it had little to do with the shaping of the event; the same could be said of the relationship between the First World War and the Bolshevik Revolution. Assigning different weights to the various necessary causes will not help much either, since it precludes qualitative differences in the nature of the "influence" exercised. Even some versions of causal pluralism can have the unintended consequence of constricting the scope of an inquiry into the interplay between elements in particular historical processes. In the case of the genesis of fascism, for example, if intellectual and ideological forces are treated as independent variables, along with social, economic, and political circumstances, it is very difficult to get at the specific characteristics of the interplay between them. The thesis that the Enlightenment was of preeminent importance in the genesis of the French Revolution cannot be considered—either for acceptance or rejection—within a causal model comprising necessary causes. The "role" of the Enlightenment in that process embraces not only an impact on particular actions but also a constitutive relationship to the event as a whole.

The reasons why many historians are not comfortable with the characterization of ideas as "causes" of events have been well stated by Gordon Wood. Noting the flaws in earlier attempts to treat ideas as "causes" of the American Revolution, he points out that such interpretations have not persuaded many people to believe that "ideas can 'cause' something like a revolution." The difficulty is that "it makes no sense to treat ideas mechanically as detached 'causes' or 'effects' of social events and behavior." He calls on historians to reject "the futile dichotomy of ideas or beliefs as causes or effects of social forces." Many historians will also find persuasive the manner in which Wood proposes to handle this conceptual problem. He suggests that "instead of asking what ideas were . . . we ought to be asking what the ideas did in a specific situation and why the historical participants used particular ideas in the way that they did." Ideas should be treated "functionally and instrumentally," since they "are important for what they do rather than for what they are."[3] The instrumental aspect of the role of ideas in history is one that requires careful attention. Wood's formulation is especially pertinent to the American Revolution. Bernard Bailyn's account of the ideological origins of the American Revolution—emphasizing the ideas of the English Commonwealthmen—fits well into this sort of framework.[4] At the same time, however, the role of ideas in the genesis of events cannot be treated exclusively in functional and instrumental terms, as reinforcing or intensifying the effects of practical forces and circumstances.

Like other historians, Keith Baker has found causal models inadequate for handling the relationship between ideas and events. In his work on the French Revolution he has broken new ground in dealing with the problems of conceptualization involved. "Understanding the ideological origins of the French Revolution," he writes, "is not a matter of establishing a causal chain linking particular ideas, individual or group motivations, and events in a series of one-to-one derivations." Moving beyond earlier formulations of the problem, Baker sets out "to identify a field of political discourse, a set of linguistic patterns and relationships that defined possible actions and utterances and give them meaning." That is, it is necessary to "reconstitute the political culture within which the creation of the revolutionary language of 1789 became possible." He rejects inquiry into the "influence" of the Enlightenment, of individual *philosophes,* or of particular ideas. On this view, "the action of a rioter in picking up a stone can no more be understood apart from the symbolic field that gives it meaning than the action of a priest in picking up a sacramental vessel." Thus, the events of the French Revolution are not to be understood in terms of a causal connection with ideas, but rather in a complex relationship to an all-embracing symbolic field, comprising competing discourses that define the range of possibilities.[5]

The role of ideas in the genesis of an event, then, cannot be characterized in causal terms appropriate to the behavior of natural phenomena. We are dealing not only with a cause-and-effect relationship, in the ordinary language sense, but also with a constitutive relationship between meanings, values, and intentions and the actions in which they are embodied. Just how that relationship can best be conceptualized is problematical. The conceptual difficulty is compounded by the fact that there are two distinct but interconnected aspects of the role of ideas in the process underlying the occurrence of an event: first, the relationship between the ideas and the event; second, the role of ideas in the origins of the cultural and symbilic forms whose relationship to the event is being examined. Thus, the analysis of the connection between the Enlightenment and the French Revolution is inextricably linked to the question of the nature and origins of the Enlightenment.

That summary, in turn, is a reminder of the *historical* character of the human world and of the processes that have shaped it. Ideas play a part in distinctively historical processes. Thus, medieval Christianity, the product of developments embracing the interplay between unique, historically created phenomena, was a dynamic element in the processes that brought into being the Enlightenment. Moreover, the historical particularity of medieval Christianity was constituted by a configuration of unique components received from the past. The assumptions underlying that sort of formulation need to be made explicit (see chapter 5, section on Historical Processes).

Human life may be said to be "historical" in a number of interconnected ways. Every society is the product of a particular history, characterized by continuity and change through time, and embodying elements created in the past. The processes that create a particular human phenomenon embrace the interplay between unique elements, themselves the product of antecedent processes of development in time. The historical world, then, manifests uniqueness, continuity and change, and the presence of the past in every present. Both parts of this book not only presuppose the historicity of human life but also are intended to describe and illustrate aspects of it. The historical dimension of human life may be characterized in terms of "uniqueness" and "pastness," the two being indissolubly connected.

One uses the word "uniqueness" reluctantly out of necessity, since it is not only ambiguous but also suggestive of an idealist ontology and epistemology. To begin with, then, it has to be said unequivocally that "uniqueness" is not claimed as a distinguishing characteristic of the being of man and his history. We can stipulate that no two snow flakes or earthquakes are identical. As described by spectrographic analysis, every star is different. Christianity, however, was *historically* unique in a number of ways: unlike a star or landscape, its components—ideas and beliefs—were also unique (lacking in the regularities of molecular and atomic structures) and were themselves the product of unique processes involving other unique phenomena; while Christianity bears significant similarities to other religious phenomena, it cannot be characterized as an instance of a type; the presence in Christianity of unique elements created in the past is different in kind from the geological structures inherited from the past that are now present on the San Andreas fault; the processes of continuity and change in history are sui generis.

Historical uniqueness or diversity may also be defined in comparison to the cultural diversity in which anthropologists are interested. There is a great deal of overlapping here. This is one of a number of reasons why so many historians have read Clifford Geertz with admiration and profit. Is there any difference between cultural diversity as conceived by the anthropologist and as it is being characterized in "historical" terms here? Historical diversity presupposes the presence of unique elements inherited from the past. Synchronic description in anthropology does not require the identification of such elements, and synchronic explanation does not require reference to the processes of continuity and change through time that created the cultural forms in a particular society. Moreover, there is another important difference in the way that anthropology handles cultural diversity. While contemporary anthropology is certainly not crudely positivist, it necessarily treats cultural particulars primarily in relation to generic human characteristics. That, after all, is the raison d'être of social science. Such an approach, however, excludes the problem of historical uniqueness (see chapter 6, section on Ahistorical Assumptions).

Ideas, beliefs, and traditions embody most directly the historical aspect of the human world: the presence of phenomena inherited from the past and created by unique processes of continuity and change through time. Intellectual forces are active ingredients in such processes, involving the creation of new forms out of the legacy of the past. To the extent that synchronic and nomological methodologies screen out the "pastness" and the "uniqueness" of human phenomena, they impose constraints on an inquiry into the role of ideas in history.

Otto Hintze approached the problem of the role of ideas in history from the standpoint of a critique of idealist historicism and an awareness of the usefulness of sociology to the study of the past.[6] Seeking to preserve the historicist grasp of particularity while divesting it of idealist metaphysics, he developed a position that is of interest at the moment, when the anti-idealist and antihistoricist pendulum has swung so far. Moreover, Hintze recognized the centrality of the problem of human freedom or "creativity" or "spontaneity" in the development of novel historical forms, a problem that tends to be pushed aside in any preoccupation with reducing the area of indeterminacy.

Recognizing the historian's primary interest in the particular, Hintze defined it in pragmatic terms, while also noting the relevance to history of the sort of knowledge that the sociologist can provide. He distinguished the historian's interest in comparison from the sociologist's: "You can compare in order to find something general that underlies the things that are compared, and you can compare in order to grasp more clearly the singularity (*Individualität*) of the thing that is compared, and to distinguish it from the others. The sociologist does the former; the historian, the latter."[7] In order to establish the particular character of an historical phenomenon, the historian has to compare it to others that are similar. Such comparison, however, presupposes common characteristics that require concepts that encompass both the general and the particular.

Rejecting the epistemology of idealist historicism, Hintze insisted that "the uniqueness of a historical event or force, its 'individuality' is not to be grasped intuitively but has to be demonstrated pragmatically." At the same time, however, he linked the individuality of historical phenomena to the exercise of freedom and creativity in the intellectual realm. And he argued that this aspect of human life cannot be explained by reference to causal regularities: "All causal analysis of historical developments must stop where it penetrates to the qualitative essence of individual life, the ultimate origin of individual events. The problem of individuality which we encounter in all strata of historical life can be pursued to earlier generations, but can never be solved." With the means at his disposal, the historian "cannot explain how individuality originates." In another essay, Hintze again emphasized the difficulty of accounting for the emergence of novel forms but held out more hope for successful inquiry: "I do not mean to deny the mysterious and inexplicable aspects of creative production. Droysen's famous 'X' remains, but to my mind historical research should aim at reducing that 'X' to a minimum. If that is not our purpose, we may as well abandon painstaking scientific research and, as Spengler put it, 'poetize' about history."[8] This passage underlines the complexity of a problem that lies at the heart of all historical inquiry: the emergence of new phenomena. The idealist tradition has tended to dispose of the problem by identifying freedom and spontaneity as intrinsic characteristics of man, ontologically distinct from the determinacy of nature. The positivist tradition has tended to ignore the existence of a problem by a methodology that postulates a degree of regularity in human life that is susceptible of scientific description and explanation.

The manner in which the historian defines the problem of freedom or spontaneity, either implicitly or explicitly, directly affects his interpretation of particular events and developments, especially his conception of the broad historical framework in which they are to be set and understood. A case in point is the astonishing originality and creativity of ancient Greece. A judgment on that problem is central to the interpretation of Western culture and its subsequent history. Jean-Pierre Vernant has offered a political and social explanation of the birth of philosophy in Greece: "The [Mycenaean] King's disappearance prepared the way . . . for two interdependent innovations: the institution of the city-state and the birth of rational thought."[9] It was the development of the *polis* that led to emergence of philosophy. Vernant's thesis has been summarized as follows: "Conflicts between the rich and the poor in the nascent *polis* led to religious ferment, which in turn led to radical, secularized thought—best seen in the poems of Solon—about the political order and the bourgeois virtues needed to sustain it."[10] Thus, the secularization and rationalization of social life "were reflected in the very existence of philosophy." We are not in a position to judge the validity of Vernant's interpretation. The value of his work is evident. The nature and extent of the explanatory claims that he puts forward are of interest, however, since they conform so closely to the paradigms of the new social history.

Malcolm Schofield's critique of Vernant's thesis identifies the kinds of difficulties that arise from the application of a social interpretation to the past. In this instance, as in others, a critic of the new social history has to contend with the fact that the precise extent of the explanatory claims being made is not clear; difficulties can readily be elided when the paradigm carries an inherent plausibility. Schofield concludes that Vernant "appears to be committed to a strong causal thesis, and for much of the book gives the impression of believing that social explanation is both necessary and sufficient for understanding the phenomenon he is concerned with." Although Vernant doubtless recognizes the problem that Miletus poses to his thesis, he does not confront it:

Does Vernant explain why philosophy should have begun in (of all Greek cities) Miletus a little after 600 B.C. and continued to flourish there alone—so far as we can tell—for some decades. Not directly, although he says a little about the decisiveness of contacts with the East in the 'unleashing' of Greek science on its career. Presumbaly he believes the question about Miletus is too particular to be of vital help in explaining the phenomenon he is concerned with. He certainly *needs* to believe something like that, for if this very specific question *is* the right way to begin tackling Vernant's larger question, then his general social explanation is no longer of the adequate form, since it points to the condition of the *polis* in general, not of one or more particular *poleis*. [11]

If the contemporary historian emphasizes the importance of the particular or even of "the unique," it is not because of an idealist epistemology, but rather because in the course of his study he has encountered countless versions of what can be called the Miletus problem. Such "unique" phenomena, which resist general explanation, often enter actively into subsequent historical developments.

In commenting on the inadequacy of a social explanation of the origins of Greek thought, Schofield argues that "it needed an inspired individual to take the step (still obscure in its intentions) of writing a philosophical treatise in prose: thus inventing genre and medium and mode of transmission in a single blow, and simultaneously creating the possibility of a tradition of philosophizing." In accounting for this startling leap forward and in speculating on the origins of Greek thought we need not only Vernant's "Durkheimian strategies," but also a concept of "the freedom and creativity of the individual." [12] Schofield's phrase identifies a problem that is fundamental to any inquiry into historical processes, especially those embracing the "long term." There are any number of familiar examples in the origins and developments of Western culture. The "freedom and creativity" of countless individuals was conspicuously present in the creation of the religion of Israel and in the "emancipation of thought from myth" in Greece. In succeeding centuries, the names of Luther and Marx, Galileo and Clerk-Maxwell come to mind. In each case, of course, their freedom was exercised within a framework of historically determined limits and possibilities. This is not a matter of the "great man theory of history," but rather a recognition of facts that tend to be screened out by paradigms that are intent on reducing the area of indeterminacy. European culture in the late eighteenth century was the end product of a long and complicated process involving the interplay between cultural and social forces and the exercise of a significant degree of "freedom and creativity." Moreover, the Europeans' response to the social order of commercial and industrial capitalism encompassed the exercise of freedom within that culture. But that political action also took place, of course, in a context of historically created constraints, both social and cultural.

The difficulty with Vernant's elegant analysis, as with much of the new social history, is that it tends to foreclose prematurely a discussion of the spectrum of possibility within a particular praxis. In order to make use of their invaluable work, we cannot accept at face value their explanatory claims or their social ontology.

Despite the dominance of causal pluralism in contemporary historiography, there is nonetheless a pervasive inclination to accord a de facto primacy to social forces in the interpretation of particular events and developments. This tendency takes a variety of forms. It is grounded, not in theory or doctrine, but rather in a realistic awareness of the massive strength of social interests, processes, and institutions and in impatience with simplistic views of the role of ideas in history. It is embedded in metaphors that suggest the firmness and solidity of social and institutional structures, in comparison to the softness and elusiveness of ideas and beliefs. It is built into paradigms that define both the questions that are asked and the kinds of answers that are deemed pertinent. This tilt toward the social assumes various forms. In some cases it is simply taken for granted that an event can be explained primarily by reference to practical circumstances, rather than to ideas and beliefs. It is frequently assumed that the ideas and beliefs present in a given situation can be explained by, if not actually derived from, practical circumstances. As W. H. Walsh has said, "the aspiration to pass beyond the sphere of ideas altogether, even the most general ideas, and to find their origin or cause in circumstances which are independent of man's thoughts remains very strong."[13] Similarly, it is often assumed that what is decisive in a given political situation is the functional imperatives inherent in the social system which not only determine the role to be played by the ideas and beliefs that happen to be present, but also tend to generate an ideological content designed to meet those needs. We can make a rough distinction between two somewhat different, but not mutually exclusive, conceptions of the social forces at work in history. Broadly speaking, the Marxist view stresses the role of economically determined social classes, whereas the Durkheimian view stresses institutionalized relationships within a social totality.

The notion that structural and institutional factors are somewhat more important than other aspects of the human world appears most prominently in the work of the new social history.[14] Since the Second World War historians using the social sciences have explored neglected aspects of the past with impressive results. They have analyzed the social matrix in which ideas develop and function. Demographic studies have been especially fruitful. Inevitably, the new social history has tended to emphasize the causal efficacy of those aspects of the historical world that it has analyzed so well. As Felix Gilbert has said, "The social historian tends to imply that a full analysis of the facts with which he is concerned might 'explain' history and even indicate future trends. . . . The implication is that only social history comes to grips with the basic factors of history; only social history is 'true history.' "[15] Commenting on American historiography, Robert Berkhofer has noted the ascendancy of a new paradigm, which stresses "behavior and social relations" and sees "the concept of society as the key to understanding American history." Thus, "the *social interpretation of history* places ideas, events, and behavior as well as institutions in the larger context of the overall social system." Moreover, Berkhofer concludes that "all social historians tend to infer ideas from social behavior."[16]

While that judgment overstates the point somewhat, there can be no doubt that the social interpretation of history assigns a distinctly subordinate role to ideas.

The *Annales* school of historians has been the spearhead of the new social history and has exercised a profound influence on its practitioners both in Europe and America.[17] The *Annalistes* exemplify the strengths of the new social history as well as its limitations. As practicing historians rather than theoreticians, they steer clear of abstract formulations. Implicit in their work, however, is a sense of the strength and pervasiveness of the social aspects of the human world. This conviction springs in part from their impatience with the narrowness of *histoire événementielle*—traditional narrative of events, chiefly political and diplomatic. They developed a broader history of society, embracing new areas that lay outside the purview of the older historiography. Their intention was to get beneath the surface of events to a more fundamental level of reality. Methodologically, they called for a more analytical history, drawing actively on the social sciences. In concentrating their research on aspects of reality that had been neglected by the older historiography, they tended to emphasize the explanatory power of these social phenomena. While the school has given a great deal of attention to *mentalités,* these have been treated within a social framework and explained by reference to the social environment. What lends weight to the *Annales* position is the extent and quality of the historical work that it has produced, as exemplified by Fernand Braudel, who has defined his methodological principles in some detail.

Braudel urged historians to move beyond the short term, "the most capricious and deceptive form of time," and pay more attention to the long term. In a number of images, he envisaged a new kind of history that would not be content with the surface brightness of events. "Unconscious history proceeds along ways that lie far beyond these flashes of light." Braudel acclaims the historiographical revolution that has consisted in "coming face to face with this semi-darkness and in making more and more room for it alongside the event, even at the expense of the event." With models drawn from the social sciences the historian can undertake "the history of the unconscious forms of social life." They enable him to travel "along the dark and unknown roads of the extremely long-term." In dealing with the long term, Braudel seeks models capable of spanning many centuries, which presupposes "certain social conditions which are precise, but which recur frequently in history."[18]

While Braudel does not formally assert the causal primacy of social forces, some such assumption is built into the paradigm underlying his work. There is point to Trevor-Roper's reference to the "social determinism" in Braudel and the other *Annalistes*. To be sure, it is an undogmatic variety, "limited and qualified by recognition of independent human vitality." But that independence is subject to the severe constraints imposed by external forces, and by the "political and intellectual deposit around them, which was similarly determined, and into which they fall."[19] Trevor-Roper's "deposit" metaphor indicates the causal relationships implicit in this approach.

The *Annalistes'* inclination to impute causal primacy to social phenomena has also received a more theoretical expression, in a manner analogous to Marxist formulations of the relationships between base and superstructure. Chaunu's account of mentalities as a third level of reality, along with the society and the economy suggests a distinctly dependent relationship. Robert Darnton notes the affinities with Marxism in Chaunu's conception of *mentalités:* "They belong to a superstructure, which rises above the more fundamental structures of the society and the economy, and therefore they develop in response to seismic shifts in the social and economic orders. This three-tiered view of change suits a historiographical tradition that has been deeply influenced by Marxism. It also lends itself to functionalist social science." Thus, the existence of separate levels is assumed, and the metaphor suggests that some levels are more fundamental than others. It follows that "cultural phenomena can be explained by demonstrating their 'structural' relations to phenomena at the other two levels."[20] Much of the new social history, also drawing on Marxism and social science, operates with a similar model of the human world.

The historiographical implications of such a conception of levels of reality can be seen in Michel Vovelle's treatment of the role of *mentalités* in "the process leading up to the French Revolution." He asks the question, "How significant is the study of pre-revolutionary *sensibilité* to the understanding of revolutionary *sensibilité* and behavior?" But he approaches that question on the basis of assumptions that severely restrict the scope of possible answers. Thus, he simply dismisses "the old interpretations," both conservative and liberal, which put "enormous emphasis on spiritual factors (we would call them . . . superstructure)." For Vovelle such archaic views are so patently inadequate that they can be disposed of summarily: "It would be all too easy to confront these historically dated interpretations with the technical problems they leave unresolved." With the same certitude Vovelle accepts the position that he perceives as having replaced outworn interpretations of the last century: "Of course today the role played by material factors in these transformations of sensibility would be stressed."[21] From this perspective he treats the Enlightenment as primarily the *mentalité* of the bourgeois elite.

Like other exponents of the new social history, Vovelle dissociates his position from mechanistic and reductionist views of social causation: "We know that dialectical relationships between different levels of reality do not take the shape of mechanically received influences." Having made that standard disclaimer, however, he warns against the tendency to treat "the field of mentalities and sensibilities" as a "mere reflection of culture and ideology." In order to avoid such cultural reductionism, Vovelle proposes closer attention to the social basis of *mentalités:* "To state the question concretely, from the point of view of what interests us here: what role did the cultural model of the bourgeois elite, contained in the body of Enlightenment philosophy, play in the transformation of eighteenth-century *sensibilité collective?*"[22] The Enlightenment is treated as an essentially "bourgeois" phenomenon. It is the "bourgeois elite" that counts. Compounding the difficulty is the fact that Vovelle is operating with social and political categories that reflect an earlier phase in the historiography of the Revolution. The bourgeoisie is in conflict with the aristocracy, and the Enlightenment is viewed as an expression of the former.

The tendency to depreciate the significance of ideas in history is not confined to any one methodological or ideological position. The following comment on fascism, for example, was made by a historian of a distinctly independent turn of mind, detached from Marxism or social science: "European fascism, then, is the political response of the European bourgeoisie to the economic recession after 1918—or rather, more directly to the political fear caused by that recession."[23] Although Marxism has contributed to a linkage between Left politics and a social interpretation of history, some conservative historians have forcefully denied a significant causal role to ideas. L. B. Namier treated mid-eighteenth-century English politics in terms of social and family interests, rather than the ideas, which had been stressed by historians in the Whig tradition. Namier has summed up his position in an apt epigram: "What matters most is the underlying emotion, the music, to which ideas are a mere libretto, often of a very inferior quality."[24] Another conservative, Maurice Cowling, has interpreted the Reform Act of 1867 from the point of view of "high politics," defined as primarily a matter of "rhetoric and manoeuvre."[25] The focus is on political elites and the devices they use to get into office and stay there. It was in criticism of Namierite interpretations that Herbert Butterfield remarked that "human beings are the carriers of ideas as well as the repositories of vested interests."[26]

The problem of the relationship between ideas and interests is central to the events and movements that will be examined in part 1 of this book.[27] Just how to define the relationship between ideas and interests in particular situations is problematical. There are cases, such as parliamentary politics in England in the 1750s or Ronald Reagan's tax reforms, where a Namierite model will work fairly well. In other historical situations and developments a more complicated model is required. In undertaking the difficult task of defining the role of ideas, we can take as given the consensus principle stated by Felix Gilbert: "After Marx the existence of a close relationship between ideas and interest can no longer be doubted and only careful analysis can determine the function of ideas in social life." In carrying out that sort of analysis, intellectual history has been assigned a consciously modest task by Gilbert, who is intent on avoiding the weaknesses of a discredited idealist interpretation while rejecting the extravagant explanatory claims of social history. While the intellectual historian cannot reconstruct the Zeitgeist, he can undertake the limited task of reconstituting "the mind of an individual or of groups at the times when a particular event happened or an advance was achieved." The importance of such an undertaking is indisputable: "Whatever one thinks of the forces that underlie the historical process, they are filtered through the human mind and this determines the tempo and the manner in which they work. It is human consciousness which connects the long-range factors and forces and the individual event and it is at this crucial point of the historical process that the intellectual historian does his work."[28] Gilbert has posed the kinds of questions that tend to be crowded off to the side in the paradigms of the new social history.

Otto Hintze's treatment of the problem is still useful because of his interest in finding a middle ground between idealism and materialism, between Ranke and Marx, in relation to concrete historical questions. As a historian of Prussia in the early modern period, he was looking into the links between Protestantism and politics, religion and capitalism, ideals and interests. He dealt with these matters not only on the basis of detailed research but also in relation to the analytical problems that they posed and to the presuppositions of analysis. In that connection, Hintze's critique of idealist historicism is of particular value, because it is specific. Dismissive references to "idealist" interpretations, without further elaboration or supporting argument, have become so common in contemporary discourse that it is necessary to specify what is objectionable. Just as it is pointless to dismiss Marx because of his "materialism," so also it is pointless to dismiss Meinecke because of his "idealism." If the valid aspects of the idealist position are to be retained, however, they have to be removed from their metaphysical matrix.[29]

Hintze firmly rejected the ontology presupposed by idealist interpretations of history. For Hintze ideas "are not transcendental forces but are inherent in society." He criticized Ernst Troeltsch for the notion that history is the arena in which ideas are actualized. "Troeltsch recognizes only one form of historical development: development governed by what he terms 'an idea,' that is, a cultural value or a unified complex of such values. Historical development, then, is a process of continual growth by which such a value is realized." The notion that values are "realized" in history presupposes metaphysical assumptions that intrude on empirical inquiry. Hintze also rejected another aspect of the treatment of ideas in the tradition of idealist historicism: "The German idealists . . . tended to see historical trends originating in a realm beyond human ken and bursting forth from the hidden regions of subconscious life in the form of sudden revelations. Troeltsch too subscribed to this view." Hintze preferred Ranke's conception of "material and intellectual tendencies of the centuries" to the narrower idealist conception of ideas realizing themselves in history. But he could not accept Ranke's belief that such tendencies had a transcendental character and existed beyond the human realm. He rejected the Rankean notion that ideas "have a life of their own and possess the force to determine the character of an age and the course of its events."[30]

Just as Hintze wished to preserve what was valid in Ranke's thought by divesting it of its "transcendental connotations," so his criticism of Marxist thought was accompanied by a recognition of valid elements:

The Marxist model of substructure and superstructure seems to me not a happy way of expressing this peculiar connection between interests and ideas. Quite apart from the fact that this simply deprives the 'ideology' of any reality of its own, it suffers from the defect of being conceived in a static spirit, whereas it is intended to illustrate the dynamic of revolution.

Hintze's conception of "a polar system of interest and ideas" was intended to emphasize the mutual interaction between the two:

In the historical sense, neither can live over the long haul without the other. Each needs the other as its complement. Where interests are energetically pursued, an ideology develops to give them inspiration, strength, and justification. This ideology is, as an indispensable part of the life process that produces action, as real as the 'real' interests themselves. Conversely, where ideas want to conquer the world, they need to be drawn by tangible interests, which in turn may often divert the ideas from their original goal or even alter and falsify them.[31]

Hintze's formulation deserves careful attention both because of its intrinsic value and also because it represents a consensus among a majority of historians and social scientists.

All human activity, political and religious, stems from an undivided root. As a rule, the first impulse for human beings' social action comes from tangible interests, political and economic. . . . Ideal interests elevate and animate these tangible interests and lend them justification. Man does not live by bread alone; he wants to have a good conscience when he pursues his vital interests; and in pursuing them he develops his powers fully only if he is conscious of simultaneously serving purposes higher than purely egotistical ones. Interests without such spiritual elevation are lame; on the other hand, ideas can succeed in history only when and to the extent that they attach themselves to tangible interests.[32]

While Hintze's formulation of the relationship between ideas and interests is valuable, it encompasses only one aspect of the role of ideas in political history. Hintze's preoccupation with the refutation of a mechanistic version of classic Marxism, combined with his dissatisfaction with idealist theories, led him to a position—similar to neo-Marxist handling of the problem—that in fact assigns a subordinate role to ideas. Having rescued ideas from the dependency required by the base-superstructure model, Hintze confines their role to processes dominated by interests. "Where interests are energetically pursued, an ideology develops to give them inspiration, strength, and justification." While interests do not directly generate ideas, they determine their function. Ideals "lend wings to these real interests, give them a spiritual meaning, and serve to justify them."[33] In the polar system of interests and ideas, the former is clearly the dominant partner. Paradoxically, another difficulty in Hintze's formulation is the result of an idealist view of ideas as entities endowed with a desire to "conquer the world"; they possess an "original goal" from which they may be diverted. In order to succeed, however, they need to be "drawn" by and they have to "attach themselves to tangible interests," which may divert them from their original goal or even "alter and falsify them."[34]

If the problem of the Enlightenment and the French Revolution is approached on the basis of Hintze's model of the relation between ideas and interests, it will result in the sort of interpretation that Georges Lefebvre has presented so effectively. But this carries us only so far. The French Revolution was significant precisely because it embodied something more than the pursuit of socially determined interests.

The relationship between culture and praxis is more complex than that described in the ideas and interests formula. To be sure, it is plain that praxis exacts conformity and acquiescence, and uses culture to provide legitimization; particular practical interests enlist ideas in their service. On the other hand, however, culture can also provide the resources for a critique of praxis and for the construction of alternatives to existing institutional arrangements. Culture can provide the basis not only for acquiescence in domination but also for resistance to the claims of authority. This aspect of culture, which has been the subject of extensive theoretical discussion in recent years, needs to be taken into account in considering the ways in which ideas exercise an influence on political developments and events.

Paul Ricoeur has suggested that while practical life compels conformity and adaptation, culture makes possible "a legitimate refusal toward adaptation." It opens up possibilities that go beyond existing praxis: "Culture is also that which unadapts man, keeps him ready for the open, for the remote, for the other, for the all." Culture is the source of criticism, protest, and the aspiration to change. Ricoeur has also described "the Utopian function of culture," rooted in the human imagination: "The imagination has a prospective and explorative function in regard to the inherent possibilities of man. It is, par excellence, the instituting and the constituting of what is humanly possible. In imagining his possibilities, man acts as a prophet of his own existence." Ricoeur reminds us that the function of the imagination cannot be reduced to "a simple projection of vital, unconscious, or repressed desires."[35] Rather, it is an expression of human freedom and consciousness.

Ricoeur's comments on the utopian function of culture have to be qualified in two respects: first, they do not apply to culture as such, but rather to Western culture in certain phases of its historical development; second, both in Europe and in other societies, the ideological and hegemonic function of culture in relation to structures of praxis and power, a genuinely universal characteristic of the human world, is never superseded or overcome by particular expressions of the utopian potentiality of culture. On the first point, we can take a passage from Tertullian, quoted by Ricoeur, as an indication of the role of Christianity in shaping the utopian dimension of Western culture: "It was necessary that the image and likeness of God be made free and autonomous in its will, since the image and likeness of God is defined by this freedom. . . . Through freedom man ceases to be a slave of nature. He comes into his own good and assures his own excellence, not as a child who receives but as a man who consents."[36] The great myth that man was created in the image of God and its development by the Church fathers and their successors has been a dynamic element in the evolution of the utopian mentality in Europe from More to Marx. On the other hand, however, the Church rationalized and legitimized the patterns of servitude and domination that pervaded feudal society. The emancipated serf who experienced the *hilaritas libertatis* achieved that cherished state despite the teachings of medieval Christianity;[37] and his sense of the blessings of liberty owed nothing to a reading of Tertullian or any other theologian.

One of the more interesting strands in neo-Marxist thought has been an emphasis on the radical potentialities inherent in culture. Marcuse, for example, has referred to "the autonomous, critical contents of culture."[38] He has deplored the gap "between the material civilization and the intellectual culture, between necessity and freedom." Applying these universal categories to modern industrial society he has argued that "the integration of cultural values into the established society cancels the alienation of culture from [material] civilization, thereby flattening out the tension between the 'ought' and the 'is,' . . . between the potential and the actual, future and present, freedom and necessity." Albert Soboul has depicted utopia, rooted in hope, as an innate tendency of the human spirit.[39] Zygmunt Bauman also has described utopia as intrinsic to culture: "Utopias are those aspects of culture (in itself a programme rather than a description of the human condition) in which the possible extrapolations of the present are explored."[40]

Critical theory presupposes an inherently critical and utopian component in man and his culture. As Geuss has described the aim of the Frankfurt School: "The positive task of the critical theory is to 'save the utopian content' of the cultural tradition, i.e. to 'separate' the underlying genuine human wants, values, needs, and aspirations from their ideological mode of expression." Thus, even ideology has "a 'utopian kernel' which it is the task of critical theory to set free." Every culture contains standards of what the good life is, which may be expressed in works of art as well as in religious and philosophical doctrines. "To a large extent these images of the good life are utopian; they describe a state of affairs which could not exist."[41] The existence of these aspects of culture, in turn, is the basis of the claim that critical theory can contribute to radical change. It is the basis of Habermas' faith that "for the species as a whole, the boundaries of reality are in fact movable," and that "parts of cultural tradition" can be changed into reality. Even illusions harbor utopia. Hence Habermas hopes that "this utopian content can be freed from its fusion with the delusory, ideological components of culture that have been fashioned into legitimations of authority and be converted into a critique of power structures that have become historically obsolete."[42]

But Habermas is not in fact describing universal characteristics of man and culture. Rather, he has invested with universality certain traits that developed in Western culture, especially modern Europe. While dreaming and hoping and imagining are intrinsically human, the particular "utopian content" envisaged by Habermas is historically specific. Its existence has to be understood in terms of the unique cultural and symbolic forms that entered into the development of Europe. To be sure, Western culture evolved in ways that bear significant similarities to developmental phases in the history of other societies. Karl Jaspers' account of the "axial" period in world history is pertinent.[43] Similarly, Habermas' typology of developmental stages in the history of various societies shows common patterns rooted in the nature of man.[44] At the same time, however, the infinite malleability of human nature, emphasized both by historicists like Meinecke and anthropologists like Geertz, has given rise to diversity that cannot be accounted for in uniformitarian terms. The utopian and radical aspirations so pervasive in modern Europe had their origin in the historically unique aspects of Western culture.

Habermas' theory of culture and utopia cannot be applied in explanation of the origins and development of radical politics in modern Europe, because the theory, along with the values and ideals that it serves, is itself the product of that history. Habermas' description of man is not an empirical construct but rather a splendid expression of a faith nurtured by Western culture and its history: by the French Revolution as transfigured by Marxism and German idealism. We turn now to 1789 and its roots in the Enlightenment and Western culture.

PART ONE

CHAPTER TWO

The Enlightenment and the French Revolution

The relationship between the Enlightenment and the French Revolution remains the classic topic for any discussion of the role of intellectual forces in history. The men of 1789 acclaimed the Revolution as a triumph of enlightened thought. Their opponents soon responded in kind by blaming the *philosophes* for the disaster. Since then denunciation of rationalist radicalism has been a staple of conservative thought. In that tradition, notably in the works of Taine and Talmon, the responsibility of the Enlightenment has been exaggerated to the point of caricature. Aware of the methodological and ideological difficulties posed by that line of interpretation, historians today are inclined to be wary of simplistic views that make too much of the Enlightenment in the etiology of the Revolution. They expect the role of the Enlightenment to be defined in relation to multiple forces in complex interaction.

We can take as given the fact that social and institutional factors were of considerable importance in the genesis of the French Revolution. There are no grounds for claiming causal primacy for the Enlightenment. It certainly cannot be identified as a "cause" of the Revolution in the sense that a virus can be identified as the cause of viral pneumonia. The Enlightenment exercised its influence only in interaction with other components of a complex situation. Within such an unequivocally pluralistic framework, however, I shall argue that the Enlightenment was of preeminent importance in the process underlying the Revolution. It was much more than just one of a number of necessary causes. The Enlightenment was a constituent that was as essential to the existence of the Revolution, as an atom of oxygen is to a molecule of water. It was also a primary ingredient that was continually active in the immensely complex process that brought the Revolution into being and shaped its character. Whereas social and institutional circumstances were capable of producing a whole range of possible events—from endemic conflict to insurrection—the Enlightenment was necessary to the French Revolution that did in fact occur.

This interpretation presupposes a conception of the nature and significance of the French Revolution that needs to be made explicit at the outset. In this instance, even more than usual, the nature of the event itself is problematical, and the problem of the character of the Revolution is inseparable from the question of its relationship to the Enlightenment. The event itself is not a "given," such as an assassination or the outbreak of a war. On the contrary, the French Revolution was a novel and unprecedented event, and is often characterized as the first "modern" revolution, the prototype of the revolutionary phenomenon that has been so prominent in world history ever since. The novel feature of the Revolution of 1789—and of revolutions since then—has been the impulse to transform the existing political and social structure so as to create a new and better order of things, based on universally valid principles. This cluster of traits sets the French Revolution apart from earlier insurrections, rebellions, revolts, uprisings, and changes of government that had been described as revolutions. The revolutionaries themselves made this claim at the time. Robespierre proclaimed the novelty of the Revolution: "All the revolutions which till now had changed the face of empire, had as their goal solely a change of dynasty or the transfer of power from one individual into the hands of the many. The French Revolution is the first which is based on the theory of the rights of humanity and on the principles of justice."[1] What needs to be explained, therefore, is the genesis of an event that was "unprecedented and unequaled in all prior history," the creation of the modern revolutionary phenomenon itself.[2]

The novel features of the French Revolution of 1789 were indissolubly linked to the unique historical characteristics of the Enlightenment, especially the notion that social and political institutions should be measured against certain "simple and incontestable principles" and brought into conformity if they fell short. The principles of revolutionary action were grounded in natural law. Man was part of an all-embracing natural order, with which his institutions ought to be in harmony. The impulse to revolutionary transformation was also linked to the belief in the possibility of progress, based on reason; and indeed in the inevitability of progress, once man's rational faculties were freed from artificial constraints. Finally, the Enlightenment embodied in new and explosive form the "utopian propensity" that had been ingrained in Western culture from the very beginning. All of these elements contributed to the development of the notion that a transforming revolution might usher in a new order of liberty and justice that eventually would embrace all mankind. From the Enlightenment came the ideas and aspirations that defined the Revolution as not merely a change in government but as a historic act, creating a new age.

This interpretation is addressed to the particular problems of description and explanation posed by the events of 1789. We cannot simply apply a formula that is adequate to handle a broad category of events such as the outbreak of war or revolution. For one thing, the outbreak of a revolution has to be dealt with differently from the outbreak of war, since the start of hostilities can be identified without difficulty. In the case of revolutions, more complex questions arise concerning the nature of the event and the relationship between the event and the intentions of the agents. Moreover, the problem of explanation varies from one revolution to another. In the case of 1688, 1776, and 1917, for example, the events can be explained to a considerable degree by reference to the intentions of the men involved, although the content of those intentions varied considerably: both Whigs and Tories set out to get rid of James II, the rebels sought independence from Britain, and Lenin was seizing power in a communist revolution. The French Revolution of 1789, however, has to be explained in different terms, for it was unplanned and unintended. (In that respect it has more in common with the outbreak of war in 1914.) What turned out to be "the Revolution" took shape "in the course of events." At the same time the nature of the event itself—especially in comparison to "revolutions" that preceded and followed—is also problematical.

In the case of the French Revolution, then, we not only have to account for the series of events that occurred between September 1788 and August 1789 but also to understand and explain the Revolution as a new mode of political action, the prototype of the revolutionary phenomenon as it has existed ever since. Thus, the French Revolution of 1789 cannot be explained by reference to specifically revolutionary intentions of the sort that were present in 1848 or 1917, for they were the product of the event, not its cause. To a significant degree, the revolutionary spirit or mentality was itself created in 1789. We are dealing with a sequence of events that "turned out to be" the French Revolution which took shape imperceptibly in the course of actions that were not aimed at the achievement of a revolution or even a rebellion. By way of explanation we have to reconstruct a strange process involving the transmutation of nonrevolutionary events into "the Revolution" and the creation of a new "revolutionary" ideology. Such an explanation, in turn, presupposes a conceptualization of the novel revolutionary phenomenon, in contrast to earlier "revolutions" to which it stands in a relationship of continuity and change.

In the immensely complex process underlying the genesis of the Revolution, two aspects of the role of the Enlightenment may be distinguished. It was constitutive of the event as a novel "modern" revolution and it was an ingredient in the process that brought that phenomenon into being. Two sequences of events composed the core of the Revolution: the creation of the National Assembly in June and the series that began with the fall of the Bastille and ends with the Declaration of the Rights of Man. In the first sequence, the latent radicalism of the Enlightenment, embodied in a nonrevolutionary *réformisme éclairé*, reinforced and magnified impulses rooted in social and political interests, while also defining the meaning of the actions being taken and pointing ahead to new possibilities. In the second sequence, which grew directly out of the first, the ideas of the Enlightenment shaped the revolutionaries' conception of themselves and their Revolution. Thus, the Enlightenment was intimately implicated in the process that produced the Revolution and the revolutionary ideology that was the primary component of the event. It was also central to the emergence of Jacobinism, the fullest expression of revolutionary radicalism.

There are a few qualifications that ought to be mentioned briefly at this point. The Enlightenment, of course, is a construct or ideal type that embraces a great range of ideas, beliefs, and attitudes. There were tensions and contradictions within that complex body of thought, as well as national variations. It was characteristic of the strength and vitality of the Enlightenment that some of the *philosophes*, notably Rousseau and Diderot, subjected many of its most cherished beliefs, including the faith in reason, to rigorous criticism. The widespread rejection of Cartesian rationalism lends point to the comment that the "revolt against reason" was a dominant characteristic of eighteenth century thought. The Enlightenment comprised not only a vigorous empiricism but also other attitudes that may be labeled "proto-romantic." The phrase "rationalist radicalism" has to be understood in this context. Finally, there was certainly no single logic or ideological direction to "the Enlightenment." At different times ideas drawn from the Enlightenment have been used to perform diverse ideological functions, conservative and reformist as well as radical and revolutionary. Yet it was the Enlightenment that provided the conceptual and ideological forms that were the essential constituents of the Revolution of 1789. It exercised its influence in dialectical interplay with social and political groupings in the context of changing events of which it was a part.[3]

PROBLEMS OF INTERPRETATION

Before developing this interpretation, it is necessary to glance at historiographical developments that define the context in which we see the event. Unlike the physicist, the historian cannot discard older hypotheses and theories on the basis of the latest research. In fact, the danger lies in overreaction against the inevitable one-sidedness of established interpretations. With respect to the problem of the relationship between the Enlightenment and the French Revolution, two historiographical developments need to be kept in mind. First, J. L. Talmon's brilliant and perverse indictment of the radical Enlightenment in 1952 evoked a widespread defense of the *philosophes*, chiefly among liberal and centrist historians, intent on the refutation of an ideologically motivated interpretation.[4] The case for the defense tended to minimize the significance of the Enlightenment in the origins of the Revolution. Second, beginning in the 1960s, the interpretation of 1789 as a "bourgeois revolution," which had achieved the status of orthodoxy in the postwar decades, was undermined by research and criticism.[5] Both exponents and critics of the Marxist interpretation tended to assign a subordinate role to the Enlightenment. Another important aspect of postwar historiography was not directly concerned with the question of the Enlightenment. Rejecting simplistic views of the uniqueness of the French Revolution, Jacques Godechot and Robert Palmer showed the presence of similar phenomena in Europe and America in the last third of the eighteenth century.[6] In somewhat different ways both the "bourgeois revolution" thesis and the social interpretation advanced to replace it also emphasize the similarities between 1789 and other revolutionary events. Only recently have historians begun to break out of the conceptual framework within which earlier conflicting interpretations have been contained.

The postwar orthodoxy, essentially Marxist in character, depicted a revolution rooted in the conflict between a capitalist bourgeoisie and a feudal nobility. The most influential exponent of this view was Georges Lefebvre. He located the "ultimate cause" of the French Revolution of 1789 in the social and institutional structure. While the nobility retained substantial privileges under the law in the old regime, "in reality economic power, personal abilities and confidence in the future had passed largely to the bourgeoisie." The Revolution of 1789 "restored the harmony between fact and law." The bourgeoisie "had developed a new ideology which the 'philosophers' and 'economists' of the time had simply put into definite form."[7]

Research during the past twenty years has undermined the neo-Marxist interpretation that reigned for so long as an unchallenged orthodoxy. It has been displaced by a more nuanced view of the social origins of the Revolution, which has eliminated the dichotomy between a feudal nobility and a capitalist bourgeoisie. A new generation of historians has shown the importance of a propertied elite of "Notables," composed of rich noblemen and bourgeois. Divisions within both the nobility and the bourgeoisie have received a great deal of attention. It follows that the origins of the Revolution of 1789 cannot be understood in terms of a clash between nobility and bourgeoisie but rather in terms of shifting relations between elites in a complex system of stratification.[8] Colin Lucas has summed up the interpretation that emerged: "The revolt of the Third Estate was a revolt against a loss of status by the central and lower sections of the elite with the approval of those elements of the trading groups which were on the threshold of the elite. It was this social group which became the 'revolutionary bourgeoisie.' "[9] Thus, the Revolution has to be understood, not as the action of a capitalist bourgeoisie, but in the context of "latent tensions" inherent in a very complicated social situation. The new social interpretation shares with the Lefebvrian orthodoxy a tendency to attribute primacy to nonideological forces in the genesis of the Revolution, although without explicit attention to the role of the Enlightenment, whereas both Lefebvre and Albert Soboul examined the problem suggestively.

George Taylor, however, one of the most effective critics of the "bourgeois revolution" thesis, has confronted the problem of the role of the Enlightenment in a thoughtful and careful way. His critique of what he calls the "irrepressible" tendency to see the Revolution as "in some sense the consequence of the Enlightenment" commands a good deal of support among historians. While rejecting economic and social factors as the key to the Revolution, Taylor emphasizes the importance of political circumstances and events, which he defines in nonideological terms. In an article based on extensive research and careful analysis, he argues that the revolution arose "without benefit of ideology" from a political and social crisis that had exposed existing institutions as "hopelessly inadequate." The struggle to overhaul a patently inadequate system generated an ideology out of the intellectual materials available. Thus, "the revolutionary state of mind expressed in the Declaration of the Rights of Man and the decrees of 1789–91 was a product—and not a cause of the crisis that began in 1787." In other words, "the revolutionary mentality was created by the crisis." The revolutionary ideology expressed in the Declaration was "an adaptation of Enlightenment words, phrases, and concepts to a revolutionary situation that the philosophers had neither intended nor foreseen."[10]

Taylor's thesis that the Revolution arose "without benefit of ideology" rests on a sharp dichotomy between ideas and beliefs on the one hand and, on the other, a political crisis, comprising events and circumstances, which generated the revolutionary mentality. Some such distinction is useful, but only up to a point. By treating an analytical distinction as if it corresponded to an ontological cleavage, Taylor has resolved in advance the very questions that need to be looked into. He has hypostatized events, as entities separate and distinct from ideas, and assigned them causal primacy in relation to the latter. Such a formulation forecloses discussion of the complex dialectical interplay not only between events and ideas but also between them and social and institutional structures.

In a variety of dichotomous formulations that are part of the conventional wisdom for many historians and social scientists, ideas are often counterposed to other aspects of the human world: interests, praxis, events, behavior, circumstances. While distinctions of that sort are necessary, they have to be handled flexibly; in rigid form they screen out the very questions that ought to be considered. Interpretations of the French Revolution abound with verbal formulas counterposing the Enlightenment to events and/or circumstances and/or interests, with the former perceived in some sort of subordinate relationship to the latter. This tendency can be seen in a current of interpretation that was prominent in the 1960s: a defense of the Enlightenment against critics who blamed it for the Terror.

Rejecting the strictures of Taine and Talmon, Alfred Cobban declared flatly that "the Enlightenment had no identifiable part in causing any of the successive revolutions between 1787 and 1795." In support of that admirably unequivocal conclusion, Cobban developed an oddly syllogistic sort of argument. Since the French Enlightenment was on the whole "lacking in systematic political theory," and "since the French Revolution was primarily a political revolution, this must cast doubt upon its supposed causal relationship with the Enlightenment."[11] In any case, Cobban went on, political theories did not cause the revolution either, but were merely used to justify an event brought on by other causes. A similar formulation was advanced by Peter Gay, who also was defending the *philosophes* against ideological criticism from the right. "In its career as the target of polemical attack, the Enlightenment has been assailed for ideas it did not hold, and for consequences it did not intend to produce."[12] Like Cobban, Gay argued that the ideas of the Enlightenment provided rhetorical justification for actions that were really determined by practical circumstances. Treating the Enlightenment primarily in relation to the rhetoric of the Revolution, however, dissolves the substantive questions that are at issue. Moreover, Gay's complaint that Tocqueville concentrates on the "trivial side effects rather than on the central purposes of Enlightenment speculation" bypasses the problem of unperceived implications and unintended consequences.

While François Furet has contributed vigorously to the critique of Marxist interpretations of the Revolution, he has also called into question other aspects of the conceptual framework within which the event has been perceived. I shall single out only two segments of his subtle and complex argument: first, his emphasis on the interconnectedness of action and thought, events and language, praxis and ideology; second, the manner in which he links changes in the symbolic realm to the novel features of the Revolution. Furet points out that the Revolution "invented a type of political discourse and practice by which we have been living ever since." It represents "the appearance on the stage of history of a practical and ideological mode of social action unrelated to anything that came before."[13] The Revolution embodied a new revolutionary discourse. To understand and explain it we have to attend closely to changes in language.

From this perspective Furet derides any inclination to treat "the most radically new and the most mysterious aspect of the French Revolution as no more than the normal result of circumstances and as a natural occurrence in the history of the oppressed." While conceding that one might "explain the revolt of most of the deputies to the Estates General by the political crisis in the Ancien Regime," he insists that the ensuing revolution cannot be explained in those terms. Similarly, while the urban uprisings of June and July can be explained in economic terms, that kind of explanation cannot account for the revolutionary *journée*. Causal analysis of that sort "does not cover the problem of the revolutionary phenomenon." It is precisely the revolutionary phenomenon as a whole that cannot be deduced from a set of social and economic causes. "A phenomenon like the French Revolution cannot be reduced to a simple cause-and-effect schema. The mere fact that the Revolution has causes does not mean that they are all there is to its history."[14] Furet's critique of attempts to explain the Revolution in terms of its social and economic "causes" applies to a broad range of interpretations, Marxist and non-Marxist. He has posed the *problem* of explanation.

Furet has a number of interesting observations about the nature of the "revolutionary phenomenon" of 1789 that cannot be accounted for as the inevitable consequence of a complex of socioeconomic causes. He identifies two sets of beliefs as constituting the very bedrock of revolutionary consciousness: "The first is that all personal problems and all moral or intellectual matters have become political; that there is no human misfortune not amenable to a political solution. The second is that, since everything can be known and changed, there is a perfect fit between action, knowledge, and morality." Henceforth, there was no limit to the beneficent possibilities of political action. "As Marx realized in his early writings, the Revolution was the very incarnation of the *illusion of politics:* it transformed mere experience into conscious acts. It inaugurated a world that attributes every social change to known, classified and living forces." The classic form of revolutionary consciousness, expressed in Jacobinism, was founded "on immanence in history, on the realisation of values in and by political action, so that those values were at stake in every conflict, were embodied by the actors, and were as discoverable and knowable as truth itself." In another formulation, Furet remarks that the "seminal idea" of the Revolution was that of the advent of a new age.[15] While Furet has not provided a definitive description of the "revolutionary phenomenon," he has put the question in the center of the problematic.

In other passages Furet identifies the "revolutionary phenomenon" with democracy in a way that blurs the distinction between them:

What sets the French Revolution apart is that it was not a transition but a beginning and a haunting vision of that beginning. Its historical importance lies in the one trait that was unique to it, especially since this 'unique' trait was to become universal: it was the first experiment with democracy.[16]

This is a misleading formulation in that the emergence of democracy can hardly be said to have been unique to France. Palmer and Godechot have shown the presence of democratic movements in Western Europe and America before and after 1789. What was unique to France was the Revolution, the new revolutionary spirit, and the new revolutionary context in which democracy developed. What France may be said to have "invented" in 1789 was not democracy, but rather the new revolutionary phenomenon, the new practical and ideological mode that Furet has described. By the same token, it follows that in characterizing the period beginning in 1760 as "the age of the democratic revolution," Palmer appears to have projected back into the 1760s and 1770s revolutionary traits that did not in fact appear until 1789. While the French Revolution was not "the first experiment with democracy," it was the first "modern" revolution.[17]

Just as Furet brings into focus the question of the nature of the Revolution, so also he illuminates the problem of reconstructing the diverse elements—events, language, social and political circumstances—that entered into the genesis of that event. His handling of the problem is skewed somewhat, however, by the intensity of his critique of the tendency to explain the Revolution by direct reference to socioeconomic causes. Having demolished that thesis, Furet develops a counterposition that appears to treat events as separate politicoideological entities, constituted by a fusion of language and action, and endowed with an independent force of their own. (There are passages in which Furet appears to be reifying language and investing it with causal efficacy.) The following formulation, for example, elides a number of important questions concerning the dynamics of the process that brought into being the Revolution of 1789: "The fact remains that the revolutionary event, *from the very outset*, totally transformed the existing situation and created a new mode of historical action that was not intrinsically a part of the situation."[18] Despite his disclaimer about causal analysis, Furet appears to be treating the "revolutionary event" as a decisive cause of the "new mode of political action," whereas these are two different descriptions of just the phenomenon that requires explanation.

By combining detailed research with new analytical and conceptual instruments, Keith Baker has carried the study of the ideological origins of the Revolution to a stage well beyond that reached by his predecessors.[19] Since his work is still in progress, only a provisional sketch is possible at this point. One theme may be singled out: Baker's exploration of the intimate connection between language and politics in their historical context in France in the second half of the eighteenth century. His purpose is not to describe the ideological causes of events, but rather to show how "the Revolution of 1789 depended, in effect, on the creation and deployment of a political language that cast many different kinds of behaviors, from aristocratic resistance to popular fears, into the same symbolic order." Similarly, Baker argues that the power of the actions taken by "the masses" in the course of the Revolution "depended on a set of symbolic representations and cultural meanings that constituted the significance of their behavior and gave it explosive force." An action such as the attack on the Bastille could "take on the meaning of an attack on despotism within the field of political discourse created in the course of the earlier events of that year."

This view of the Revolution, in turn, rests on a conception of "politics as constituted within a field of discourse" and of "political language as elaborated in the course of political action." Hence Baker's study of ideological origins is concerned not so much with the *philosophes* as with the broad political debate that emerged out of the institutional and ideological conflicts in France in the mid-eighteenth century. His purpose is not to trace the history of unit ideas but rather "to identify a field of political discourse, a set of linguistic patterns and relationships that defined possible actions and gave them meaning," and "to reconstruct the political culture within which the creation of the revolutionary language of 1789 became possible."[20] In order to understand the Revolution of 1789, then, it is necessary to analyze revolutionary language and the whole field of discourse in which it was located. Baker is conducting that analysis in the context of French society and politics.

This chapter operates on a narrower front and deals with only one aspect of the intellectual and ideological origins of the French Revolution. It concentrates on 1789 as "the first modern revolution" and on components of the Enlightenment that entered into the genesis of that event and of the new revolutionary ideology.

ENLIGHTENMENT RADICALISM

The Enlightenment was a complex entity comprising multifarious ideas and beliefs that had developed at different stages in the long history of Western culture. We shall single out a few interconnected components that entered into the genesis of the French Revolution and the revolutionary ideology. First and foremost was a rationalist radicalism rooted in seventeenth-century science: the triumph of reason in the mastery of nature might be repeated in the social and political world. The Enlightenment also embodied older elements that had been renewed and transformed in the course of the scientific and intellectual revolution of the seventeenth century: above all, concepts of natural law and natural rights. In politics and morals there were self-evident truths by which human action should be guided. The Enlightenment idea of progress, interwoven into every aspect of the French Revolution, had its origin in the impact of science on inherited religious and humanistic traditions. Since reason and virtue were inextricably linked, the destruction of artificial restraints on the mind would lead to liberation as the ultimate goal of a progressive history rooted in human nature itself. Finally, new and more intense forms of utopianism, deeply rooted in Western culture, were present in the Enlightenment and the Revolution. The idea of a revolutionary transformation and a new beginning had its origin in this cultural tradition.

The core of the distinctive cognitive and normative structure of the Enlightenment, as defined here, is expressed in the belief in "natural right and the law of reason," a conventional phrase that occurs in a remonstrance of 1774. Such a belief is compatible with a diversity of social and political ideas. The specific content of the political thought of the Enlightenment—the vision of a society of free men equal in rights, ideas of popular sovereignty, conceptions of representative government, notions of economic freedom—was not intrinsically related to its distinctive conceptual structure. Thus, various institutional and ideological phenomena presupposed by French political culture in the mid-eighteenth century—notably the existence of parliamentary government in England along with the liberal ideology associated with it— had no necessary connection with the Enlightenment as such. Similarly, ideas of popular sovereignty, so prominent in French political discourse throughout the pre-1789 generation, had their immediate origins in political and institutional developments in England and America, as R. R. Palmer has shown. (More remote intellectual and ideological origins of such ideas long antedated the Enlightenment.) French political culture contained elements from still another ideological tradition—a republicanism rooted in civic humanism and antiquity that received a new formulation in the ideas of the English Commonwealthmen—that was the product of a history antedating the Enlightenment. Finally, the American Revolution, the product of a history of its own, was the source of important ideological and political components that entered into the genesis of the Revolution of 1789. In the interpretation that follows, we take these disparate elements as given, and consider them primarily in relation to the Enlightenment, with which they were adventitiously linked in historical conjuncture.[21]

As conservative critics have pointed out from the very beginning, a prime source of the latent radicalism of the Enlightenment was a rationalist approach to politics, the novel notion that social and political institutions should be measured against rationally formulated standards and brought into conformity with them. This principle cut the ground from under traditional justifications of the status quo and introduced a new impulse to change. It was literally subversive, because it raised the question of the legitimacy of existing institutions by demanding that they be examined in the light of universally valid principles. In this spirit, the Declaration of the Rights of Man announced that henceforth the demands of citizens would be based on "simple and incontestable principles," since rational men can recognize "the aim of all political institutions." Edmund Burke's extravagant complaint identifies the inherently subversive character of Enlightenment rationalism:

They have "the rights of man." Against these there can be no prescription. . . . Against these their rights of man let no government look for security in the length of its continuance, or in the justice and lenity of its administration. The objections of these speculatists, if its forms do not quadrate with their theories, are as valid against such an old and beneficent government, as against the most violent tyranny, or the greenest usurpation.[22]

Marx also recognized the radical dynamism inherent in the Enlightenment: "Just as *Cartesian* materialism passes into *natural science proper*, the other trend of French materialism leads directly to *socialism* and *communism*. There is no need for any great penetration to see from the teaching of materialism on the original goodness and equal intellectual endowment of man, the omnipotence of experience, habit and education, . . . how necessarily materialism is connected with communism and socialism."[23] Centrist and reformist interpretations of the *philosophes* have tended to deradicalize them. Franco Venturi's balanced judgment captures the radicalism inherent in their relentless critique of established ideas and institutions: "It was precisely the abstractness, the universal validity of their principles, the element of negation in their revolt—with which they and the whole of the Enlightenment were endlessly reproached by conservatives—which made them autonomous and led them to the conclusions they derived from their experience in the great decade of the *Encyclopédie*."[24]

Lending strength to the theories that Burke found so appalling was the tradition of natural law, in new scientific form. Closely linked to the notion that society should be judged by rational principles and that politics should be guided accordingly was the belief in an order of nature, governed by natural law. The human world was perceived as part of a single natural order, with which man's institutions ought to be maintained in harmony. Natural law defined what was in accord with reason and nature. The adjective "unnatural" lent its weight to criticism which held that a given institution violated certain self-evident principles. Here was an additional impetus to renovation and change: what was unnatural should be brought into line. Moreover, by virtue of the strength of the natural law tradition, the principles by which the existing order was to be judged enjoyed an exalted metaphysical status which they do not possess today. The same is true of the whole concept of "rights" which lay at the heart of eighteenth-century liberal ideology. They too had a special ontological and epistemological character as an integral part of the "reality" of the universe.[25]

The Enlightenment belief in the objective existence of moral truths, natural rights, and self-evident principles reflected its distinctive position in the history of thought. On the one hand, the Enlightenment represented the final destruction of the medieval thought structure and the clear emergence of the "modern" world view. Resolutely empiricist in outlook, the *philosophes* rejected not only scholasticism but also Cartesian rationalism and the metaphysical impulses that went with it. On the other hand, various metaphysical assumptions central to the natural law tradition had by no means disappeared; in fact the Enlightenment endowed them with a new luster. Thus, the *philosophes* continued to believe in the existence of moral truths as part of natural law, susceptible of formulation with a certainty comparable to that of mathematics and science. Such truths were now asserted with even greater confidence, for they were believed to be based on empirical data, scientifically and rationally analyzed. Even when utilitarianism began to displace natural law theory, a widespread tendency in the second half of the eighteenth century, the confidence in man's ability to arrive at valid normative principles remained. Thus, the new radicalism latent in the Enlightenment rested on the survival of the natural law tradition in empirical and scientific form. While Cartesian rationalism had been formally repudiated, the belief in the existence of moral and metaphysical truths persisted in new guise. From this source came a confidence in the possibility of formulating "incontestable principles" as guides to politics. Precisely because of the rejection of the old rationalism, the new "empiricism" was able to provide a more solid basis for the belief in man's ability to discover moral truths. As Georges Lefebvre observed, Cartesian metaphysics had been eliminated, but not metaphysics itself.[26] Robert Darnton has pointed out that "if there was any 'radicalism' among the abbés and petits marquis of the synthetic Enlightenment, it was their faith in natural law." The abbé Raynal denounced slavery because he considered it 'contrary to the law of nature." The *philosophes* justified many other proposals by reference to what they considered "eternal, immutable values."[27]

Condillac illustrates the way in which many of the *philosophes* managed to reconcile a belief in natural law with a "rejection of rationalist metaphysics and epistemology in favor of empiricism." While preserving the epistemological status of natural law as universally knowable and applicable, Condillac shifted the means of its discovery from reason to experience. Although he denied that the truths of natural law were accessible to man through mere reflection, he took for granted their existence and accessibility: "There is, then, a natural law; that is to say, a law having its foundation in the will of God, and which we discover by the sole use of our faculties. There are no men who are absolutely ignorant of this law. . . . The means we have for discovering this law must not be confused with the principles that give it its authority. Our faculties are the means for knowing it; God is the sole principle from which it emanates. It was in him before he created man.

It is what he consulted when he moulded us, and it is what he wants us to be subject to."[28]

In one way or another the *philosophes* were able to resolve to their satisfaction the antinomy described by Cassirer: "How does the necessity and immutability of the concept of law agree with the proposition that every idea is derived from the senses, and that, accordingly it can possess no other and no higher significance than the various sense experiences on which it is based?"[29] Voltaire was aware of the problem and resolved it with a formula that preserved the substance of natural law theory while detaching it from the notion of innate ideas: "Yet it seems to me, nevertheless, certain that there are natural laws with respect to which human beings in all parts of the world must agree. . . . God endowed man with certain inalienable feelings; and these are the eternal bonds and the first laws of human society."[30] Central to the faith of the Enlightenment was the belief that there are moral truths, discoverable through man's reason and other faculties, which ought to provide the basis for the progressive improvement of mankind. Some such belief as that, together with other aspects of Enlightenment thought, was a primary constituent of the French Revolution.

The radical potentialities inherent in the Enlightenment sprang not only from the rationalist "presumption" denounced by Burke but also from perfectionist and utopian impulses present in Western culture throughout its history. Conservatives in the Burkean tradition have exalted the old regime, as the product of a gradual and organic development, embodying a collective wisdom beyond the reach of individual reason. What Burke and Talmon were unwilling and unable to see, however, was the radical Enlightenment in similar terms. The *philosophes* embodied values, ideals, aspirations, hopes, myths, and principles that had been nurtured by Western history. As an admirer of the manners and ethos of the aristocracy, Burke saw the court of Marie Antoinette and the feudal institutions of the old regime as the expression of a romanticized history. But his social and ideological situation prevented him from seeing Rousseau and Voltaire as a culmination of the moral and intellectual development of Western culture.

The notion that man might build an ideal city or a heavenly city in this world was deeply rooted in the two great traditions on which

Western culture rested. It was part of a more general ideal of perfection to be achieved not only in the next world but in this one. In his survey of the history of the idea of perfection, John Passmore has shown the origins of this notion in both Greek and Jewish culture, the fusion of these disparate elements in Christianity, and the subsequent interplay between them in medieval and early modern Europe. A salient component of the Greek legacy was "the idea of metaphysical perfection, and the ascription of that perfection to a Supreme Being, whether the Being was distinguished from or identified with Nature." In medieval Europe the idea of perfection, like other aspects of Western culture, developed in a Christian matrix. But the presence of specifically Greek elements within Christianity needs to be emphasized, since so much has been made of the Christian origins of the perfectionist and progressive orientation of modern Western thought and since its emergence has often been depicted in terms of the secularization of religious ideas. Hence it is well to keep in mind Passmore's point that various Greek conceptions of perfection were at different times and in different ways both "incorporated into and rejected by" diverse forms of Christianity.[31]

While the Christian origins of the idea of progress are of evident importance, it is necessary to reject one-sided accounts of a direct linear relationship between Christianity and the Enlightenment, with the latter depicted as a secularization of the former. This sort of oversimplification is lucidly presented in Löwith's arresting formulation:

> The Christian scheme of history and the particular scheme of Joachim created an intellectual climate and a perspective in which alone certain philosophies of history became possible which are impossible within the framework of classical thinking. There would be no American, no French, and no Russian revolutions and constitutions without the idea of progress and no idea of secular progress toward fulfillment without the original faith in a Kingdom of God, though one can hardly say that the teaching of Jesus is manifest in the manifestos of these political movements.[32]

Löwith argues that the progressive view of man and his history "originates with the Hebrew and Christian faith in a fulfillment" and ends with "the secularization of its eschatological pattern." Löwith's comment on the New Testament is pertinent, provided that it is taken as only one element in a complex process. "The mere fact that Christianity interprets itself as a *new* Testament, superseding an old one and fulfilling the promises of the latter, necessarily invites further progress and innovations either religious or irreligious and antireligious—hence the derivation of secular irreligions of progress from the eschatology of the church, together with their theological pattern." The words "necessarily" and "derivation" in that sentence represent the sort of one-sided, "idealist" interpretation that has evoked a reaction that depreciates the role of ideas in history. In Byzantium, Christianity invited neither progress nor innovation. In Western culture it did contribute significantly to the eighteenth-century impulse to innovation and to its faith in progress, but only in interplay with various other factors, both social and cultural.

Provided that we eliminate any hint of a single logic working itself out, we can recognize the centrality of Christianity in the process that shaped the perfectionist, utopian, progressive, and eventually revolutionary aspects of Western culture in the different phases of its development. Isaiah Berlin has set the ideas of the Russian Populists of the nineteenth century in a historical framework of Christian belief: "This great Utopian dream, based on simple faith in regenerated human nature, was a vision which the Populists shared with Godwin and Bakunin, Marx and Lenin. Its heart is the pattern of sin and fall and resurrection—of the road to the earthly paradise the gates of which will only open if men find the one true way and follow it."[33]

Preeminent in the Christian legacy to Western culture was the notion that man had been created in the image of God and that he was destined to achieve his godlike potentialities in this world as well as in the next. That idea lay at the heart of perfectionist, progressive, and utopian impulses that entered so actively into the political and ideological history of modern Europe.[34]

Intertwined with the perfectionist strand in Western culture has been a utopian impulse that found expression in a vast literature. Like the idea of perfection, it was rooted in both of the great traditions that entered into the making of Christian Europe. In their magisterial study, the Manuels have described a "profusion of Western utopias unequaled in any other culture." They have traced the "utopian propensity" in the Western world and the myth of a heaven on earth that lies at the heart of it. They characterize utopia as a "hybrid plant, born of the crossing of a paradisiacal other-worldly belief of Judeo-Christian religion with the Hellenic myth of an ideal city on earth." The complex and changing interrelationships between these mutually reinforcing yet contradictory myths shaped the development of utopian thought. Out of this tradition came More's *Utopia*, which introduced the word and the literary form that was to become so pervasive in the sixteenth and seventeenth centuries. The new genre became the vehicle for imaginative accounts of the perfect society. Although still "profoundly Christian," these modern utopias envisaged a "man-made paradise on earth," a usurpation of divine omnipotence. The old vision of perfection had been transferred into the utopian imagination.[35]

By the beginning of the eighteenth century Europe possessed a huge stock of utopian writings. In the course of the century there took place a further proliferation of utopias, which changed their character in the new social and intellectual setting. Many utopian writers dropped the fictional framework and spoke directly to the reformation of mankind. The locus of fantasy shifted from nonexistent places to a future envisaged as within reach of human action. By the end of the eighteenth century a new branch of utopian thought was in evidence: "In these rationalist, systematic utopias whose province was the whole world, the means of reaching utopia was transformed from an adventure story or a *rite de passage* to Elysium into a question of political action: How do you change a present misery into a future happiness in this world?"[36] Just as the Enlightenment helped to turn utopian thought in a new direction, so it was itself affected by the untrammeled fantasies of that genre.

The *philosophes* stood in an ambivalent relationship to the utopians. On the one hand, on the conscious level, they were critical and even contemptuous of the older utopians. There is a significant difference between utopians like Morelly or Deschamps and *philosophes* like Voltaire or Diderot, as indicated in the title of an article on that theme, "Les Utopistes contre les Lumières."[37] The *philosophes* prided themselves on the sort of realism expressed in Rousseau's comment to Mirabeau the elder in 1767: "Your system is very good for the people of utopia, it is not valid for the children of Adam."[38] He defended himself against the charge that *The Social Contract* should be relegated to the "land of chimeras" along with Plato's Republic. At the same time, however, the writings of the *philosophes* were very much in the utopian tradition. Rousseau, Condorcet, and others fit readily into the Manuels' analytical framework. Baczko distinguishes between the true utopians—such as Meslier, Deschamps, Morelly—who were serious about their utopias, and for whom utopia was a profession of faith, from Voltaire and Diderot, who wrote utopian works, in which this was merely a literary device. The *Lumières* and *Utopistes* shared a great deal of common ground. It has been suggested that they represent two faces of the thought of the century. Their attitudes are not so much opposed as complementary. Both were concerned with changing reality. In the case of the utopians, their dream envisaged another society, often one in which social hierarchy and private property had been eliminated. But the *philosophes'* vision of reform also was based on dream and anticipation.[39]

The utopian form enabled writers to carry Enlightenment principles to egalitarian extremes that went well beyond the position taken by the *philosophes*. In 1761 Dom Deschamps took the ideas of the young Rousseau and made them the basis of a communist utopia characterized by the abolition of private property and the elimination of all artificial constraints. The construction of the perfect society was simply a matter of applying sound metaphysical principles. "It is enough to replace moral inequality and property with moral equality and the community of goods to efface all the moral vices that reign over humanity."[40] By means of a revolt of the heart and the spirit it was possible to transfer "our paradise to the only place where we can establish it, I mean in this world."[41] A generation earlier the Curé Jean Meslier had depicted a communal utopia without private property that was to be achieved by violence if necessary. He argued that nature had made all men equal. In violation of this natural equality, private property was at the root of human ills. When the poor came to understand these truths they would rise up and destroy "the odious yoke of their tyrannical Government."[42] In a quieter tone the Abbé Mably also depicted an ideal society in which private property had been abolished. "I believe that equality, the modesty of our needs, preserves in my soul a tranquillity that opposes the birth and growth of passions."[43] In a dialogue Mably has a character state blandly, "I think that no one will contest the obviousness of this proposition, that where no property existed there would not be any of its pernicious consequences."[44] On the one hand, Mably doubted the practical feasibility of the creation of an ideal society, since "men are now too depraved ever to be able to have a wise polity." On the other hand, he could also exhort the people to rebellion: "Choose between revolution and slavery, there is no half-way house."[45] In the most famous of the communist utopias, the Abbé Morelly argued cogently from Enlightenment premises that one can easily conceive of a society in which it is impossible for man to be "depraved or wicked."[46]

The utopian writings are not significant as a source of ideas that "caused" the Revolution or that were "applied" in it. Bronislaw Baczko's warning against simplistic formulations of the relationship between utopias and the Revolution is very much to the point. (His observations are also pertinent to any conception of a linear relationship between ideas and events.) The utopian writings do not contain "omens or horoscopes" of the Revolution. Their authors neither foresaw nor desired such an event. If the utopias prepared minds for that event, they did so indirectly. What Baczko finds totally lacking is the idea of renewal or regeneration to be produced by a political and social revolution.[47]

Yet the utopian literature of the eighteenth century and the attitudes and ideas embedded in it represented an important aspect of the cultural matrix of both the Enlightenment and the French Revolution. In the most general terms, it can be said that the utopias manifested that sense of unlimited possibility that was transferred into politics in 1789. They contributed to the fact that during the Revolution "all seemed possible." The utopian literature had made commonplaces of the most radical notions, familiarized their readers with alternatives to existing society, popularized and even routinized criticism of the established order. In addition, the utopian genre provided a format in which the radicalism of the Enlightenment was pushed to its farthest extreme.[48]

The *philosophes* were neither utopians nor revolutionaries. As Cassirer put it, the Encyclopedists "wanted to ameliorate and to cure." They would have been satisfied merely to eliminate the worst abuses while moving forward gradually. Despite trenchant criticism of the old regime, "this will to reform neither explicitly nor implicitly rose to revolutionary demands."[49] A recognition of the *philosophes'* reformism, however, should not be permitted to obscure the subversive and radical implications of Enlightenment thought as a whole. What is noteworthy is the mixture of overt reformism and latent radicalism. The *philosophes* were moderate in their specific proposals but radical in temper. Diderot is a case in point.

The specific proposals advanced by Diderot remained well within the bounds of modest reform. Yet his doctrine of political authority was "peculiarly audacious" nevertheless.[50] It was audacious not so much because it demanded limitations on authority in a country formally committed to monarchical absolutism but rather in the uncompromising assertion of inherently subversive principles. The first sentence of Diderot's article, "Political Authority," distills the latent radicalism of the Enlightenment: "No man has received from nature the right to command others."[51] He casually takes for granted assumptions which, if adopted as principles of action, would cut the ground from under every government of his day. Only legitimate governments are entitled to obedience; and legitimacy must be justified by reference to nature and reason. Thus, the proposition that "true and legitimate power necessarily has limits" is radical not only because of the proposal to limit power, but because of the premise that men are obliged to obey only when power is "true and legitimate."

Diderot's radicalism also sprang from the assumption that beliefs and institutions should be in harmony with the "law of nature." The trenchant criticism fostered by the Enlightenment—and exemplified so vividly in Diderot—was not something adventitious, merely reinforcing socially determined radical impulses. On the contrary, it was of the very essence of a radicalism which could not have been created merely by the discontents of displaced elites, or by literary men suffering from censorship. In the *Supplement to Bougainville's Voyage*, Orou, speaking for Diderot, opposes the universal truths of the law of nature to the beliefs and practices of the Europeans: "Would you like to know what is good and what is bad in all times and places? Pay close attention to the nature of things and actions, to your relations with your fellow creatures, to the effect of your behavior on your own well-being and on the general welfare. You are mad if you believe that there is anything in the universe, high or low, that can add or subtract from the laws of nature. Her eternal will is that good shall be chosen rather than evil, and the general welfare rather than the individual's well-being. You may decree the opposite, but you will not be obeyed." Orou finds the chaplain's precepts "contrary to nature and contrary to reason," and his laws "contrary to the general order of things." Diderot on a number of occasions made the point that the civil law and the law of nature cannot be permitted to be "in contradiction" without the gravest consequences. In an open letter in 1761 Diderot stated that in a healthy society laws and political obligation must be in harmony with the "law of nature" and not in opposition to it.[52] In this instance Diderot attacked the religious basis of authority and argued, as before, that it could be based only on nature.

Rousseau was not typical of the Enlightenment; nor was his thought a "cause" of the Revolution of 1789. Yet he is essential to an understanding of the Revolution and its genesis, because he explored more profoundly than anyone else the radical intimations and possibilities within European culture in the middle of the eighteenth century. It has been said that among the *philosophes* only Rousseau manifested a "truly revolutionary impulse."[53] Provided that the word "revolutionary" is not taken in a literal and anachronistic sense, such a judgment underlines the point that it was Rousseau above all who expressed the radical implications and potentialities of Enlightenment thought.

At the heart of Rousseau's political thought is his conception of the nature of man. The truly distinctive characteristic of man is freedom: "It is not so much understanding which constitutes the distinction of man among the animals as it is his being a free agent." And "it is above all in the consciousness of this freedom that the spirituality of his soul is shown."[54] Related to freedom is a second quality that also distinguishes men from the animals—"the faculty of self-perfection." Setting out "to form conjectures, drawn solely from the nature of man," Rousseau was relentless in the pursuit of the conclusions that followed. The temper of his thought is as important as its specific content. Confronting the most fundamental social and political questions on the basis of reasoned principle, he goes wherever his reason leads him. It is not just a matter of rejecting the traditional religious and metaphysical sanctions for social and political hierarchy. Rousseau is actively hostile to all forms of domination and subordination. At the very outset of the second Discourse, he defines moral or political inequality as "the different privileges that some men enjoy to the prejudice of others, such as to be richer, more honored, more powerful than they, or even to make themselves obeyed by them." In showing the origins of inequality so defined, Rousseau assumes a position of uncompromising opposition. He refuses even to consider the question of "whether those who command are necessarily worth more than those who obey." He dismisses it as the sort of question that slaves might discuss in the hearing of their masters: it is not suitable for "reasonable and free men who seek the truth."[55] For Rousseau, it is plain that such men will not put up with the traditional forms of inequality or their justification.

The familiar sentences of the *Social Contract* set the tone: "Man is born free, and everywhere he is in chains. Many a man believes himself to be the master of others, who is no less than they, a slave. How did this change take place? I do not know. What can make it legitimate? To this question I hope to be able to furnish an answer." What is noteworthy is not merely the question posed, but also the certitude with which Rousseau presents his answer: "These principles derive from the Nature of Things and are founded upon Reason." The tone matches the substance. Only a legitimate government is entitled to obedience, and Rousseau—like so many of his contemporaries is contemptuous of traditional injunctions to obedience: "Obey the Powers that be. If that means Yield to Force, the precept is admirable but redundant. . . . All power comes from God. Certainly, but so do all ailments. Are we to conclude from such an argument that we are never to call in the doctor?"[56] Not at all. Since "no man is under obligation to obey any but the legitimate powers of the State," the doctor should be called in to determine, on the basis of reason and the nature of things, whether the government is entitled to obedience.

Rousseau's discussion of property as the source of man's misfortunes exemplifies the uncompromising radicalism of his thought. Bluntly, and almost casually, he makes his point in the first two sentences of the second part of the *Discourse on Inequality:* "The first person who, having fenced off a plot of ground, took it into his head to say *this is mine* and found people simple enough to believe him, was the true founder of civil society. What crimes, wars, murders, what miseries and horrors would the human race have been spared by someone who, uprooting the stakes or filling in the ditch, had shouted to his fellow-men: Beware of listening to this imposter; you are lost if you forget that the fruits belong to all and the earth to no one!" At the end of a long catalogue of human afflictions, Rousseau writes: "All these evils are the first effect of property and the inseparable consequence of nascent inequality." In this situation there began to arise, "according to the diverse characters of the rich and the poor, domination and servitude, or violence and rapine." As soon as the rich had experienced "the pleasure of domination," they thought only of "subjugating and enslaving their neighbors: like those famished wolves which, having once tasted human flesh, refuse all other food and thenceforth want only to devour men."[57] This is the spirit of the left. In Rousseau we can see it coming into existence in the matrix of Enlightenment thought.

Rousseau's account of the origins of government carries his critique of domination one stage further. Since the rich also suffered from the "perpetual war" that ensued, it was they who offered order and justice to the poor: "Let us unite to protect the weak from oppression, restrain the ambitious, and secure for everyone the possession of what belongs to him." The offer was accepted with alacrity by "crude, easily seduced men," who had too much avarice and ambition to be able to do without masters for long. "All ran to meet their chains thinking they secured their freedom." In the guise of a summary of the origins of social and political institutions, Rousseau delivers a devastating indictment of the established order:

Such was, or must have been, the origin of society and laws, which gave new fetters to the weak and new forces to the rich, destroyed natural freedom for all time, established forever the law of property and inequality, changed a clever usurpation into an irrevocable right, and for the profit of a few ambitious men henceforth subjected the whole human race to work, servitude and misery.

The last words of the second discourse sum up the radical critique latent in Enlightenment thought. Rousseau denounces "the sort of inequality that reigns among all civilized people" on the grounds that "it is manifestly against the law of nature, in whatever manner it is defined, that a child command an old man, an imbecile lead a wise man, and a handful of men be glutted with superfluities while the starving multitude lacks necessities."[58]

Despite this devastating critique of the established order, however, the second discourse contains no proposals for change. The object of attack is society as such. Hence it is possible to conclude, as Cobban did, that Rousseau's thesis is that since society is the source of human ills the only remedy for a man is to withdraw altogether and flee the corruption inherent in the social state. Such a message also appears to be present in *Emile*, with its emphasis on an educational program designed to overcome the deadly effects of society on the individual.[59]

In the *Social Contract*, however, Rousseau takes a much more favorable view of the possibilities of politics and social life. Men have their destiny in their own hands. A polity based on sound principles will enable man's true nature to find expression. "The passing from the state of nature to the civil society produces a remarkable change in man; it puts justice as a rule of conduct in the place of instinct, and gives his actions the moral quality they previously lacked." In return for surrendering some of the advantages that he enjoyed in the state of nature, man gains far greater ones: "His faculties are so exercised and developed, his mind is so enlarged, his sentiments so ennobled, and his whole spirit so elevated that, if the abuse of his new condition did not in many cases lower him to something worse than what he had left, he should constantly bless the happy hour that lifted him for ever, from the state of nature and from a narrow, stupid animal, made a creature of intelligence and a man."[60] Rousseau's account of the legislator and his task is a splendid statement of the sort of political radicalism that the Enlightenment infused into the history of modern Europe. "Whoso would undertake to give institutions to a People must work with full consciousness that he has set himself to change, as it were, the very stuff of human nature; to transform each individual who, in isolation, is a complete but solitary whole, into a part of something greater than himself, from which, in a sense, he derives his life and his being."[61] Political action could solve the most intractable problem and even transform human nature itself.

The contradiction between the *Social Contract* and other writings of Rousseau has been dealt with variously by historians. Following Lanson and Cassirer, we are emphasizing the unity of his thought. Rousseau's description of his own "great principle" points the way: "That nature has made man happy and good, but that society corrupts him and makes him miserable." This echoes Voltaire's comment that man is not born wicked; he becomes so as he becomes sick. Unlike Voltaire, however, Rousseau concluded that the evil that had been done by society might also be purged by it. Politics would be the means of remedy and transformation. In the *Confessions* Rousseau noted his gradual realization that "everything was basically related to politics" and that governments must be designed "to shape the most virtuous, the most enlightened, the wisest, and, in short, the 'best' people, taking that word in its noblest meaning." In Cassirer's formulation, it was by assigning this great ethical task to politics that Rousseau "accomplished his truly revolutionary act." Guided by reason and good will, men have it within their power to overcome the sins of the past. Cassirer has summed up the conviction, central to every radical movement since, that Rousseau educed from his culture: "In its present form society has inflicted the deepest wounds on humanity; but society alone can and should heal those wounds."[62] Only in the framework of the Enlightenment could such an intense and demanding radicalism have developed.[63]

Rousseau, then, illustrates the radical and utopian aspects of the Enlightenment that were a primary ingredient in the development of the revolutionary spirit from Sieyès to Robespierre. The affinities between Rousseauism and Jacobinism are unmistakable. It was the radical Enlightenment, which received its most brilliant expression in Rousseau, that shaped the revolutionary tradition that France transmitted to nineteenth-century Europe.

When we turn to the role of the Enlightenment in the genesis of the Revolution, however, we cannot draw any sort of direct line from Rousseauist radicalism to the events of 1789 or to the revolutionary spirit that developed in the course of those events. The dominant ideology in France in the 1780s was a *réformisme éclairé* of a different temper.[64] The decisive ideological fact was the presence of a wide range of views expressed in the concepts and language of the Enlightenment. Both opponents and defenders of the monarchy, *parlementaires* and bourgeois, operated within the same field of discourse. The chief agency for the spread of these ideas for a whole generation before 1789 was not primarily the treatises of the *philosophes* but rather sustained political debate, rooted in institutional and ideological conflicts. Keith Baker, in a subtle analysis of three texts from that debate in the mid 1770s—by Malesherbes, Turgot, and Saige—has shown the presence of competing modes of discourse.[65] Considerable ideological diversity within a consensus framework was still conspicuous in 1787–89. There was no single logic or teleology at work. In a sense, it was the absence of revolutionary or protorevolutionary ideas that made possible the unanticipated emergence of what turned out to be a revolutionary situation. Only in the course of events did the latent radicalism of the Enlightenment contribute to the emergence of the Revolution and a new revolutionary ideology.

In the fluid situation created by the events of 1787–88 and the calling of the Estates General, Enlightenment ideals and principles that had become platitudes during the previous generation took on new life during the intense political conflicts that ensued. Although there was little talk of revolution, there was a constant reference to the need for "regeneration." Conceptual and ideological forms that had long been in existence, reinterpreted in the wake of the American Revolution, made possible the novel and unprecedented revolution that took place in France in 1789. While the Enlightenment did not cause the French Revolution or bring it about, it provided the conceptual and symbolic forms that were essential to the event and to the revolutionary ideology. Its explanatory significance lies in the fact that the social and institutional structure in France in the 1780s was compatible with various patterns of conflict. Only the Enlightenment—along with other ideological and historical forms antecedent to the institutional situation—could create the possibility of Revolution in that social and institutional context.

1789

The Enlightenment did not play any single, identifiable role in the genesis of the French Revolution. It was involved in the process in various ways, in dialectical interplay with disparate social and political groups in circumstances that changed in the course of events. Moreover, each of the major events that began with the convening of the

Assembly of Notables in 1787 can be accounted for, to a considerable extent, in social, political, and institutional terms without reference to the Enlightenment: a financial crisis led to the decision to call a meeting of Notables; the *révolte nobiliaire*, which forced the calling of the Estates General, reflected the interests and traditions of the nobility; the ruling of the Paris *parlement* in September 1788 evoked a predictable response from the bourgeoisie, whose actions led to the creation of the National Assembly; royal and noble resistance was a primary "cause" of the insurrectionary activity that culminated in the fall of the Bastille; both urban riots and rural insurrection had direct social and economic "causes." In what sense, then, can it be said that the Enlightenment was central to the process that brought into being the French Revolution of 1789?

Since what turned out to be the French Revolution was unplanned and unintended, we have to reconstruct a process through which actions directed to nonrevolutionary ends became or developed into that unique event. I shall consider the role of the Enlightenment in relation to two clusters of events that were at the center of the process: first, the transformation of the National Assembly in June; second, the fall of the Bastille and its aftermath. In those events I shall describe two interconnected aspects of the role of the Enlightenment: in influencing both the nobility and bourgeoisie to take actions and to envisage goals that went beyond socially determined interests; and in defining and constituting the novel "revolutionary" character of the events of the summer of 1789. Shortly after the fall of the Bastille the men who now saw themselves as revolutionaries defined their Revolution and its principles in the language and ideas of the Enlightenment, which were already embedded in the various events that followed the calling of the Assembly of Notables. It was as an integral component of the events of 1787–89 that the Enlightenment exercised an influence. In July and August of 1789 the new conception of the Revolution emerged from events of which the Enlightenment was a part. This was not a theoretical activity. The Revolution was defined and conceptualized in the course of action. But the action was inseparable from the ideas interwoven into it. And those ideas were not intrinsic to the social and institutional structure.

The interpenetration of ideas and action can be seen at the very beginning. The nobility created what turned out to be a revolutionary situation by compelling the King to call the Estates General. It acted in pursuit of traditional interests. The ideas of the *Lumières* were secondary. By virtue of its acceptance of those ideas, however, the nobility propagated the ideological ingredients that became part of a revolutionary situation and entered into the making of the Revolution. The nobility proclaimed Enlightenment principles not only during the *révolte nobiliaire* but throughout the middle decades of the century. It participated actively in an intense political and social debate based on Enlightenment premises. Established beliefs had lost their prescriptive authority. Moral and political principles had to be justified by appeals to reason and experience. Among both the nobility and the bourgeoisie there developed a belief in the need for reform and improvement. The educated classes accepted a reformist consensus that transcended the differences between individual *philosophes*. As Furet and Richet put it, "All the intellectual effort of the century converges toward a critique of the Church and of despotism, toward tolerance, liberty, equality, the rights of man." The majority of the men who guided opinion in the spring of 1789 had learned that "it is necessary to believe in progress and in education and that the road to human happiness passes through the transformation of the ancien regime." Furet and Richet conclude that "by the 1770's the battle was won among the cultivated public; the ancien regime, religious and political, had been reduced to silence"[66]

It was the parlementary nobility who carried the ideas of the Enlightenment into the political realm in the most direct and forceful way. In a continuing attack on royal "despotism" the *parlement* of Paris invoked the social contract and natural law. The *remontrances* issued in Paris and in the provinces were much more influential than the *philosophes* in spreading disrespect for the monarchy. The *parlements* lodged Enlightenment ideas in political discourse and action. In the *Grandes Remontrances* of April 1753 the *parlement* of Paris proclaimed itself the guardian of "a kind of contract" between the sovereign and the people and argued that "if subjects owe obedience to kings, kings for their part owe obedience to the laws." The *parlement* of Toulouse in 1763 announced that the law must be subject to "the free consent of the nation." By 1788 the *parlement* at Rennes was speaking the language of the Declaration of the Rights of Man: "That man is born free, that originally men are equal, these are truths that have no need of proof." It appealed not only to natural law but also to the general will: "One of the first conditions of society is that the individual will shall always yield to the general will." The Rennes statement was merely repeating the commonplaces of the *réformisme éclairé* that had been propagated by the *parlementaires* for a generation.[67]

Recent research has emphasized the reformist outlook of the nobility on the eve of 1789. It has been argued that the "principles of 1789" were more prominent in the cahiers of the second estate than in those of the third. As Doyle has remarked, "Most surprising of all is the degree to which the nobility as a whole were prepared to consider the claims of the third estate sympathetically."[68] To be sure, the nobility continued to pursue its traditional interests. The ideas of the *Lumières* were useful instruments in the long-standing struggle with the monarchy. Yet it would be misleading to characterize the role of the Enlightenment in narrowly functionalist terms, as providing a rationalization and legitimation of class interests. Nor had the nobility surrendered to new values and beliefs generated by the bourgeoisie. As the embodiment of the *conscience collective* of Europe in this phase of its history, the Enlightenment exercised an influence that transcended the interests of any one class. The dynamism of Enlightenment rationalism intensified—and, to a degree, radicalized—the antimonarchical movement renewed in 1787 in response to Calonne's summons to the Notables.

Having forced the King to call the Estates General the nobility also set the stage for the entry of the bourgeoisie into a turbulent debate and agitation that reached a climax in the creation of the National Assembly in June. In September of 1788 the *parlement* of Paris ruled that the Estates General would be constituted as in 1614, with three orders, each with one vote and the same number of members. The *révolte nobiliaire*, whose appeals to principle had been accepted at face value by the bourgeoisie and the common people, now appeared as no more than yet another manifestation of aristocratic self-aggrandizement. Sieyès' pamphlet expressed the fury of the bourgeoisie. These events are part of the answer to the question posed by Doyle, in reponse to the sometimes extravagant claims of revisionist historiography: "If the nobility and the bourgeoisie had so much in common, why did they become such implacable enemies in 1789?"[69] They became enemies, in part, because the ruling of the Paris *parlement* made it clear that the principles proclaimed by the nobility presupposed the persistence of its social and political hegemony. These developments, in turn, contributed to the events of June.

On June 10 the deputies of the Third Estate took what has been characterized as their "first revolutionary step." They voted 493–41 to invite the nobility and clergy to verify credentials in common, and to proceed independently even if the other two orders declined the invitation. Thus they made plain that they would ignore legal and constitutional precedent and act unilaterally to give France a new constitution. "On this date," Doyle has written, "the bourgeoisie became revolutionary; and the transfer of power which lay at the heart of the French Revolution began." A few days later, joined by a few deputies from the clergy, the third estate declared itself to be a National Assembly. On June 20 the Assembly took the tennis court oath not to disband until its self-defined task was finished. It declared that "the National Assembly has been called upon to draft a constitution for the kingdom, effect the regeneration of public order and maintain the true principles of the monarchy." The members vowed not to separate "until the constitution of the kingdom shall be laid and established on secure foundations."[70]

What was the connection between the Enlightenment and the illegal and unconstitutional actions taken by the respectable and law-abiding deputies of the Third Estate in the middle of June? As in the case of the nobility in 1787–88, the Enlightenment reinforced and magnified impulses rooted in practical circumstances. It did so in a rather paradoxical way, however. On the one hand, it can be said that the deputies were so insistent in June precisely because of the formally moderate and nonrevolutionary character of their demands. They took their stand in behalf of consensus beliefs that had been the commonplaces of political discourse for a generation. They were outraged at the violation of those principles by those who had been proclaiming them for so long. At the same time, however, they were inspirited and emboldened by the rationalist radicalism of the Enlightenment. They were acting in behalf of self-evident truths and incontestable principles.

The role of the Enlightenment in the genesis of the events of June can be seen in two men who took the lead in the formation of the National Assembly, Joseph Mounier and the Abbé Sieyès. Mounier, who also helped to draft the Declaration of the Rights of Man, was the more moderate of the two. He had proposed the tennis court oath in order to head off Sieyès' suggestion that the National Assembly move to Paris, where it would be under popular protection. By October he found himself far to the right on the political spectrum and soon went into exile. Precisely because he was a reformer, not a revolutionary, Mounier exemplifies the latent radicalism of *réformisme éclairé*.

In February of 1789 Mounier urged the doubling of the third on the basis of the principles of consensus liberalism that had been propagated during the previous generation. He remained firmly committed to "the independence of the crown and the maintenance of its prerogatives," including the royal veto. On the question of the composition and organization of the Estates General and the need for a new constitution, however, Mounier called for swift and decisive action: "I shall not be so foolish as to think that the fundamental bases of the constitution must be laid down slowly; we must profit from the favorable moment, for liberty is like fortune; it easily escapes from the indolent. . . . Frenchmen, make haste to build the foundations of a constitution in the torrent of despotism while its flow is still diminished." Solidly conservative, albeit in the progressive Whig mode that was to flourish across the Channel, Mounier nevertheless took a radical line on the great issues that confronted France at the beginning of 1789: "The coming Estates General will be useless if the orders are not joined together and the votes counted by head." The reason that he gave indicates the extent to which a moderate and conservative leader of the Notables had arrived at a position, nourished by Enlightenment liberalism, that made the revolutionary action in June appear as no more than a modest proposal that would commend itself to responsible men. Deliberation by head "can alone procure a constitution for us," and "we must therefore either accept this form or resign ourselves to remaining slaves of the ministers and the aristocracy." The familiar denunciation of despotism took on a new significance in the changed ideological and political situation in the spring of 1789. Mounier was appealing to the people in terms that went well beyond conventional

attacks on ministerial despotism: "Good citizens will not think it possible to hesitate. They will judge that to become free they must risk
the so-called inconveniences of deliberation by head; that the worst of
evils is to languish in servitude after having had the hope of liberty."[71]

Mounier called for a second chamber in which the distinction between the three orders has been abolished. Confident that his proposal
included safeguards against radical change—the royal veto and the upper chamber—he invoked principles that led readily to the formation
of a National Assembly in June:

We must, if we wish to enjoy liberty for any length of time, renounce this
unfortunate mistrust that divides the orders; and we must see in a gentleman
merely a citizen who has been decorated, who is interested as the most obscure of men in resisting arbitrary power, demanding good laws, and remaining free.[72]

Mounier called for the elimination of "the barbarous designations of
commoners and Third Estate." In conformity with "true principles,"
no attention should be paid to a citizen's rank. Sieyès voiced the same
principles, but in a more radical spirit.

Sieyès' pamphlet, *What Is the Third Estate?*, achieved an extraordinary popularity during the months of debate that preceded the convening of the Estates General. In addition to doubling of the third and
vote by head, he called for the next step that followed logically:

There you have enough to demonstrate the obligation that the Third Estate is
going to have to form by itself alone a National Assembly, and to authorize,
in the name of reason and equity, the claim that this order may have to delib-
erate and vote for the entire nation without exception.[73]

That sentence encapsulates much of the revolution of June and July.
"In the name of reason and equity" is not a rhetorical flourish, but an
expression of Enlightenment assumptions that made radical actions
appear necessary, natural, and in conformity with the truth. Sieyès
confidently rested his case on the validity of his principles. While conceding that "such principles will appear *extravagant* to most readers,"
he promised that he would press forward, since his own role, like that
of all patriot writers, "consists of presenting the truth." He took an
exalted view of that role: "If everyone were to think *the truth*, there

would be no difficulty about making even the greatest changes if they offered socially useful objectives. What better can I do than to aid with all my strength to spread this truth that prepares the way?"[74]

The Enlightenment had no direct influence on the sequence of events that followed the formation of the National Assembly. At the end of June, the King, at the behest of the Court nobility, initiated military action that was clearly intended to destroy the Assembly. The fall of the Bastille, the decisive event in the transition from the events of June to the Revolution of July, represented the successful defense of the National Assembly by the bourgeoisie, supported by the urban masses. It had been preceded by quasi-insurrectionary activity in various cities that had been occurring sporadically but extensively throughout the year. In a number of places municipal power had already been taken over by bourgeois groups. As Godechot puts it, "The Parisian rising of July 14th, resulting from the provincial insurrectional movements which had begun the previous January, provoked in turn a great national revolutionary impulse."[75]

The fall of the Bastille and the events surrounding it were immediately recognized as an "important and extraordinary revolution which cannot fail to bring about a considerable change in the political system of France." The words were those of the Ambassador of Saxony on July 19. The Portuguese Ambassador reported that "in all the world's annals there is no mention of a revolution like this one. . . . If he had not witnessed it he would not dare to describe it, for fear the truth should be considered as a fable." What set this insurrection apart in the eyes of the Portuguese ambassador was the dramatic character of the events that unfolded in the greatest country in Europe: "A King of France in an army coach, surrounded by the bayonets and muskets of a large crowd, finally forced to display on his head the cockade of liberty." A report to Kaunitz in Austria also depicted a mass uprising on a scale that had never occurred before: "However unbelievable the Revolution that has just been accomplished may appear, it is none the less absolutely certain that from now on the city of Paris has assumed the role of a King in France, and that it can, if it pleases, send an army of forty to fifty thousand citizens to surround the Assembly and dictate the laws to it."[76] These observers were recording the occurrence of a spectacular version of the sort of "revolution" that had been anticipated and even predicted. A lawyer in Nantes wrote in February of 1789: "The Revolution will certainly take place in Brittany without trouble and without civil dissension if we are helped by the government, with stress and trouble if we lack the necessary support." A few months before another resident of Nantes perceived a revolution as having occurred already: "The dazzling insurrection in the city of Nantes came along to precipitate the Revolution. A newly created nobleman renouncing his privileges, a crowd of distinguished citizens signing a petition and bearing it in pomp to the *hôtel de ville,* opulent merchants contributing funds to send twelve deputies to Versailles: all these extraordinary happenings produced a sort of explosion."[77] On June 9 Arthur Young had described "nests and hotbeds of sedition and revolt" in Paris.[78] As the men of July defined the nature and significance of their Revolution, however, they infused it with a new content that went beyond the traits depicted in the ambassadorial accounts.

Along with the older notion of revolution as an insurrection producing a considerable change in the political system, the revolutionaries—as they now perceived themselves—also proclaimed the Revolution as a great historic event that would usher in a new order, based on immutable principles of truth and justice. This was what Robespierre had in mind when he rejoiced, in a letter written at the end of July, that "the present Revolution has made us see in a few days the greatest events that the history of men can present."[79] An English doctor in Paris accepted the revolutionaries' view of events in an enthusiastic letter to his wife: "I have been witness to the most extraordinary revolution that perhaps ever took place in human society. A great and wise people struggled for freedom and the rights of humanity; their courage, prudence and perseverance have been rewarded by success, and an event which will contribute to the happiness and prosperity of millions of their descendants has taken place with very little loss of blood, and with but few days' interruption to the common business of the place."[80] The men of 1789 saw themselves engaged in a great historic enterprise, in the vanguard of reason and progress. The aim of their revolution was nothing less than the establishment of "the empire of justice and liberty on earth." Thus, in the course of events in July hitherto separate notions of "revolution" were fused into the conception of the French Revolution proclaimed by the revolutionaries.

A national insurrection would create a new order of things, based on the rights of man.

Beginning at the end of July, the uprising of the peasants in the countryside radicalized the Revolution that was being acclaimed by the bourgeois revolutionaries in the cities. The rural insurrection led to the August decrees and "the abolition of feudalism." As a result of mass action, in which the Enlightenment was not a causal factor, the Revolution now comprised not only constitutional reform but also sweeping changes in social and economic institutions. By the end of August, a fully developed revolutionary ideology had come into being. These developments, in turn, imparted a revolutionary character to the Declaration of the Rights of Man, whose text repeated principles that had become commonplace in the 1770s and 1780s. The Enlightenment was constitutive of the revolutionary ideology and the Revolution.

In a speech on the suffrage question, prepared for delivery to the Constituent Assembly in 1791, Robespierre celebrated the "glorious insurrection that saved France" and urged the Assembly to remain true to its principles and continue its "sacred mission." The speech is a convenient summary of the nature and significance of the Revolution as viewed by a broad spectrum of revolutionary opinion at the end of 1789. He reminded the deputies that they were leading a people "passing rapidly from servitude to liberty" and "a new order of things." They were the men called upon to carry out France's revolutionary mission: "Eternal Providence has summoned you alone since the origin of the world to re-establish on earth the empire of justice and liberty, in the heart of the most vivid enlightenment that has ever instructed the public reason, in the midst of the almost miraculous circumstances that it has seen fit to assemble, in order to assure you the power to give man his happiness, his virtues, and his basic dignity."[81]

We have concentrated our attention on the bourgeois revolutionaries, the chief agents in the making of the Revolution, defining its character, and shaping the revolutionary ideology in its various forms. The Enlightenment was interwoven into the outlook and actions of the bourgeoisie and their interpretation of the Revolution. Yet the "urban masses" (an umbrella term whose all-inclusiveness is useful at this point) provided essential support. In the defense of the National Assembly that culminated in the fall of the Bastille, the common people provided the shock troops who took to the streets. The bourgeoisie relied heavily on such support. In the first of the great *journées*, as in those that followed, the *menu peuple* were in vanguard. The municipal uprisings earlier in 1789 and the *révolte nobiliaire* also had been supported by rioting and popular disturbances.

In accounting for the activity of the urban masses in the June and July of 1789 there is no need to spend much time on the Enlightenment. In this instance economic conditions exercised a direct influence on behavior. Bread riots were a frequent occurrence in the eighteenth century. In the summer of 1789 the common people were once again protesting against immediate and intolerable deprivation. Both before and during 1789 there is a clear correlation between price levels and riotous behavior. As Furet puts it, the grain or tax riot was "a relatively classic occurrence under the ancien regime." One could explain "the popular urban uprisings of June-July by the economic crisis, the price of bread, unemployment, the commercial treaty between England and France, and so forth."[82] Urban riots and insurrections were common throughout Europe, especially after the middle of the century, in such cities as London, Naples, Madrid, Geneva, Lyon, and Amsterdam.

It would be a mistake, however, to interpret the behavior of the *menu peuple* exclusively in terms of an instinctive response to economic deprivation. Even the protests of the mid-century expressed what has been called "the moral economy of the crowd," and are not to be understood simply as a blind reaction to hunger and want. George Rudé has noted "the inherent, intrinsic traditional body of ideas and beliefs arising within the direct experience or folk-memory of the common people." The bread riots at Dijon in 1775 represented that sort of elemental protest, "innocent of any political intrusion," and without links to the ideas of the *philosophes*. By the 1780s mass protest of this sort, expressing a range of attitudes from anger to "moral economy," became linked to public events, which contributed to the development of political consciousness among the common people. Even before 1789 such activity often assumed a political cast. As early as 1784 crowds in Dijon were shouting "Vive le Parlement." In support of the *révolte nobiliaire* and in the attack on royal "despotism" popular slogans voiced the ideas of the Enlightenment. There was a further *prise de conscience* as the common people of Dijon shifted their allegiance to the National Assembly. In other cities also, especially in Paris, a similar pattern occurred: the emergence of a popular political consciousness, first in response to the agitation of the nobility and then to the pamphlet campaign of the third estate.[83] All of the events that contributed to the education of the common people embodied the language and ideas of the Enlightenment. In addition, moreover, as Robert Darnton has shown, an especially radical and subversive version of the familiar ideas of the *philosophes* was being purveyed in the underground press in the 1780s.[84] While these ideological and symbolic forms did not "cause" the mass uprisings of 1789, they were important ingredients in the process that shaped the Revolution.

The fall of the Bastille and the popular uprisings that accompanied it were important first and foremost for political and military reasons, in defending the National Assembly against the threat of force.[85] Underlying that joint action were the social links between middling bourgeoisie and the upper working classes along with shared political ideas and attitudes. But those events were also important in molding the iconography and ideology of the inchoate Revolution, as an uprising of "the people" in behalf of universal principles. The participation of the masses was visible confirmation of the claim to universality that lay at the core of the nascent revolutionary ideology. That participation and its ideological celebration were facilitated by a discourse based on the Enlightenment. Ideological and symbolic forms contributed not only to joint action by diverse social groups but also to the emergence of a view of the Revolution as an enterprise of "the people" building a new social and political order incorporating the rights of man. Thus, the events of July not only defended the "Revolution," but also helped to define the characteristics that were to constitute it as a primary component in the political consciousness of Europe.[86]

While the urban masses in the summer of 1789 played an important but essentially supportive role in relation to the decisive initiatives taken by bourgeois revolutionaries, even then their presence contributed to the emergence of a more militantly populist and activist ideology, which found expression in September in the *Ami du peuple* so different in temper not only from the cahiers but also from the Declaration. Moreover, in the next few years the *sans-culottes*, organized in their sections, intervened aggressively to radicalize the Revolution. Their activity paved the way for the coming to power of the Jacobins in 1793.

JACOBINISM

The new revolutionary mentality that took shape in the course of events in the summer of 1789 received its fullest expression in Jacobinism. To a large extent it was through Jacobinism that the French Revolution exercised a direct influence on the development of radical politics and ideology in Europe. Robespierre embodied and articulated the mystique of revolution that became the hallmark of the far left. The Jacobins took seriously the new ideology, considered the principles of 1789 as truly universal, and set out to apply them accordingly. They conceived of "completing" the Revolution by carrying out its fundamental principles. Contributing to these ideological developments was the social basis of Jacobinism, in a middling bourgeoisie hostile to the classes above them. But the dynamism of Jacobinism and its revolutionary faith was rooted in the rationalist radicalism of the Enlightenment. There is an unbroken ideological continuity from Sieyès and the National Assembly to Robespierre and the Convention.

The rationalist radicalism at the core of Jacobinism is vividly present in Sieyès. Early in 1789 he drew an apt distinction between administrators and philosophers, criticizing those who "confuse the measured and cautious conduct of the administrator . . . with the freedom of the philosopher." Sieyès left no doubt about his preference for the philosopher: "His duty is to introduce sound social principles, in direct proportion to the number of minds that are corroded by feudal barbarism. When the philosopher is driving a road, he is concerned with *errors;* to make progress he must destroy them without pity." Sieyès' Legislator looks much like his philosopher. He must rid himself of the "frightful experience of the centuries" and think of true principles. Sieyès acclaimed a principle that Burke was to find so appalling: "Reason has no love for mystery; it acts only by means of a great expansion; only by striking everywhere does it hit the mark. . . ." He rebuked those who talk "nonsense about what they call the importance of practice and uselessness or perils of theory." The aim of such rationally ordered change was nothing less than the "regenera-

tion" of France, a word with utopian and religious overtones. It recurs
in Sieyès and has been characterized as "one of the most abused words
of 1789." A primary aim of the Estates General was "national regeneration." The aspiration to radical regeneration was even more pronounced a few years later. In all these ways the ideological affinities
between Sieyès and Robespierre are clear. There is something to be
said for the suggestion that the course of events between 1789 and 1794
may be understood, in part, in terms of "the radicalization of an ideology in accordance with the laws of its own dynamism."[87]

By 1791 Robespierre had already defined the essentials of Jacobinism in terms of a full commitment to the principles of 1789. Judging
the work of the Constituent Assembly against "the principles of equality and justice," he found it wanting. From this perspective he denounced the distinction between active and passive citizens and demanded the revocation of the decrees establishing a monetary
requirement for the suffrage. The form of his argument—and much
of its substance—has echoed in various forms on the Left ever since.
Robespierre proposed to do nothing less than test the offending decrees against the "immutable laws of human society." Judged in the
light of such "self-evident truths," the decrees stood condemned as
"the most flagrant violation of the rights of man." In an idiom that
was to recur in different form in the next century, he inveighed against
the "absurd contradictions" inherent in the distinction between active
and passive citizens. He appealed to "the unchangeable principles that
the eternal legislator has himself engraved in the hearts of men." He
even argued that the decrees did not really need to be formally re-
voked: "they are essentially void, because no human power, not even
yours, was competent to inscribe them." "It is to the immutable decrees of the eternal legislator placed in the reason and hearts of all men
before you ever inscribed them in your code that I appeal against the
dispositions which infringe them and must disappear before them."[88]

Robespierre combined the rationalist universality of the principle of
equal political rights with a populist assault on "the rich and the powerful." While his denunciation reflects the latent hostility of the middling bourgeoisie toward the social strata above them, the intensity of
Robespierre's critique, so characteristic of the socialist movements of
the nineteenth century, also reflects a rationalist eagerness to carry

general principles to their logical conclusion. The principle of equal rights, rigorously applied, underlay Robespierre's attack on "this extreme inequality of fortunes that concentrates all wealth in the hands of the few." A paragraph dealing with equality of rights ends with this ringing conclusion: "To place the public authority entirely in the hands of the rich, is therefore to flout all the principles that govern society." Unfortunately, however, the rich and powerful "have reasoned otherwise." They have built their case and the constitution on "absurd and cruel prejudices." These had to give way to the empire of reason.[89]

The Enlightenment is woven into the texture of Robespierre's famous speech of February 5, 1794. "It is time to mark clearly the aim of the Revolution," he said. Like other revolutionaries, he acclaimed the link between the revolution and the thought of the century: "We wish in a word to fulfil the course of nature, to accomplish the destiny of mankind, to make good the promises of philosophy, to absolve Providence from the long reign of tyranny and crime." They would substitute "the empire of reason for the tyranny of custom." Fundamental to Robespierre's radicalism is a vision of the regenerative power of political revolution. Through revolutionary action the principles of philosophy can be put into practice, thus transforming not only the political and social order but human nature itself: "We wish an order of things where all low and cruel passions are enchained by the laws, all beneficent and generous feelings awakened; . . . where distinctions arise only from equality itself; . . . where industry is an adornment to the liberty that ennobles it, and commerce the source of public wealth, not simply the monstrous riches for a few families." While Robespierre's hostility to "monstrous riches" can hardly be interpreted as a deduction from the premises of the Enlightenment, it is set in the context of a rationalist radicalism that requires action to deal with conditions that are perceived as an evident violation of the principles of justice. His utopianism rests on rationalist foundations. There is no limit to what the revolution can achieve: "We wish to substitute in our country morality for egotism, probity for a mere sense of honor, principle for habit, duty for etiquette, . . . a people magnanimous, powerful, and happy for a people lovable, frivolous, and wretched—that is to say, all the virtues and miracles of the Republic for all the vices and puerilities of the monarchy." Thus, his aim is nothing less than "the dawn of universal felicity."[90] The grandiloquent language is not mere rhetoric, providing a form for something more fundamental. It expresses the extravagant hopes that entered into the radical phase of the Revolution and which also constituted the heart of the left at the moment when it came into being.

Robespierre admired the ideas of Rousseau, which are interwoven into his social and political thought. The connection is significant, provided that it is not interpreted in terms of "influence." Albert Soboul's discussion of the relationship between Rousseauism and Jacobinism provides a useful approach. As a Marxist he puts heavy emphasis on the social basis of Jacobinism in the middle strata of the bourgeoisie. Like other historians, he notes that Rousseauism had little direct effect on the policies put into effect by the Jacobins in 1793–94, when the exigencies of events and circumstances were decisive. Having established those limits, however, Soboul describes links to Rousseau. Although the constitution of the year 1793 was suspended before taking effect, it was "incontestably elaborated in the spirit of the *Social Contract*." Although the Jacobins' debt to Rousseau did not include the adoption of specific doctrines or theories, it was considerable nevertheless: "Even more than by a theory derived from Rousseauism, Jacobinism is defined by a political temperament and still more by a revolutionary technique; but what does it owe here to the author of the *Social Contract?* From Jean-Jacques to the Jacobin the link *[parenté]* is not illusory." Affinities of political temperament linked Rousseau and the Jacobins: "In both one finds the same certainty of being right, the same pride, the same passionate attachment to principles—the same rigidity of attitude, often masking, in the case of the Jacobin a fluidity of doctrine. Finally, intolerant, sectarian, they both apply themselves to a passionate quest for unity."[91] The shared characteristics of Rousseauism and Jacobinism derived from the Enlightenment of which both were an expression.

It was not 1789 that so profoundly affected the consciousness and politics of Europe in the nineteenth century, but rather the radical revolution of 1792–94 and the revolutionary ideology of Jacobinism. The Revolution exercised its influence most directly and pervasively by way of Marxist socialism. It was chiefly in this remarkable and ambiguous body of thought—dedicated to the proposition that bourgeois ideology and institutions were the primary obstacle to the emancipation of mankind—that the revolutionary myth entered into the history of Europe and the world in the twentieth century.

CHAPTER THREE

Marxism and Revolution

The extraordinary impact of Marxism on the history of the modern world is plain enough. It shaped the character of socialist and working-class movements in Europe at the end of the nineteenth century and provided the ideological foundations for the two great revolutions of the twentieth century. Although these events and developments were affected by social and institutional forces, Marx's ideas were central to the processes that produced them. The ironic disjunction between Marx's aspirations and Soviet reality poses the problem of the role of ideas in history concretely and insistently. While there is bound to be disagreement about the nature and significance of the influence of Marxism, there can be no doubt about its magnitude.

The impact of Marxism on the history of Europe is a standing refutation of any theory of history, including Marx's, which implicitly or explicitly asserts the primacy of socioeconomic or "material" forces and assigns a subordinate role to ideas. In fact, what is noteworthy about the historical influence of Marxism is the extent to which it ran against the grain of patterns determined by the social and economic structure. The development of industrial capitalism did not produce a revolutionary proletariat but rather a working class predisposed to what Lenin called "trade union consciousness." To the extent that the consciousness of the proletariat was determined by social being—as required by Marx's theory of history—it was nonrevolutionary; to the extent that the proletariat became revolutionary (in the Marxist sense) it became so as a consequence of the French Revolution, as interpreted by Marx. What turned out to be historically effective was the myth that lies at the core of Marxist doctrine: "It is not a question of what this or that proletarian, or even the whole proletariat, at the moment *regards* as its aim. It is a question of *what the proletariat is*, and what, in accordance with this *being*, it will historically be compelled to do."[1] It was the acceptance of this myth, not capitalism, which was responsible for the support given by a segment of the European working class to a revolutionary socialist program at the turn of the century. Similarly, the occurrence of a "proletarian revolution" in Russia took place despite the primitive state of industrial development. The revolutionary politics of twentieth-century Europe owed much more to Marxism than to capitalism.

Unlike the Enlightenment, Marxism was the unique product of the thought of a single individual, who took a complex intellectual inheritance (of which the Enlightenment was an important component) and out of it constructed a coherent, all-embracing ideological system. Whereas the Enlightenment was the expression of a phase in the history of European culture and society, Marxism was the creation of one man. (Engels, of course, was an invaluable coadjutor.) Hence it represents a very different kind of intellectual force, illustrating another aspect of the role of ideas in the historical process: the ability of an individual to create new forms out of the unknown possibilities latent in the cultural legacy he has received from the past. Marx exemplifies, in extreme form, the presence of unpredictable freedom and creativity in history. The example of Luther also comes to mind, as it did to the young Marx: "Germany's revolutionary past is theoretical, it is the Reformation. Once it was the monk's brain in which the revolution began, now it is in the philosopher's."[2] Luther is remarkable in that he was the initiator of the events whose theological basis he had articulated. Whereas Luther's ideas reflect preexisting theological patterns in late-fifteenth-century Europe, Marx created an intellectual and ideological system of striking originality that became the dominant form of socialism in the course of the nineteenth century.

The fact that Marx, unlike Luther, did not participate in the events and developments in which his ideas were involved magnifies the difficulty of assessing the impact of Marxism on the political history of modern Europe. Whereas the nature of the connection between the Enlightenment and the French Revolution or between late nineteenth century European culture and fascism can be established with a fair degree of precision, one can do no more than sketch a range of possibilities in assessing the influence of Marxism. At the simplest level, there is the matter of the gap in time between the formulation of Marxist doctrine and its embodiment in socialist movements. Whatever Marx's influence on the Bolshevik Revolution, it was exercised only indirectly through Lenin and Leninism. In addition, of course, a multitude of other historical developments intervened before Marxism played a part in the events of the twentieth century. One's conclusions must have an even more tentative and provisional character than usual. Having said that, however, the fact remains that it is quite impossible to understand the history of the modern world without considering the "role" or "influence" of Marxism. Hence there are a number of questions that have to be asked, even if the answers remain elusive.

THE IMPACT OF MARXIST SOCIALISM

Marx constructed a socialist theory of great intellectual and moral power by fusing into a coherent whole ideas and beliefs derived from disparate traditions of Western culture. It has often been noted that Marxism was a synthesis of French politics and German philosophy. In addition to the radical imperatives inherent in the Enlightenment and the French Revolution, Marxism embodied the even more exalted aspirations that had developed within Christianity and German idealism.[3] From Hegel and the young Hegelians came the ultimate goal of Marx's socialism, the total liberation of humanity, the overcoming of alienation, "the realization of philosophy." This vision of human emancipation went beyond the *philosophes'* notion of the elimination of artificial restraints on human activity. Marx was the most utopian of the utopian socialists. But he distinguished himself from his predecessors by the claim that his program was grounded in the objective forces of history. And it was his theory of history, drawing on the Enlightenment and German historicism, that welded the disparate components of his socialism into a cohesive whole. The highest ideals of Western culture were linked to a revolutionary tradition that promised immediate practical results. The proletarian revolution, based on the Jacobin model, was depicted as the predestined culmination of an historical process determined by the most powerful material forces.

This interpretation, emphasizing the importance of the specific content of Marxism in relation to competing forms of socialism, may be counterposed to other views which, in one way or another, tend to depict socialism as the direct consequence of industrialization or industrial capitalism or modernization. Schumpeter's account of the capitalist origins of socialism is a case in point: "Capitalism creates a critical frame of mind which, after having destroyed the moral authority of so many institutions, in the end turns against its own; the bourgeois finds to his amazement that the rationalist attitude does not stop at the credentials of kings and popes but goes on to attack private property and the whole system of bourgeois values."[4] Over against this sort of interpretation, there is much to be said for Talmon's warning against deriving specific ideological and political patterns directly from the Industrial Revolution: "It was not that the Industrial Revolution by engendering new conditions gave rise to new ideas. The French Revolution, its ideas and traumas, conditioned men to experience and interpret in a way that would have been quite unthinkable had the technological and social-economic changes taken place earlier."[5] What was decisive was the conjuncture of social, intellectual, and ideological developments.

Early-nineteenth-century socialism was above all a utopia, a profoundly radical response to the first impact of industrialization and urbanization. That response was shaped not only by the Enlightenment and the French Revolution but also by the Counter-Enlightenment and the reaction against liberal individualism. Hence a profusion of socialist ideas and theories emerged in the second quarter of the nineteenth century. By the end of two decades of unprecedented ideological ferment it was by no means clear whether any one of the various versions of socialism would become dominant and, if so, whether it would exercise a significant influence on the outlook and behavior of the new working class.

By the end of the eighteenth century, socialism was an inevitable next stage in the development of the new radicalism that had taken shape in the course of the eighteenth century. That is, some men of the left were bound to come to the conclusion that the principles of liberty and equality, and perhaps the "postulate of a rational order," required the transformation of the emerging industrial society into something radically different. Even without the French Revolution the radical Enlightenment would have contributed to the emergence of some sort of socialist doctrine. The socialism of Robert Owen or Louis Blanc rested on ideological foundations that presupposed reformist action. The Revolution, however, added the possibility of revolutionary socialism, in the mode of Babeuf or Blanqui. In addition, very different intellectual and ideological forces entered into the development of socialist utopianism. The romantic critique of liberal individualism lent itself to the socialist affirmation of communal, organic, and collectivist values. The socialist vision of Fourier and Saint Simon differed substantially from that of Blanc or Blanqui. Moreover, socialists who differed on other matters joined in perceiving liberal economics and classical political economy as the chief ideological bulwark of the capitalist system. The forms of *vormärzlich* socialism in the 1840s were multifarious indeed.[6]

By virtue of its intellectual and moral power Marxism became the preeminent form of socialism in Europe. By the end of the nineteenth century, it had established its dominance among intellectuals and in the mass parties of the industrial working class. It was Marxism that kept alive revolutionary socialism at a time when both socioeconomic and ideological forces fostered laborism and reformism. Marx's version of socialism left its distinctive imprint on mass movements that otherwise would have assumed a different character. In the final section I shall consider two aspects of the impact of Marxist ideas: the adoption of a Marxist program by the German Social Democratic party and the influence of Marxism on Leninism and the Bolshevik Revolution.

Once we move beyond the obvious fact that Marxism has exercised a prodigious influence on socialist and working-class movements, the problem of specifying the nature of that influence and assessing its significance is formidable indeed. First of all, it affected and entered into a host of events and movements, each the product of historical processes comprising a multitude of elements. Second, Marx's thought was an immensely complex entity, encompassing doctrines that were often contradictory; it was not static, but changed over time. There is no single logic that can be identified. Third, by the end of the nineteenth century there was a number of authentic "Marxisms," each emphasizing different aspects of Marx's thought and each reflecting particular historical circumstances. A case in point is the familiar problem of defining the relationship between Marxism and Leninism.

Within Marxism, which doctrines were of importance from the standpoint of historical consequences? The answer to that question is likely to be affected by the historian's ideological and philosophical orientation. An obvious danger, drawing a straight line from Marxism to the Gulag, is easily avoided, since it embodies a simplistic view of the historical process. Marxism clearly did not embody an immanent logic, entailing specific consequences. At the same time, however, it would be a mistake to rule out inquiry into the question of the practical implications of Marxist doctrines. The evident contradiction between Marx's aspirations and the character of the regime established by the Bolshevik Revolution is part of the historical reality. The question of the nature of the connection between Marxist doctrine and the political history of the twentieth century is one that no historian can ignore. As a philosopher has put it, "the one thing that most readers have always wanted to learn from books about Marxism is how much responsibility Marx must bear for the authoritarian character of regimes that claim to follow his doctrines."[7] While the historian cannot assess that kind of "responsibility," in the moral or legal sense, he has to consider the question of the role of Marxism in the process that brought into existence the totalitarian regimes that proclaim his doctrines.

We shall single out three interconnected components as fundamental to an understanding of the impact of Marxism on European history: the theory of history, the doctrine of class struggle, and the concept of revolution. These ideas stood in a relationship of tension and even contradiction to Marx's goal of human emancipation. The crux of the matter was Marx's ambivalent relationship to liberalism and the French Revolution. On the one hand he wanted to carry forward the revolutionary sequence that had been stopped by Thermidor; and the *Communist Manifesto* included a ringing reaffirmation of the libertarian aim of the Enlightenment and the French Revolution—a society in which the free development of each is the condition for the free development of all. At the same time, however, Marx reviled bourgeois liberalism as an ideological obstacle that had to be removed. As George Lichtheim has emphasized, Marx presented his socialism as an alternative to liberalism: "If liberalism represented a vision of the social whole encompassing philosophy, history, politics, and economics, then Marx's formulation of socialism was the only alternative doctrine that was both coherent and universal. For Marx challenged liberalism not in this or that respect, but all over the field."[8] The materialist theory of history and the doctrine of class struggle led Marx to denounce as bourgeois specific principles and practices—the notion of individual rights, the apparatus of parliamentary government, and fundamental liberal values—that were in fact prerequisite to the kind of society that Marx had in mind.

On this view, then, Marxism contained internal contradictions that contributed to the defeat of his project for human emancipation. If we wish to account for the unintended consequences of Marx's thought, we have to look not only at external developments but also within the doctrine itself. To be sure, a great deal depended on circumstances. The Marxism of Kautsky differed from Rosa Luxemburg's, and both those versions differed profoundly from Lenin's. These divergent Marxisms played their part in very different situations in Germany and in Russia. But the contradictions that lay at the very core of Marxism and the manner in which they were dealt with, as the doctrine was interpreted and reinterpreted, were to have practical consequences.

In dealing with the impact of Marxism, we confront irony on a number of different levels and in different forms. First of all, there is the matter of unintended consequences on a vast scale: the establishment of a totally repressive regime on the basis of an ideology that aspired to a total liberation hitherto confined to dreams about the next world. Moreover, those unanticipated results were not unconnected to aspects of the doctrine itself. External circumstances were not solely responsible. In addition, the contradictions in Marxism cannot be characterized as flaws or errors or weaknesses that Marx ought to have noticed and corrected. On the contrary, they were rooted in the strengths of the system. Marx's critique of the utopian confidence in rational persuasion and his conception of the measures necessary to deal with a recalcitrant bourgeoisie after the conquest of power were grounded in a realistic appraisal of human nature and the historical situation of his day. Similarly his relentless attack on liberalism sprang from a moral intensity that has often been compared to that of an Old

Testament prophet. Having constructed a system that embodied the most exalted ideals of Western culture, Marx found bourgeois liberalism totally corrupt by comparison. That intuition was reinforced by the materialism of a brilliant theory of history. In sum, in assessing the relationship between Marx's ideas and Soviet totalitarianism, the historian must take as his point of departure the judgment that in the middle of the nineteenth century Marxism represented a reformulation of the highest ideals of Western culture, applied to the new society being created by industrialization and urbanization.

There is a final irony in the fact that when Marx himself came to apply his doctrines to European politics, he expressed a clear preference for social democratic solutions. His own interpretation of "Marxist socialism" leaned toward the ballot box where possible. Lichtheim's account of the views of the "mature Marx" depicts a firm social democrat; the idea of dictatorship of the proletariat is tangential at best.[9] Shlomo Avineri has argued quite persuasively that even in the 1840s Marx was committed to the substance of democratic politics.[10]

THE DEVELOPMENT OF MARXISM

From this perspective I shall sketch two aspects of the development of Marx's thought in the 1840s: first, the manner in which he drew on the intellectual and ideological resources of Western culture to construct a socialist theory of remarkable coherence and power; second, the formulation of the doctrine of proletarian revolution in the *Communist Manifesto*, with particular attention to tensions and contradictions within Marxism.

Marx began his intellectual career as a young Hegelian. From that starting point he moved into a searching analysis of the questions posed by the socialist ferment of the 1830s. He developed a socialist theory that combined the revolutionary traditions created in France with the religious and intellectual traditions of German idealism. As a result, Marxism raised to a higher power the socialist aspirations inherent in the conjuncture of the French Revolution and the Industrial Revolution. Marx assigned to revolution the far more ambitious task of transforming man and his world in an apocalyptic fusion of theory and practice. Human nature itself would be transformed.[11] As a young Hegelian, Marx approached social and political questions in the context of a broader interest in the nature and destiny of man. His initial radicalism encompassed not only politics but all established beliefs and practices. In his doctoral dissertation he articulated themes reflecting the outlook of the young Hegelians that were to remain at the core of his thought throughout his life. The "realization of philosophy" required the actualization of the freedom that is the essence of man. It is the noblest task of philosophy to contribute to the total emancipation of humanity.

To the astonishment of even his left Hegelian friends, Marx chose the preface of his doctoral dissertation to proclaim radical criticism as the chief business of philosophy. "Prometheus," he wrote, "is the foremost saint and martyr in the philosopher's calendar. . . . The creed of philosophy is the creed of Prometheus—'In a word I detest all the gods.' This is her device against all the deities of heaven or earth who do not recognize as the highest divinity the human self-consciousness itself." He took as the epigraph to the dissertation Prometheus' reply to Hermes, whom Zeus has sent to him: "Better do I deem it to be bound to this rock than to spend my life as Father Zeus' faithful messenger." Like Prometheus, it was man's destiny to be free. Although freedom was his very essence, he was in fact unfree. That fact, in turn, posed the problem of philosophy, whose activity is "criticism which measures individual existence against essence, particular actuality against the Idea." The "realization of philosophy" required the actualization of the Idea. "In its drive to realize itself, [philosophy] enters into tension with everything else." Thus, "the realization of philosophy in opposition to the world" entails "the liberation of the world from non-philosophy." Wherever he looks, therefore, the philosopher sees a "world to be made philosophical." Rejecting the tendency of orthodox Hegelian philosophy to explain existing reality as rational and to show the presence of the Idea in the world, Marx praised the sort of philosophy that took the form of "critique, that is, philosophy turning itself against the exterior world." Here also he used a Promethean analogy: "Like Prometheus, who stole fire from heaven and began to build houses and settle on earth, so philosophy, which has evolved so as to impinge on the world, turns itself against the world that it finds." As a philosopher defined in these terms Marx set out to build a system that would achieve nothing less than the "realization of philosophy."[12]

The task of philosophy, Marx wrote in 1843, is to unmask all forms of human alienation and thus contribute to "universal emancipation" and "total freedom." Man as he actually exists is alienated from his true essence. "The human essence possesses no true reality," because freedom has not been actualized. Hence the concept of alienation is the complement to the concept of freedom in Marx's thought. In the young Hegelian mode, Marx saw the critical analysis of alienation in its various forms as the prime prerequisite to the "complete redemption of humanity" that represented the realization of philosophy. He praised philosophy for having made a good start through the critique of religion as "the holy form of human self-alienation." Religion "is the imaginary realization of the human essence, because the human essence possesses no true reality." Hence "the abolition of religion as the illusory happiness of the people" would make possible "the demand for their real happiness." The next step was the exposure of "self-alienation in its unholy forms." The essay on Hegel was a contribution to the transformation of "the criticism of theology into the ciriticism of politics."[13]

While the call for the criticism of politics was still very much in the young Hegelian tradition, Marx was at the same time moving in a new and "Marxist" direction. However trenchant the criticism, mere thought was insufficient to accomplish radical change. Action was necessary. Even in 1843 he had concluded that that action must come from the proletariat. Commenting specifically on Germany, Marx argued that "no class of civil society has the need for, or capability of achieving, universal emancipation until it is compelled to by its immediate situation, by material necessity and its own chains." The proletariat, a class in chains, "cannot emancipate itself without emancipating itself from all other spheres of society and thereby emancipating these other spheres themselves." Marx defined the role of the proletariat in terms that reflected the abstract and philosophical outlook of the young Hegelians: "The emancipation of Germany is the emancipation of man. The head of this emancipation is philosophy, its heart is the proletariat. Philosophy cannot realize itself without transcending the proletariat, the proletariat cannot transcend itself without realizing philosophy."[14]

In the early 1840s Marx absorbed the socialist ideas of Owen, Saint-Simon, Fourier, and Cabet. He now approached the problem of human emancipation in the context of socialist thought. While appropriating the socialists' critique of capitalism and vision of the future, Marx tried to escape their utopianism. Where the utopian socialists proposed to rely on rational persuasion, Marx proposed political action by a proletariat destined by history to bring about a socialist revolution. He presented socialism not as the achievement of humanitarian ideals but as the end product of an historical process determined by material forces.

Even in 1843 Marx emphasized the importance of "material necessity" as a spur to action for the proletariat which had come into existence as a result of the "industrial movement." He described "the negation of private property" as a principle inherent in the proletariat. A year later, in the 1844 Manuscripts, these new themes were even more prominent. Emphasizing the economic forms of man's self-alienation, he argued that "economic alienation is that of real life." Hence its abolition disposes of all kinds of alienation, including religious. "The positive abolition of private property and the appropriation of human life is therefore the positive abolition of all alienation, thus the return of man out of religion, family, state, etc. into his human, i.e. social being." It followed that communism and the abolition of private property would lead to the overcoming of alienation and the realization of philosophy. Communism represented "the positive abolition of private property and thus of human self-alienation and therefore the real reappropriation of the human essence by and for man." Thus the "realization of philosophy" had been translated into a specific social program to be achieved by a particular social class. But the grandiose objective remained: "This is communism as the complete and conscious return of man conserving all the riches of previous development for man himself as a social, i.e. human being. Communism as completed naturalism is humanism and as completed humanism is naturalism."[15]

In 1844 and in the works that followed, the ultimate aim of socialism for Marx was nothing less than the overcoming of alienation and the actualization of the freedom that constitutes man's true essence. From the Christian tradition, by way of Hegel, Marx derived a more radical and absolutist conception of human emancipation than that of the *philosophes*.[16] With good reason Marxism has been characterized as a "secularized eschatology." Marx was the most utopian of socialists because his ultimate objective was defined in terms that approximated Christian aspirations to perfection through divine grace. Marxism embodied quasi-religious aims that were present in attenuated form in utopian socialism or in the Enlightenment. Marxist socialism represented a great deal more than an extension of Jacobin radicalism and egalitarianism.

The profoundly utopian character of Marxism was masked by the materialism of the theory of history and the doctrine of revolution connected with it. In fact, a prime source of its ideological appeal was the claim that unlike "utopian socialism" it was grounded on an objective analysis of the material forces governing the course of history. Whereas the "utopian socialists" hoped to win converts to their ideals and persuade reasonable men of good will to act justly, Marx claimed that socialism would be achieved through a proletarian revolution based on the class struggle. Thus, the most utopian of aspirations were clothed in the rhetoric of realism and materialism. The proletarian socialist revolution was the inevitable end product of an historical process determined by economic and social forces. Marx's theory of history held together the diverse components of his socialist doctrine.

In 1844 Marx was already working toward the theory of history that was to impart such force to his socialism. "The whole movement of history, therefore, both as regards the real engendering of this communism, the birth of its empirical existence, and also as regards its consciousness and thought, is the consciously comprehended process of its becoming."[17] Here the economic emphasis is only incipiently present, for in the *Manuscripts* his view of history is closely linked to his conception of man as a free and conscious being. In this vein he praises Hegel's *Phenomenology* because it depicts "the self-creation of man as a process."[18] Earlier in the *Manuscripts* Marx wrote that "what is called world history is nothing but the creation of man by human labour," and cited this as evidence of man's "self-creation." This view of man and his history bears on Marx's socialist theory in two ways. First, man has not yet achieved control of his history. As a free and conscious being, he ought to be in control of his destiny, but he has not yet achieved that control; in fact his history has contributed to his self-alienation. At the same time, however, history offers the possibility of transforming man as he is into what he ought to be, into his true essence. All that is required is a free and conscious control of history. A few years later, however, Marx's fully developed theory of history put so much emphasis on the socioeconomic determinants that free action was reduced to recognizing forces that must be helped along.

In the *German Ideology* Marx developed at length the theory of history that was to be the foundation of every aspect of his socialist doctrine. While that theory was a prime source of intellectual and ideological strength, it also embodied the contradictions that lay at the core of the system. Both aspects of the theory were shaped by the depth and intensity of his reaction against the young Hegelians and the position to which he himself had been committed only a few years before. On the one hand, he moved beyond the philosophical-critical orientation of the "German ideologists," and grounded his socialism in social and economic reality. On the other hand, however, the momentum of his dialectical reaction carried him to the point where he affirmed the primacy of social and economic forces. As a result, human freedom in history was reduced to recognizing the presence of objective forces and cooperating with them.

A main theme of the *German Ideology* is the point that communism is not to be regarded as an ideal that ought to be striven for and put into practice, since it is in fact the inevitable end product of history, as determined by economic and social forces. "Communism is for us not a state of affairs which is to be established, an ideal to which reality will have to adjust itself. We call communism the real movement which abolishes the present state of things. The conditions of this movement result from the premises now in existence." As in 1844 the aim of communism is depicted as the overcoming of human alienation, but the latter is now defined even more in specifically economic and social terms and its abolition is to be achieved through an historical process whose dynamic is to be found in the same forces. The "social power" that operates as "an alien force" outside individuals, who are ignorant of its origin and goal and unable to control it, is defined as "the multiplied productive force," which in the final analysis "turns out to be the world market." By a sort of providential materialism, however, history has also produced two "practical premises" that will make possible the abolition of alienation: first, the great mass of humanity is being rendered propertyless, to such an extent that they find that alien power intolerable and are prepared to make a revolution; second, the universal development of productive forces is making the propertyless mass into a universal phenomenon. Up to the present men have become "more and more enslaved under a power alien to them," and which has been erroneously conceived of as a "dirty trick on the part of the so-called universal spirit." In fact, the world market is ultimately responsible. And Marx holds that it has been "empirically established" that "by the overthrow of the existing state of society by the communist revolution . . . and the abolition of private property which is identical with it, this power, which so baffles the German theoreticians, will be dissolved." Then "the liberation of each single individual will be accomplished in the measure in which history becomes transformed into world history." Although the utopianism of 1841–43 was still very much in evidence, it now rested on a materialistic base:

In the present epoch, the domination of material conditions over individuals, and the suppression of individuality by chance, has assumed its sharpest and most universal form, thereby setting existing individuals a very definite task. It has set them the task of replacing the domination of circumstances and of chance over individuals by the domination of individuals over chance and circumstances. . . . This task, dictated by present-day conditions, coincides with the task of the communist organization of society.[19]

The revolutionary role of the proletariat became the centerpiece of the all-embracing philosophy of history expounded in the *German Ideology*. But the essence of the proletariat—its "being" or *Wesen*—was identical to that described in 1843 before Marx had developed historical materialism:

Only the proletarians of the present day, who are completely shut off from all self-activity, are in a position to achieve a complete and no longer restricted self-activity, which consists in the appropriation of a totality of productive forces and in the thus postulated development of a totality of capacities. . . . This appropriation is further determined by the manner in which it must be effected. It can only be effected through a union, which by the character of the proletariat itself can again only be a universal one, and through a revolution, in which, on the one hand, the power of the earlier mode of production and intercourse and social organization is overthrown, and, on the other hand, there develops the universal character and the energy of the proletariat, without which the revolution itself cannot be accomplished; and in which, further, the proletariat rids itself of everything that still clings to it from its previous position in society.[20]

The description of the proletariat in this passage is not based on an empirical examination of the relations of production. Rather, it is a restatement, in materialist language, of an abstract, philosophical concept of the proletariat. In this instance, and in others, the fusion of German idealism with the "realism" of a materialist theory of history enhanced the power of Marx's socialism.

Since the *German Ideology* remained unpublished until the twentieth century, its ideas exercised an influence through other writings, above all the *Communist Manifesto*, a stunning programmatic formulation of the socialist theory that Marx and Engels had developed in the 1840s. In a few remarkable pages they depicted the proletarian socialist revolution as the culmination of European history. Then they called on the proletariat to assume their revolutionary mission. They described the proletarian revolution that would overthrow the bourgeoisie and transform capitalism into socialism. The tone of this brilliant tract is briskly realistic and antiutopian. Yet the nature of the proletariat and its revolutionary mission is defined in absolutist terms derived from German idealism. The *Manifesto* displays the ideological strength of Marxism along with the tensions and contradictions within it.

In a memorable passage Marx summoned the proletariat to destroy capitalism in much the same way that the bourgeoisie had destroyed feudalism. "What the bourgeoisie, therefore, produces, above all, is its own grave-diggers. Its fall and the victory of the proletariat are equally inevitable." Just as feudalism had given way to capitalism, so the latter would be transformed into socialism. As a result of economic forces generated in feudal society the bourgeoisie constructed a new social order and conquered political power; in place of feudal relations of property stepped "free competition, accompanied by a social and political constitution adapted to it, and by the economical and political sway of the bourgeois class." A similar movement was going on in Europe in the middle of the nineteenth century. Economic forces being generated in bourgeois society were in the process of creating a new society, in which classes themselves would be abolished. "The weapons with which the bourgeoisie felled feudalism to the ground are now being turned against the bourgeoisie itself. But not only has the bourgeoisie forged the weapons that bring death to itself; it has also called into existence the men who are to wield those weapons—the modern working class—the proletarians.[21]

In the *Manifesto* Marx describes the character of the proletarian revolution. From the standpoint of an assessment of the practical implications of Marxism, his conception of the conquest of political power by the proletariat is of fundamental importance. It is at this point that Marx's theory makes direct contact with practice. What sort of revolution does Marxism entail? What measures are to follow the revolutionary seizure of power? These questions, of course, cannot be taken literally. The *Manifesto* is not a handbook or field manual. Moreover, as noted above, Marxism embraces a variety of ideas and policies; Marx himself was convinced that the revolution would take different form in England and in Germany. While keeping these qualifications in mind, however, the historian nevertheless has to determine the conception of revolutionary practice, implicit and explicit, in the cardinal document of Marxism as a revolutionary creed. Marx's conception of the proletarian revolution must be understood in conjunction with his theory of history and the principle of the class struggle.

The sort of revolution envisaged in the *Manifesto*—a seizure of power in the Jacobin mode—is clearly a rather despotic affair, based on the realistic assumption that the bourgeoisie was unlikely to acquiesce meekly in the conquest of power by the proletariat. The burden of Marx's argument is that the proletariat will seize power and hold it by whatever means are necessary. As a critic of various forms of "utopian socialism," Marx was aware of the need for drastic measures in order to pull off the revolution. His bellicose metaphors are not mere rhetoric; they reflect his conviction, woven into the fabric of his thought, that the bourgeoisie is the enemy and must be dealt with accordingly. Thus, the statement that the first step in the revolution is to "raise the proletariat to the position of ruling class," given Marx's account of the nature of class rule, is a call for the use of coercive measures. When he demands the centralization of the means of production in the hands of the state, he defines the latter as "the proletariat organized as the ruling class." In the beginning such centralization cannot be accomplished "except by means of despotic inroads on the rights of property, and on the conditions of bourgeois production."[22] This description of the immediate aftermath of the conquest of power by the proletariat has to be understood in the light of his definition of political power as "merely the organized power of one class for oppressing another." Although Marx does not refer to the "dictatorship of the proletariat" in the *Manifesto*, it can plausibly be argued, as Lenin did, that the substance of the doctrine is there.

Marx's conception of revolution cannot be understood in purely pragmatic terms as a description of the means required to achieve socialism in countries where democratic institutions did not exist; nor can the despotic character of the revolution be interpreted primarily as a realistic measure intended to prevent counterrevolution. In this instance, as in others, Marx's manifest realism is accompanied by a latent utopianism. His conception of revolution was based on the events in France transfigured by German philosophy. Marx conceived of revolution as a fusion of theory and practice that would effect an apocalyptic transformation of man and society.[23] This view of revolution, so central to Marxism, is not easily squared with the sort of "revolutionary transformation" that might be brought about by legislative enactment after the election of a communist government by a majority in a democracy. It is difficult to conceive of Marx's apocalyptic vision of revolution being achieved in any but a dictatorial context.

While the language of the *Manifesto* is realistic and hardheaded, the content reflects the metaphysics of German idealism. Given the *Wesen* of the proletariat, its revolutionary action necessarily brings about a miraculous transubstantiation of the entities involved. After his account of the manner in which the proletariat will revolutionize the means of production following the conquest of political power, Marx writes: "When, in the course of development, class distinctions have disappeared, and all production has been concentrated in the hands of associated individuals, the public power will lose its political character. Political power, properly so called, is merely the organized power of one class for oppressing another." The argument is definitional and conceptual. By its very nature a revolution by the proletariat cannot embody such "political power," for the whole point of a communist revolution is to abolish classes and the political expression of class rule. In the next sentence, however, Marx takes note of the fact that the conquest of political power will be followed by various measures of a "despotic" sort, including the sweeping away of aspects of the old order by force. He combines that realistic judgment with the utopian prophecy that proletarian despotism will be self-dissolving: "If the proletariat during its contest with the bourgeoisie is compelled, by the force of circumstances, to organize itself as a class, if, by means of a revolution, it makes itself the ruling class, and, as such, sweeps away by force the old conditions of production, then it will, along with these conditions, have swept away the conditions for the existence of class antagonisms and of classes generally, and will thereby have abolished its own supremacy as a class."[24]

Marx's conception of a revolution, both in the *Manifesto* and in his thought as a whole, also has to be understood in relation to the doctrine of class struggle and its implications. The centrality of that doctrine, both in the call to action and in the theory of history, affects every aspect of his socialism. Marx preached class war as the primary means, in the short run, for achieving the revolution and the classless society. This is forcefully set forth in a passage toward the end of the *Manifesto* where a comment on the German situation in 1847 reveals quite clearly the practical and ideological implications of the doctrine of the class struggle. After pointing out that in Germany the Communists will fight side by side with the bourgeoisie against the absolute monarchy and the feudal squirearchy, Marx adds a characteristic comment:

But they never cease, for a single instant, to instill into the working class the clearest possible recognition of the hostile antagonism between bourgeoisie and proletariat, in order that the German workers may straightaway use, as so many weapons against the bourgeoisie, the social and political conditions that the bourgeoisie must necessarily introduce along with its supremacy, and in order that, after the fall of the reactionary classes in Germany, the fight against the bourgeoisie itself may immediately begin.

The frequent references to struggle, weapons, battle are not mere metaphors: they reflect an essential element in Marx's view of man and society. When Marx writes that the bourgeois, the middle-class owner of property "must, indeed, be swept out of the way, and made impossible,"[25] the language has an ominous ring.

Another consequence of the doctrine of class struggle is Marx's relentless attack on every aspect of what he took to be bourgeois values and ideology. Not content to show the disparity between professed ideals and social reality, he depicted "bourgeois notions of freedom, culture, law, etc." as "but the outgrowth of the conditions of your bourgeois production and bourgeois property." A "selfish misconception" had led the bourgeoisie to "transform into eternal laws of nature and of reason the social forms springing from your present mode of production and form of property."[26] He pressed home his attack with the fervor of an Old Testament prophet. His critique still has great moral force: it was an important source of the strength of his thought and of its great appeal. But the very absoluteness and vigor of his critique introduced ambiguities into the heart of his thought. Much of what he denounced was indispensable to the sort of society that he was trying to create. As in the case of the dictatorship of the proletariat, major elements of his socialist theory—unless modified—would be obstacles to the achievement of the utopia he dreamed of.

In his denunciation of capitalism and the bourgeoisie Marx inveighed against liberalism and liberal democratic institutions. The theory of rights so central to the liberal traditon evoked some of his most scornful attacks. In 1875 he contemptuously dismissed "ideological nonsense about right and other trash so common among the democrats and French Socialists."[27] This was not merely the rhetorical excess of a polemical outburst. It reflected a reasoned conviction that had been present in his thought from the very outset.

In the 1843 essay "On the Jewish Question," Marx described at great length the limitations of the conception of human rights embodied in the Declaration of the Rights of Man of 1789 (which appeared as the preamble to the constitution of 1791) and in the Declaration of the 1793 constitution. Marx argues that "the so-called *rights of man,* as distinct from the *rights of the citizen,* are simply the rights of a *member of civil society,* that is, of egoistic man, of man separated from other men and from the community." "Civil society" (*bürgerlich Gesellschaft*), a Hegelian term, denotes the realm of economic and social activity. Marx's thesis is that the abstractly defined rights of the Declaration are not in fact universal rights of "man," but rather a statement of the particular rights of the individuals who compose civil society: above all, the rights of such individuals to pursue their own selfish interests. In the 1793 Declaration, he points out, liberty is defined as "the right to do everything which does not harm the rights of others." What is involved here, Marx argues, is "the liberty of man regarded as an isolated monad, withdrawn into himself." In the Declaration, then, the right of man to liberty "is not founded on the relation between man with man, but rather upon the separation of man from man." Such rights embrace only "the *circumscribed* individual, withdrawn into himself." Similarly, the right of man to property is no more than "the right of self-interest." Thus, the right to freedom, together with its application in the right of property forms the basis of civil society. "It leads every man to see in other men, not the *realization*, but rather the *limitation* of his own liberty."[28]

Marx's hostility to traditional liberal conceptions of natural rights was reinforced by a theory of history that traced all ideals and values to social or material circumstances and denied them autonomy and independent validity. This thesis cut two ways. On the one hand, it served to undermine the liberal claims to the universality and validity of their doctrines by reducing them to expressions of class interest. This further weakened any lingering commitment to the substance of the liberal theory of rights. On the other hand, the materialistic theory of history ruled out the conscious formulation of alternative ideals that would replace the inadequate liberal conceptions. Marx would have no truck with idealistic or utopian theories and insisted that his own doctrines were the product of the material forces of history. He combined extreme hostility to the principles and institutions that bore the taint of bourgeois liberalism with a denial of the relevance of ideals to human action.

REVISIONISM, LENINISM, AND REVOLUTION

The practical consequences of the tensions and contradictions within Marxism appear in extreme form in the Bolshevik Revolution, since Leninism accentuated the authoritarian and illiberal aspects of Marx's thought. Events in Russia have to be understood, however, in the context of the development of Marxism in the German Social Democratic party in the generation preceding the 1914 war. Like the Mensheviks in Russia, the Social Democrats in Germany committed themselves to the revolutionary socialism of Marx and then diluted it in various ways.

At Erfurt in 1891 the German Social Democratic party abandoned the Gotha program of 1875 and replaced it with the doctrines of Marxism. In a series of intense doctrinal debates at party congresses between 1898 and 1902 the SPD reaffirmed its Marxist character and rejected a reformist version of socialism. The debates drew a sharp distinction between a non-Marxist, reformist, liberal-democratic socialism, as expounded by Bernstein, and the revolutionary, class struggle socialism of Marx. They provide a succinct statement of revolutionary Marxism, as understood by the leadership, in contrast to other versions of the road to socialism.[29]

Bernstein asked the SPD "to make up its mind to appear what it is in reality today: a democratic, socialistic party of reform." Spelling out the full implications of that position, he treated socialism as the fulfillment of liberalism: "With respect to liberalism as a great historical movement, socialism is its legitimate heir, not only in chronological sequence but also in spiritual qualities." Liberalism was more than bourgeois liberalism; the constitution of 1793, the logical expression of the liberalism of that period, was not an obstacle to socialism. Bernstein envisaged socialism as growing out of existing liberal democratic institutions. "The liberal organizations of modern society are distinguished from those [of feudalism] exactly because they are flexible, and capable of change and development. They do not need to be destroyed, but only to be further developed. For that we need organization and energetic action, but not necessarily a revolutionary dictatorship."[30] He depicted democracy as an alternative to violent revolution. It must be built up gradually from below. Bernstein had not revised Marxism. He had transformed it into democratic socialism.

In rejecting Bernsteinian revisionism the party defined its Marxist character in unequivocal terms. The party congress in 1899 passed a resolution proclaiming that "the party rests as before on the principle of the class struggle." It was the historic mission of the working class to conquer political power and bring about the socialization of the means of production. In his speech introducing the resolution, Bebel left no doubt about the party's commitment to the essential principles of Marxism. "I say once again, we are in essence a revolutionary party." All tactics were directed to one final goal, the creation of a socialist society through the conquest of political power by the proletariat. The purpose of the party was to "render the work class more *kampffähig* in our great struggles."[31] At Dresden in 1903 the SPD again defined itself as a Marxist revolutionary party, rather than a party of socialist reform. Rejecting a policy of "advances within the existing order," the SPD's tactics rested on "the class struggle" and the "conquest of political power." The party was "revolutionary in the best sense of the word" and would not be "content to reform bourgeois society."[32]

The full theoretical formulation of orthodox Marxism as opposed to revisionism was provided by Karl Kautsky. At the party congress of 1898, speaking in reply to Bernstein, he argued that the development of socialism could not be achieved "peacefully and without catastrophe." Bernstein's tactics were suitable to England, not Germany. Kautsky elaborated on that theme in 1902 in *The Social Revolution.* What distinguished social revolution from social reform is "the conquest of political power by an hitherto oppressed class." He emphasized that "society can only be raised to a higher stage of development through a catastrophe." Democracy was invaluable as a means of "ripening the proletariat for the social revolution. . . . Democracy is to the proletariat what light and air are to the organism; without them it cannot develop its powers." The conquest of political power by the proletariat "makes possible a higher form of the revolutionary struggle."[33] In rejecting Bernstein's revisionism Kautsky brought into the foreground the Marxist doctrines of class struggle, revolution, and conquest of political power by the proletariat. His views corresponded closely to the position taken by Engels in the 1890s.

In the course of the decade that preceded the outbreak of the 1914 war, Kautsky's Marxism became increasingly deterministic. Confident of the inevitability of triumph of proletarian socialism, orthodox Marxists tended to concentrate on immediate political issues and to postpone consideration of revolutionary action. This theoretical development paralleled the growth of de facto reformism within the SPD and the trade unions.[34] While Marxist formulas remained intact, they were in fact being emptied of their revolutionary content. Among the Social Democrats in Germany and the Mensheviks in Russia, the revolutionary seizure of power had moved to the periphery of orthodox Marxism. Marxist doctrine had been adapted to the democratic traditions of 1789 and 1848 and to the subsequent growth of parliamentary institutions.

It has been argued, with some plausibility, that after the collapse of the German Empire in November 1918, an SPD committed to the activist Marxism of the *Manifesto* might have created a social and economic order more conducive to the survival of Weimar democracy. Marx had seen the need for swift and radical action in order to prevent counterrevolutionary action by the sort of social forces that were so powerful on the German right in the 1920s. While counterfactual speculation of this sort has a useful function in historical analysis, it requires an extended consideration of possibilities and choices. We shall leave the matter there without further discussion, noting merely that the primary reason for the reluctance of the vast majority of the Social Democrats to undertake revolutionary action was the Bolshevik Revolution, which was based on a Leninist ideology that diverged from the Marxism of both the Social Democrats in Germany and the Mensheviks in Russia.[35]

By the first decade of the twentieth century both in Germany and in Russia the dominant forms of Marxism were variants of Kautsky's position. While still committed to the goal of the proletarian socialist revolution and rejecting Bernsteinian reformism, most Marxists had come to take a long-run view, emphasizing the strong current of socioeconomic determinism in Marx's thought. Wary of the danger of a premature insurrection of the Blanquist type, they were convinced that the full development of capitalism and the maturing of the proletariat must come first. The bourgeois revolution must precede the socialist revolution. This sort of analysis was particularly applicable to Russia, whose economic and political institutions were less developed than in Europe. The Mensheviks applied to Russia the orthodox Marxism of the turn of the century and developed a two-stage theory of revolution, which continued to guide their policies in the spring and summer of 1917.[36] Lenin, of course, had formulated another version of Marxism and took a very different view of the situation after the February Revolution.

Central to Lenin's revision of Marxism was a rejection of the myth that a revolutionary proletariat is the inevitable end product of the economic and social development of capitalism. He recognized that in fact the forces of production in capitalist society tend to produce "trade union consciousness" rather than revolutionary consciousness in the proletariat. He drew the conclusion that revolutionary consciousness would have to be instilled in the proletariat from outside. His conception of a vanguard party was adapted to that end and to leading the proletariat in the conquest of political power. It required formidable intelligence and originality to establish this position in the face of prevailing forms of Marxist orthodoxy. The relationship between Marxism and Leninism is a conspicuous example of the complex and dialectical way in which ideas enter into historical processes. Lenin did not simply accept an established doctrine and apply it in a particular situation. What he appropriated he shaped and modified on the basis of his experience and reflection.

Lenin's version of Marxism reflected the influence of the Russian revolutionary tradition, especially the Russian Jacobins. From this vantage point he took the *Communist Manifesto* as his primary text and expounded an activist, voluntarist, antideterminist Marxism. Throughout his life he denounced the opportunists who "omit, obscure, or distort the revolutionary side of this theory, its revolutionary soul."[37] In 1902 in *What Is To Be Done?* Lenin forcefully defended his position against opponents who had criticized him for "belittling the significance of the objective or spontaneous element of development." Expressing his own views in the terminology of Russian debates on the subject, Lenin took his stand on the side of "consciousness" against spontaneity. "Hence, our task, the task of Social-Democracy, is to *combat spontaneity*, to *divert* the working-class movement from this spontaneous, trade-unionist striving to come under the wing of the bourgeoisie, and to bring it under the wing of revolutionary Social-Democracy."[38]

A second distinctive aspect of Leninism was its intensely authoritarian and antiliberal character. Lenin seized on the doctrine of the dictatorship of the proletariat, defined it in the most despotic terms, and lodged it at the core of Marxism. Throughout his life Lenin prided himself on taking a "hard" line against the "softs" who were inclined to liberal and democratic principles. Here also his links to the Russian revolutionary tradition are pronounced. The authoritarian thrust of Lenin's Marxism, in turn, raises two questions that are pertinent to an inquiry into the role of ideas in the history of modern Europe. What is the connection between Leninism and the character of the regime that was established by the Bolshevik Revolution? What was the role of Marxism in shaping the character of that regime? Lenin's *The State and Revolution* bears directly on both those questions. Writing in the summer of 1917, Lenin described in detail the characteristics of the proletarian dictatorship that he intended to establish, and he took great pains to defend his position on the basis of its fidelity to Marxism.[39]

The regime that Lenin established after the seizure of power corresponds directly to the dictatorship of the proletariat described in *The State and Revolution*. He explains the essence of that dictatorship by reference to the "forgotten words" of Marxism, the definition of the postrevolutionary state as "the proletariat organized as the ruling class." On this doctrinal basis Lenin builds his description of the dictatorship of the proletariat. "The state is a special organization of force: it is an organization of violence for the suppression of some class. What class must the proletariat suppress? Naturally, only the exploiting class, i.e., the bourgeoisie." Lenin makes it plain that the period of repressive dictatorship will persist long after the elimination of bourgeois resistance to the revolution: "The proletariat needs state power, the centralized organization of force, an organization of violence, both to crush the resistance of the exploiters and to *lead* the enormous mass of the population—the peasants, the petty bourgeoisie, and semi-proletarians—in the work of organizing a socialist economy." Lenin justified on the grounds of necessity the revolutionary state that he intended to establish: "We are not utopians, we do not 'dream' of dispensing *at once* with all administration, with all subordination." Such anarchist dreams reflect a lack of understanding of the Marxist conception of proletarian dictatorship. "No, we want the socialist revolution with people as they are now, with people who cannot dispense with subordination, control and 'foremen and accounts.' The subordination, however, must be to the armed vanguard of all the exploited and working people, i.e. to the proletariat." There will be "strict, iron discipline backed up by the state power of the armed workers."[40]

The dissolution of the Constituent Assembly in January 1918 was based on pragmatic considerations, and there is no need to "explain" it by reference to Leninist or Marxist theory. Lenin recognized that the Bolsheviks were in a minority and that democratic processes were incompatible with the survival of his revolution. He acted realistically, with the lesson of 1848 in mind. It is also the case, however, that democratic institutions were incompatible with the repressive regime that Lenin characterized in *The State and Revolution* for the long period of transition to communism. In the Theses on the Constituent Assembly in December 1917, Lenin restated the need for a dictatorship, which he described as "a higher form of democracy than the usual bourgeois republic with a Constituent Assembly." In any case, "the interests of this revolution stand higher than the formal rights of the Constituent Assembly."[41] Thus both the imperatives of practical necessity and the requirements of Leninist theory led inexorably to the establishment of a dictatorial regime that was unlikely to be transformed or dismantled.

The establishment of the Cheka was also a response to political pressures and circumstances, but the institutionization of terror went well beyond such practical considerations. A newly established authoritarian regime confronted with opposition was bound to take strong action to suppress it. After the outbreak of civil war, the most severe countermeasures were required if the regime was to survive. Having noted that, however, the fact remains that in *The State and Revolution* and in other statements as well, Lenin displayed a doctrinal enthusiasm for violence and terror in support of the revolution. Terror began before the Civil War. While initially confined to counterrevolutionaries, it soon was extended to all oppostion parties, plus the proletariat and peasants. Doctrine reinforced practical necessity.

On a brief vacation in Finland early in 1918 Lenin drafted two articles in which he called for an intensification of proletarian violence in order to crush the resistance being offered by "the exploiters" and "their intellectual menials."[42] Although he decided not to publish these drafts, they present a vivid picture of his views at the time. He exhorted the revolutionary workers and peasants to accelerate their efforts to eliminate the corrupt remnants of capitalist society: "The workers and peasants are breaking their resistance—unfortunately not yet firmly, resolutely and ruthlessly enough—*and will break it.*" As soon as possible these parasites had to be rendered "harmless to socialist society." Lenin recommended a variety of ways to achieve "the single common aim—to cleanse the land of Russia of all sorts of harmful insects, of crook-fleas, of bedbugs—the rich, and so on and so forth." In some areas they might be put in prison, in others set to work cleaning latrines. "In a third place they will be provided with 'yellow' tickets after they have served their time, so that all the people shall have them under surveillance as *harmful* persons, until they reform." Lenin justified the most extreme measures as a means of destroying the malignant vestiges of capitalism.

The voluntary and conscientious cooperation, marked by revolutionary enthusiasm, of the masses of the workers and peasants in accounting and controlling *the rich*, the crooks, the idlers and hooligans can alone conquer these survivals of accursed capitalist society, these dregs of humanity, these hopelessly decayed and atrophied limbs, this contagion, this plague, this ulcer that socialism has inherited from capitalism.

There is a connection, then, between Leninist doctrine and the repressive regime established by the Bolshevik Revolution. The precise character of the connection, considered in relation to the multifarious factors and circumstances involved, is problematical. We have to stop well short of treating the Stalinist regime of the 1930s as the logical consequence of Leninism. Robert Tucker's critique of Solzhenitsyn's tendentious interpretation of the unpublished articles of 1918 is well taken: "While Lenin was indeed a principled advocate of revolutionary terror, forced labor for opponents of the regime, etc., it may be questioned whether the terror of the civil war period (1917–21) was either quantitatively or qualitatively the same phenomenon as the Stalinist terror of 1929–39 and later."[43] Stephen Cohen has made a plausible case for an even greater discontinuity between Leninism and Stalinist Russia.[44] Lenin certainly would have been appalled by the events of the 1930s. Like Marx, Lenin envisaged the eventual creation of a totally free society, characterized by participatory democracy, as the end product of the proletarian revolution. *The State and Revolution* contains an idyllic picture of the communist utopia. Moreover, Lenin's policies after the consolidation of power and the elimination of resistance indicate a clear intention to move Russia in a less authoritarian direction. He appears to have considered the N.E.P. as part of a liberalization process in the political sphere as well as the economic. Finally, whether we consider the Leninist regime of 1918 or 1923, there can be no doubt that Stalin carried to a perverse and hideous extreme the system that he inherited. But it must also be said that the Leninist system lent itself to such perversion. Tucker's characterization of Lenin as "a principled advocate of revolutionary terror" underlines the close connection between certain Leninist ideas and Stalinist practice.

The existence of such a connection, in turn, raises the question of the relationship between Marxism and those aspects of Leninism that contributed to the establishment of an authoritarian and repressive regime. One can begin with Lenin's claim that his ideas were truly Marxist and that his opponents' views were nothing more than an opportunistic "doctoring" of Marxism. His "prime task," he wrote in *The State and Revolution,* was "to re-establish what Marx really taught on the subject of the state."[45] Lenin is certainly correct in his contention that the views he set forth in *The State and the Revolution* are authentically Marxist. It follows, then, that there is a direct link between Marxism and the regime that emerged from the Bolshevik Revolution. October 1917 represented an undeniably Marxist revolution. Marx's ideas were an essential ingredient in the processes underlying the Bolshevik Revolution and its consequences. On the other hand, it is also clear that Lenin singled out those aspects of Marxism that were congenial to an illiberal authoritarian outlook shaped by the Russian Jacobins. The social democratic side of Marx was eliminated. Plekhanov's position was much closer to the spirit of Marx and Engels than was Lenin's. And Plekhanov's critique of the Russian Jacobins in 1883, on the grounds that their ideas could only lead to a patriarchal or Peruvian communism, is also applicable to Leninism.[46] Moreover, immediately after the Revolution there were Bolsheviks, such as Kamenev and Zinoviev, who interpreted Marxism in a democratic and pluralistic fashion. Thus, although there is no tidy answer to the question of the relationship between Marxism and the regime established by the Bolshevik Revolution, the presence of an important connection is indisputable.

The question of the relationship between Marxism and Stalinism is even more difficult, since it involves a consideration of the mediating role of Leninism, as well as practical circumstances in the process. In recognition of the degree of complexity to be dealt with, historians prefer to concentrate on questions that are likely to yield more conclusive answers. At a symposium sponsored by the Rockefeller foundation a few years ago, the problem of the relationship between Marxism and Stalinism was addressed not by the historians but by two philosophers, who arrived at diametrically opposed conclusions. Their handling of the question is illuminating because they concentrate so directly on the assessment of the practical implications of Marxist doctrine along with the analytical problems involved.

Leszek Kolakowski begins his essay, "Marxist Roots of Stalinism," by considering the proper way of shaping the question, "How were the Stalinist system of power and the Stalinist ideology related to Marxism?"[47] He rejects the question, "Was the Stalinist system causally generated by the Marxian theory?" on the grounds that "no society has ever been entirely begotten by an ideology or may ever be accounted for by ideas of people who contributed to its origin." Taking "causally generated" to entail the claim that the causes adduced were sufficient to have produced the phenomenon, Kolakowski prefers the "commonsense platitude" that societies "have always been molded by what they thought about themselves, but this dependence has always been partial only." In the rest of the essay, he refrains from considering any kind of "causal" link between Marxist doctrines and Stalinist practice. Instead, Kolakowski asserts a very close connection between Marxism and Stalinism by returning an affirmative answer to two rather different questions: "Was (or is) the characteristically Stalinist ideology that was (or is) designed to justify the Stalinist system of societal organization a legitimate (even if not the only possible) interpretation of Marxist philosophy of history? This is the milder version of my question. The stronger version is: Was every attempt to implement all basic values of Marxian socialism likely to generate a political organization that would bear marks unmistakably analogous to Stalinism?"

Kolakowski argues that it was "both Marx's anticipation of perfect unity of mankind and his mythology of the historically privileged proletarian consciousness which were responsible for his theory's being eventually turned into an ideology of the totalitarian movement: not because he conceived of it in such terms, but because its basic values could hardly be materialized otherwise." This is bound to strike the historian as a rather abstract and even intellectualistic formulation of the connection between Marxism and Stalinism, apart from the problem of assessing the importance of intervening events and circumstances. It rules out even the possibility of a non-authoritarian system based on Marxist principles. Moreover, it is questionable whether Kolakowski's second question can be answered historically.

Mihailo Markovic also begins his essay on "Stalinism and Marxism" with a consideration of the problem of formulating the questions so as to make the issue "more rationally debatable and more theoretically interesting."[48] He poses two questions: "Does Stalinism have any roots in Marxism, and if it does how strong are they? . . . What is the nature of its link with Marxism?" He concludes that the link between Stalinism and Marxism was weak and tenuous. He dismisses the notion that Stalinist ideology and practice is "a *necessary* practical consequence of Marxist theory." He argues that "Stalinism and Marxism differ essentially both in their critique of capitalist society and in their approach to socialism"; although Stalinism clearly "has some roots in Marxism," it represents a radical distortion of the doctrine.

Putting aside the details of Markovic's argument, it is clear that he is dealing with a philosophical or doctrinal issue rather than a historical question. From this perspective he denies the existence of a significant link between Marxism and Stalinism: "When taken in totality, Marx's views do not give any ground for such distorted interpretations." Kolakowski, however, makes a good case for an antithetical conclusion. But even if the historian recognizes that Stalinism represents Marxism transmogrified, he still has to look into the nature of the connection between them, especially the question of the extent to which certain elements in Marx's thought may have "contributed to," without in any sense "causing," the ideological and political developments of the 1930s.

While the sort of analysis performed by Kolakowski and Markovic is indispensable, it can do no more than provide a basis for further inquiry into the question of the influence of Marxism. If it becomes the dominant approach, it can lead to the kind of error embodied in

J. L. Talmon's assertion of a direct link between the Enlightenment and "totalitarian democracy." Although historical connections are not narrowly "causal," neither are they of a purely logical or conceptual character. In his commentary on the papers read at the conference, Robert C. Tucker does not spend much time on the question of whether Stalinism was "the logical or inevitable end-product" of Marxism. Instead, he concentrates on the more complex historical developments that came in between: Lenin's version of Marxism and the establishment of a single-party dictatorship under his leadership after the Revolution. Tucker takes into account the "circumstantial explanation" of Stalinism and also reminds us of the importance of Stalin's personality. His paper is aptly entitled, "Some Questions on the Scholarly Agenda."[49]

Throughout this discussion of the Bolshevik Revolution and its consequences nothing has been said about the role of the revolutionary rank and file. This omission should not be construed as a depreciation of their importance. In a book that illustrates the value of "history from below," Alexander Rabinowitch has described the nature and significance of the direct contribution to the success of the revolution made by factory workers, soldiers, and sailors. He concludes that "the relative flexibility of the party, as well as its responsiveness to the prevailing mass mood, had at least as much to do with the ultimate Bolshevik victory as did revolutionary discipline, organizational unity, or obedience to Lenin."

Revising received interpretations, Rabinowitch points out that the phenomenal success of the Bolsheviks in 1917 can be attributed, not so much to the party's tight organization and unity, which has been exaggerated, but rather to its "relatively democratic, tolerant and decentralized structure and method of operation, as well as its essentially open and mass character—in striking contrast to the traditional Leninist model." In the Bolshevik organization in Petrograd there was "continuing free and lively discussion and debate over the most basic theoretical and tactical issues." Rabinowitch has also described the vigorously expressed views of Bolshevik moderates who advocated a Constituent Assembly and a broadly based socialist government. All of this is evidence of the possibility of a democratic, non-authoritarian outcome of the Bolshevik Revolution.[50]

When we consider the question of how it happened that the Petrograd workers contributed to the success of a revolution that led to the creation of a political and social order that was the opposite of what they intended—and of what Marx had dreamed of—we have to take a close look at Marxist doctrine and its inner contradictions. This chapter has argued that Marxism was an "active ingredient" in the process that led to the establishment of Soviet authoritarianism. That metaphor is intentionally general. It allows room for a good deal of debate about the "role" of Marxist ideas and the complex process in which they were involved.

The Bolshevik Revolution contributed as much as any one event to the spread of fascist movements in Europe after the war. Fascism was explicitly directed against communism and proletarian socialism. But the role of Marxism in the genesis of fascism was more complex. The antirevisionist left in pre-1914 Marxism—exemplified in Lenin, Sorel, and Mussolini—operating in the cultural climate of fin-de-siècle Europe, was an active ingredient in the process that created fascism. It is also the case, of course, that the primary roots of fascism were in the counterrevolutionary tradition that began with the rejection of the principles of 1789. Neither the far left nor the new right were "causes" of fascism, but they were historically connected with it as elements in the process that produced it.

CHAPTER FOUR

The Genesis of Fascism

Ideas and beliefs were primary ingredients in the process that brought fascism into being. We cannot begin to understand what fascism was or how it came into existence unless we attend closely to the role of ideas, beliefs, and traditions in shaping and constituting it. While social and institutional circumstances were necessary preconditions of the emergence of fascism and influenced its development, intellectual and ideological forces provided the specific elements that shaped its character and constituted its essence. We can distinguish analytically between three such forces: the distinctive cultural climate of pre-1914 Europe, ideological traditions that developed in the century following the French Revolution, and nationalism.

Just as the French Revolution and the Enlightenment were indissolubly linked, so fascism was inextricably connected with the intellectual climate of pre-1914 Europe. Salient aspects of fascism had their origin in the remarkable cultural configuration that emerged toward the end of the nineteenth century—characterized by a radical rejection of established values and beliefs and a glorification of struggle and violence. In that cultural milieu the specific components of fascism took shape in the course of a complex interplay between nationalism and ideologies of right and left, each the product of a unique history. These diverse elements entered into novel and often paradoxical combinations that defined the character of the new phenomenon. The protofascist currents that developed before the First World War comprised not only traits of the new right but also antibourgeois and anticapitalist attitudes and an impulse to radical change that reflected, in perverse form, the traditions of the left. Mediating these disparate elements was an intense nationalism. In the genesis of fascism we find a juxtaposition of nationalism and socialism and a convergence of the extreme right and far left, in a culture that was in revolt against the heritage of the Enlightenment.

From these disparate intellectual and ideological forces came the constituents that were essential to the existence of fascism in its historical uniqueness. While various aspects of pre-1914 Europe contributed to the emergence of fascism, ideas and beliefs composed the specific ingredients that entered into the phenomenon itself. In fact, to say that fascism was a "reflection" of pre-1914 culture is to use a metaphor that does less than justice to the relationship between them. Nor is it adequate to say that the former was "derived from" or "rooted in" the latter. Even these metaphors understate the role of intellectual forces. Particular ideas, beliefs, and traditions characteristic of pre-1914 Europe affected not only the form of fascism but its content, its concrete historical reality. And the word "affected" in this context implies a much closer relationship than that between a separate cause and effect. Intellectual forces played something more than a reinforcing or intensifying role. While social and institutional factors were of obvious importance in the process, they were quite insufficient by themselves to produce fascism.

This emphasis on the constitutive role of intellectual forces may be contrasted to a distinction that is sometimes made between the "ideas" and the "realities" of fascism. Walter Laqueur, for example, has observed that Ernst Nolte is "more interested in the ideas of fascism than the realities." From this premise, he concludes that "the search for genetic ties and origins should never be pressed too hard."[1] As a warning against a simplistic view of the intellectual origins of fascism, Laqueur's point is well taken. The retrospective philosophical rationalization provided by Giovanni Gentile along with an account of "intellectual origins," can hardly be accepted as the "reality" of fascism. On the other hand, however, anti-Semitism was obviously an integral part of the "reality" of National Socialism. Fascism was a collage of myths, illusions, delusions, hopes, resentments, aspirations, and even "ideals." The injunction not to press too hard the search for their origins is a self-denying ordinance that the historian cannot afford to accept.

Even historians who are not prepared to draw a stark distinction between the "ideas" and the "realities" of fascism are nevertheless inclined, for good reasons, to be wary of "intellectualistic" interpretations that attribute overriding importance to the ruminations of intellectuals. In defining their view, however, they may end up rather close to Laqueur's position. A case in point is Robert Paxton's thoughtful review of Zeev Sternhell's study of fascist ideology in France between the wars.[2] He classifies Sternhell with "Ernst Nolte, George Mosse, and others who treat fascism as an ideology." In the course of his review Paxton distinguishes sharply between fascist ideology or rhetoric and fascist practice: "One wants to know whether fascist practice, as well as fascist ideology, impregnated interwar France." Paxton's primary emphasis is on practice, as counterposed to ideology. His own approach, defining fascism in social and political terms, represents the views of many historians:

It is a more fruitful approach to define as fascism precisely that alliance constructed by Hitler and Mussolini between a mass following thirsting vaguely for national unity and energy ("revolution" in a very limited sense) and old power blocs, an alliance built on a common hatred of Marxian socialism. On this reading, the kind of intellectuals studied by Sternhell seem more the victims than the apostles of fascism. The heart of the matter is whether the fascist movements managed to root themselves in society as the defenders of threatened interests, by what they did as well as by what they said.

While the utility of this approach has been demonstrated, in the writings of Paxton and others, it should not be permitted to foreclose other lines of inquiry into the nature of fascism and the historical processes that produced it.

What exactly is the problem here? A distinction between ideology and practice is unexceptionable. Every historian has to consider the question of the relationship between fascist ideology and practice in Mussolini's Italy. The same sort of question is equally pertinent to the "people's democracies." Difficulties arise, however, when a useful analytical distinction is transformed (either explicitly or implicitly) into an ontological claim concerning the nature of the phenomenon under study. The notion that the "reality" of fascism is embodied in its "practice," as counterposed to its ideology, ideas, or rhetoric begs a number of important questions. (For a discussion of the problem of defining the constitutive relationship between language and social reality, see the first section of the next chapter.) Considering the matter merely from the point of view of common sense and ordinary language, it would appear to be rather difficult to describe the essential characteristics of fascism, fascists, or fascist movements without close attention to their ideas and beliefs, or to dissociate fascist "practice" from the ideology with which it is so intimately connected. Moreover, while the analytical distinction between ideology and practice is indispensable to the interpretation of fascist regimes, it gives rise to serious difficulties when applied to fascist movements. Furthermore, a dichotomous distinction between practice and ideology is often linked to the further assumption that the fascist phenomenon is socially constituted, and that ideas affect only the form and not the content. Such an assumption, in turn, prejudges questions that ought to be settled by empirical inquiry into the historical processes involved. If one assumes that the essence of fascism consists of a socially constituted "practice" or "reality," then intellectual forces are automatically relegated to a subordinate role in the process that produced it.

A related issue is raised in the passage from Paxton quoted above. On the one hand, it is clear that the impact of fascist movements, including their success or failure, was directly affected by socio-economic interests; the "old power blocs" enlisted fascism in defense of their threatened interests. On the other hand, it is also clear that fascism came into existence independently of the landowners of the Po valley or the industrialists of the Ruhr. The question of the genesis of fascism—the sudden appearance of a novel phenomenon all over Europe after the first World War—has to be treated in its own terms apart from the use to which it may subsequently have been put. In dealing with such a quintessentially "historical" problem, the nature of the phenomenon has to be defined in the course of empirical inquiry, along with the character of the disparate forces whose interplay produced it.

The analysis of the formative influence of intellectual forces is especially important in the case of fascism, because problems of description and explanation are so closely intertwined. The nature of fascism remains problematical and has been the subject of continuing discussion and debate. Hence it is quite impossible to talk about "causes" or "origins" without defining the character of an exceedingly complex and protean phenomenon. At the same time, however, a full historical analysis of the genesis of fascism is essential to an understanding of its distinctive traits. In order to deal with the interconnected questions of "what" and "why" close attention to ideas, beliefs, and traditions is required, because they were both constituents of fascism and also ingredients in the process that produced it. Thus, any *description* of the distinctive characteristics of fascism must distinguish it from and define its relationship to similar movements. Such a description, in turn, necessarily entails an examination of the intellectual and ideological forces involved in the genesis of fascism. The problematical and indeed paradoxical character of fascism is expressed in the title of Eugen Weber's article, "Revolution? Counterrevolution? What Revolution?" and in the debate to which it is addressed.[3] It is precisely the juxtaposition of counterrevolutionary and revolutionary traits, of elements of right and left, of nationalism and socialism that is of the essence of fascism. In order to describe fascism in its historical uniqueness, and to understand the process that produced it, we have to look into its relationship to the intellectual and ideological traditions of Europe in the early twentieth century.

PROBLEMS OF INTERPRETATION

Since historians are agreed in rejecting monocasual or reductionist interpretations, we can concentrate on the questions at issue concerning the genesis of fascism: the nature and significance of intellectual forces in interaction with social and institutional structures. We do not have to deal with mutually exclusive positions, but rather with a continuum of interpretations, differing in assessments of significance. At one end lies Stanley Payne's impeccably pluralistic synthesis, which brings problems of conceptualization into full view. At the other end of the spectrum lie those interpretations that unequivocally affirm the primacy of praxis in the genesis of fascism. In between there is a great deal of variation, with formally pluralistic principles often accompanied by a tendency to tilt the balance in favor of social and institutional factors.

Payne's multicausal analysis provides a good point of departure. "Fascist ideology and culture," he writes, "deserve more attention than they normally receive, for fascist doctrine, like all others, stemmed from ideas, and the ideas of fascists had distinct philosophical and cultural bases, despite frequent assertions to the contrary." He treats cultural variables as of equivalent importance to the social and political: "The chief cultural variables were the doctrines of intense nationalism, militarism and international Social Darwinism in the forms that became widespread among the World War I generation in greater central Europe, coupled with the contemporary philosophical and cultural currents of neo-idealism, vitalism, and activism and the cult of the hero." The cultural crisis of 1890–1914 was one of the major historical antecedents of fascism and other forms of authoritarian nationalism. Cultural changes, in turn, encouraged the expansion of right authoritarian nationalism and the growth of "more revolutionary new forms of collectivist nationalism." These new ideas and attitudes played a reinforcing and intensifying role, contributing to the acceptance of various forms of authoritarian nationalism, of which fascism was one. "The new cultural mood . . . contributed to the proliferation and acceptance of new doctrines of authoritarian nationalism, whether of the rightist or revolutionary varieties."[4]

We shall argue that intellectual forces not only contributed to the proliferation and acceptance of fascism but also were essential to the creation of the phenomenon itself: their role in the process went well beyond that of reinforcing the influence of social and political variables.

This interpretation may be contrasted to the position taken by Geoffrey Barraclough. He has argued with admirable explicitness that if we are to understand the history of modern Germany, we must give "due precedence to social realities." For Barraclough "the almost obsessive preoccupation with the origins of National Socialism, particularly with its intellectual origins, has long outlived its usefulness." He deplores the "intellectualist bias" inherent in the notion that "the moving force of history is ideas, rather than social relations, or fundamental structural changes." He broadens his critique to include a misplaced emphasis on "causes and origins," as opposed to a structural or synchronic analysis. To be sure, Barraclough's warning against "intellectualist bias" should be kept in mind. The "intellectual origins" of fascism can easily be treated in a superficial and sterile manner. Postwar studies of the origins of National Socialism were little more than attempts to rummage through German history in search of material for an indictment. From a rather different ideological vantage point, Giovanni Gentile set out to give Italian fascism philosophical respectability. A. J. Gregor's recent study of the intellectual origins of Italian fascism seems bent on persuading his readers to view the phenomenon more seriously, if not in a more favorable light than before. Such tendentious approaches are not helpful. But historians like Zeev Sternhell and David Roberts have provided solid studies of the role of ideas in the genesis of fascism without the faintest suggestion that "the moving force of history is ideas."[5]

In one form or another, the social ontology presupposed by Barraclough's thesis is quite pervasive. It underlies Arno Mayer's comment on the prehistory of fascism: "For like the laboring class the lower middle class generates and keeps generating a separate culture, ethos, life-style and world view."[6] Such a formulation excludes an independent role for ideas, which do no more than perform a function required by a "reality" defined in social and institutional terms. Yet some such view of the human world runs through the historiography of fascism. Assumptions of that sort, even when embedded in a formally pluralistic setting, foreclose an examination of the role of ideas. Similarly, a distinction between form and content, even when only implicit, lends itself to a conclusion that privileges praxis. Thus, the historian who distinguishes between the "realities" and the "ideas" of fascism will find it very difficult if not impossible to consider the problem of the role of intellectual forces in the genesis of fascism. Similarly, a narrowly functionalist view of social processes will exclude a priori an independent role for ideas, beliefs, and traditions. Finally, a conception of historical causation that presupposes a sharp distinction between cause and effect will also tend to inhibit an empirical examination of the problem.

Although an explicit denial of the significance of ideas and beliefs in the genesis of fascism is rare, there is a tendency, among interpretations that vary in other respects, to assign a very heavy weight to social factors. On the whole, intellectual forces lie in a dusty corner of the dominant paradigms. A glance at the historiography of fascism reveals a long-standing preoccupation with the social and economic circumstances in which it developed. Whereas the relation between the Enlightenment and the French Revolution has been of major interest to observers and historians from the very beginning, the role of intellectual forces in the genesis of fascism has remained on the periphery. F. L. Carsten's summary of recent interpretations of fascism makes clear the extent to which an interest in the social composition of fascist movements has thrust other matters into the background. He concludes that "no fundamentally new interpretations of fascism have been put forward by the modern historians and political scientists." The main questions throughout have been "where did the mass following of the fascist parties come from, and which social groups tended to support them?"[7]

In the various social interpretations of fascism, a secondary role for ideas and beliefs is built into the conceptual framework. A case in point is Arno Mayer's account of fascism as a counterrevolutionary phenomenon whose essential characteristics were determined by the need to defend capitalism against the threat of proletarian socialism. The doctrines of fascism were dictated by the requirements of social and political conflict. Ideas and beliefs were developed in order to meet the needs of action. "As of the 1870s," Mayer writes, "it became increasingly clear that to be effective the struggle against Socialism required a distinct popular ideology." In due course there emerged the kind of ideology and program capable of mobilizing "mass support among highly diversified crisis strata." Counterrevolutionary leaders developed the ideas necessary to build a mass base. Thus, it is not significant whether the ideology of these leaders was a new invention or a rediscovery of an earlier doctrinal dispensation. The point is that "the style as well as the substance of their appeals is prescribed by the nature of the adherents they propose to rally." Thus, Mayer derives counterrevolutionary doctrines directly from the nature of the mass base of the movement. "Counterrevolution is essentially a praxis. Its political doctrine is in the nature of a rationalization and justification of prior actions. It is a pseudo doctrine." The specific characteristics of fascist ideology require no further explanation. We are told that "one of the chief earmarks of counterrevolutionary ideology is that it exalts passion to the near paralysis of man's reasoning faculties and potentials."[8] A pseudo doctrine does not require much explanation in any case. All that the historian needs to do is identify the inexorable requirements of counterrevolutionary praxis.

Mayer's account of fascism as primarily a counterrevolutionary phenomenon has been rejected as an oversimplification by historians. In his historiographical survey, Carsten concludes that historians and political scientists "seem to be agreed in using the term 'fascist revolution,' while they are also aware that the fascist movements contained counterrevolutionary elements."[9] At this juncture, however, we are not concerned with the details of Mayer's thesis, but rather with the fact that it is not possible to come to grips with his interpretation without confronting the problem of ideas and beliefs as constituents and causes of fascism. Any serious consideration of Mayer's position necessarily entails the examination of phenomena that lie outside the purview of a social interpretation. The notion of counterrevolution itself cannot be satisfactorily defined primarily in terms of praxis. From this perspective Eugen Weber's trenchant critique of Mayer is instructive. Noting radical and revolutionary aspects of fascism that do not square with the notion that it was fundamentally an antileft movement, he argues that fascism was not a counterrevolution but "a rival revolution." He advances a fundamentally different conception of what fascism was all about, that is, of the ideas and beliefs that constituted its essence. Weber argues that "belief in revolution for its own sake is one more thing radical Left and Right seem to have in common." They shared "the ultimate revolutionary promise: *changer la vie*." Weber emphasizes the common characteristics of the radical left and right and traces them to the same sources: "The great revolutionary creeds of the twentieth century were (among other things) all inspired by Social Darwinism, Nationalism, fascism, communism, all reflect belief in the survival of the fittest: in terms of nation (or of race, itself a confused notion of the nineteenth century), or in terms of class."[10] Putting aside the question of the validity of Weber's sweeping counterthesis, it is clear that his critique of Mayer leads directly into an examination of the ideas and beliefs of fascism and the thought world of which they were an expression.

It goes without saying that a description of fascist ideas, attitudes, and beliefs cannot serve as an adequate account of the nature and genesis of the phenomenon. Any interpretation of fascism must show the role of social forces, especially the lower middle class that provided its mass support. Fascist movements had their base in the diverse social strata located between the propertied bourgeoisie and the proletariat. The lower middle classes were of obvious importance in the genesis of the movement. Fascism catered to the anxieties, frustrations, and aspirations of social groups that felt threatened by proletarian socialism and by the massive structures of industrial and commercial capitalism. Hence fascism has to be understood, in part, as a petty bourgeois *ressentiment* movement, rooted in the social, economic, and political circumstances that existed in Europe in the first third of the twentieth century. Socially determined discontents and resentments were active ingredients in the genesis of fascism. Carsten sums up the standard account of the social basis of fascism. As a result of economic development before 1914, "the position of the lower middle classes, which in most towns formed the bulk of the population, was threatened on the one hand by the process of concentration in industry and trade, the foundation of larger and larger enterprises, and on the other by the rise of the working classes and their vociferous demands for equality and political rights." Large segments of the lower middle classes feared that their position would be undermined or their traditional ways of life eroded. Carsten suggests that in considering the origins of fascism we must look first to these groups. Although they did not come close to power before 1914, "their ideologies were to be carried over into the post-war period when they were to thrive in a far more promising climate."[11]

A rather different view of the relationship between fascism and the lower middle class has been presented by Renzo de Felice. While his interpretation is one-sided and tendentious, it underlies the complexity of the historical process involved and of the social and intellectual forces at work. Although his primary emphasis is social, he rejects the thesis that "the middle classes were becoming *déclassé*, proletarianized, and to avoid this fate they rebelled" and that fascism is to be conceived of as a movement of those people who were being pushed down, "a movement of failures." Against the established interpretation, de Felice argues that "Fascism as movement was the idealization, the desire of an emerging middle class." It was in large part "the expression of an emerging middle class, of bourgeois elements who, having become an important social force, attempted to participate and to acquire political power." Denying that the primary factor in the genesis of fascism was a lower middle class threatened with proletarianization, de Felice argues that fascism was, on the contrary, "the attempt of the petite bourgeoisie in its ascendancy—not in crisis—to assert itself as a new class, a new force." That is, we are dealing with "a class seeking to gain power and to assert its own function, its own culture, and its own political power against both the bourgeoisie and the proletariat. To put the matter briefly: they wanted a revolution. The revolution of the middle classes is extremely important." Hence fascism must be conceived of in more positive terms, whose "class aspects" should be emphasized. It appealed to "those sectors of the petite bourgeoisie that desired a greater participation in and direction of the political and social life of the country." [12]

De Felice's novel conception of the role of the lower middle classes is closely linked to an interpretation of the nature of fascism that also departs sharply from the traditional view. Distinguishing between fascism as "movement" and as "regime," he takes a rather favorable view of the former. Emphasizing the positive aspects of the movement— "that part of fascism that has a certain vitality"—he relegates the nasty aspects of the phenomenon to the regimes in power. Although de Felice denies that his interpretation represents a "positive evaluation of it, an evaluation of merit," the context and his reference to the "moral component" in fascism clearly implies that he expects his readers, who presumably are nonfascists committed to the consensus liberal-democratic values of the 1970s, to regard the aspirations of the "movement" as by no means totally alien. In fact, he identifies fascism as a movement of renovation and renewal very much in the tradition of 1789: "Fascism is the impulse to renew, to interpret certain needs, certain stimuli, and certain themes of renovation. It is that spark of revolutionary fervor that there is within fascism itself, and that tends to construct something new." [13]

Precisely because of its one-sidedness—and originality—de Felice's interpretation brings a number of important issues into the foreground. First of all, while it is well to be reminded that fascism cannot be explained as the expression of a lower middle class threatened with proletarianization, there is little reason to accept the counterthesis that the movements represented the "idealization" of its aspirations as "an important social force." What does emerge clearly is that the relationship between the lower middle class and fascism is complex and problematical. Moreover, that relationship cannot be defined primarily in terms of the social and economic characteristics of the lower middle class. Whether we are interested in accounting for the political outlook and behavior of the lower middle class or for the genesis of fascism, we have to examine the total historical configuration that resulted from the conjuncture of disparate developments before the First World War. One decisive fact is that the political emergence of the lower middle classes occurred in a particular ideological and intellectual milieu, the product of a history that was independent of that social group. While de Felice is in error in linking the lower middle class directly to the tradition of 1789, he has recognized the need to bring ideological factors into the picture. The social and economic characteristics of a class determine no more than the general outline of its outlook. The outlook and behavior of a social group at a particular time and place are affected by the interplay between its socioeconomic characteristics and ideological traditions inherited from the past.

De Felice's depiction of fascism as a relatively benign phenomenon, a lower middle-class version of the principles of 1789, along with his emphasis on the "positive" aspects of fascism is open to objection not only as a whitewashing of a movement that is alien to liberal democratic values, but also as a misrepresentation of the essence of the phenomenon. By the same token, de Felice's interpretation underlines the importance of the question of the nature of fascism. What is striking and novel in fascism is the extent and magnitude of its rejection of values and beliefs that had been established in Western culture for centuries. We have to keep in mind what an extraordinary movement it was. The nihilistic and destructive attitudes at the core of fascism have a special significance for the lower middle class that provided the mass base of the movement. Ordinarily that class is wedded to established values and traditions. The petite bourgeoisie tends to defer to the Establishment in all its forms. At the very least, therefore, its relationship to fascism must be said to be problematical. To be sure, the lower middle class was caught up in social, economic, and political circumstances that undermined its normal inclinations. What was decisive in the genesis of fascism, however, was not these circumstances, although they were a necessary precondition, but the intellectual and ideological setting in which the social and political crisis occurred.

INTELLECTUAL AND IDEOLOGICAL ORIGINS

There were two aspects of the role of intellectual forces in the genesis of fascism: first, certain salient features of European culture in the period 1890–1914; second, the interplay between nationalism, the new right, and the far left in that milieu.

Two interwoven strands in the culture of pre-1914 Europe entered directly into the process underlying the emergence of fascism: a widespread revolt against established liberal and humanitarian values along with the affirmation of countervalues of "activism" and social Darwinism. Toward the end of the nineteenth century there took place a ferocious attack on the consensus ideals of the Enlightenment—liberal, democratic, rationalist, humanitarian, progressive. Europe went through a profound intellectual and moral crisis, unprecedented before or since. As Zeev Sternhell has observed, "for the first time in modern history the work of the greatest minds of their age was used to attack the principles underlying not only bourgeois society and liberal democracy but an entire civilization founded on faith in progress, on the rationality of the individual and on the postulate according to which the ultimate purpose of all social organization is the good of the individual." [14] The result was *une véritable crise de civilisation*. It was in this milieu that fascism took shape.

To be sure, pre-1914 Europe was characterized by an enormous cultural and intellectual diversity. We have to keep in mind Carl Schorske's warning: "What the historian must now abjure, and nowhere more so than in confronting the problem of modernity, is the positing in advance of an abstract categorical common denominator—what Hegel called the *Zeitgeist*, and Mill 'the characteristic of the age.' " [15] Schorske's brilliant account of fin-de-siècle Vienna illustrates the need to undertake "the empirical pursuit of pluralities as a precondition of finding unitary patterns in culture." Historians have just begun to describe the common cultural patterns beneath the multifariousness of the cultural and intellectual life of pre-1914 Europe. While recognizing the difficulties of conceptualization, however, there can be no doubt that cultural and intellectual phenomena characteristic of the period were fundamental to the genesis of fascism. We can refer to the culture of pre-1914 Europe as a form of historical shorthand, so long as we take note of diversity and complexity, of conflicting and contradictory currents.

We have chosen five disparate figures, each from a different country, to illustrate aspects of the culture of pre-1914 Europe that entered into the genesis of fascism. They are not presented as significant causes or influences or as protofascists. One of them was not even European. All of them, however, illustrate pervasive ideas and attitudes that were essential ingredients in the creation of fascism.

Vilfredo Pareto, a major figure in European sociology in the early twentieth century, is noteworthy for the vehemence and intensity of his attack on the traditional humanitarian values of Western culture. At the same time he was obsessed with decadence and degeneracy, whose chief symptoms he took to be the sentiments of benevolence and good will. In a typical sentence, he expressed these views in the diction that pervaded so much of the thought world of pre-1914 Europe:

> If European societies were to model themselves on the ideal dear to the humanitarians, if they should go so far as to inhibit selection, to favour systematically the weak, the vicious, the idle and the ill-adapted—the 'small and humble' as they are termed by our philanthropists—at the expense of the strong, the energetic who constitute the elite, then a new conquest by new 'barbarians' would by no means be impossible.[16]

Humanitarianism was a prime symptom of the decadence of elites: "A sign which almost invariably presages the decadence of an aristocracy is the intrusion of humanitarian feelings and of affected sentimentalizing which render the aristocracy incapable of defending its position."[17]

Social Darwinist categories mingle with a fin-de-siècle obsession with decadence: "When a living creature loses the sentiments which . . . are necessary to it in order to maintain the struggle for life, this is a certain sign of degeneration, for the absence of these sentiments will, sooner, or later, entail the extinction of the species. The living creature which shrinks from giving blow for blow and from shedding its adversary's blood thereby puts itself at the mercy of this adversary." Readiness to use force was a sign of virility; humanitarianism was soft and effeminate. "Any elite which is not prepared to join in battle to defend its positions is in full decadence, and all that is left to it is to give way to another elite having the virile qualities it lacks." Pareto was especially concerned about the decadence of the bourgeoisie. He hoped that their "stupidly humanitarian feelings" would be replaced by something more virile.[18]

Pareto is of interest precisely because of his ambiguous and ambivalent relationship to fascism and its genesis. On the one hand, he viewed it with considerable sympathy and exercised an influence on its development. In 1923 he wrote that "France will be able to save herself only if she finds her Mussolini."[19] On the other hand, he started out as a free trade liberal in the 1890s and retained a number of liberal attitudes throughout his life. Raymond Aron has argued that "if Pareto can be interpreted as a Fascist . . . he can also be interpreted as a liberal. . . . To do him justice, he recommended intellectual liberalism to those who govern, not only because he believed in it, but because he felt that freedom of inquiry and thought is indispensable to the advance of scientific thought, of the logico-experimental mode of thought, and that in the long run society as a whole is benefited by the development of logico-experimental thought."[20] Without entering into the question of the nature and authenticity of Pareto's liberalism, including the extent to which it was in fact compatible with other attitudes and principles that were fundamental to his outlook, it can be said that the presence of such contradictory elements in his thought is a reminder that fascism has to be understood not as a purely demonic force but in part as a perversion of liberal values and principles.

Vacher de Lapouge is of much lesser intellectual stature than Pareto. A doctrinaire social Darwinist, he developed an Aryan racism that won few adherents. Yet he is of considerable historical interest, because he expressed coherently and vividly a cluster of ideas and attitudes that were a part of the culture of pre-1914 Europe. The following passage has a special resonance when read in conjunction with more muted and imprecise expressions of a sensibility shaped by social Darwinism.

Every man is related to all men and all living creatures. Therefore there are no human rights, any more than there are . . . rights of the armadillo. As soon as man loses his right to be a separate entity in the image of God, he no longer has any more right than any other mammal. The idea of justice is in itself an illusion. Nothing exists but violence.[21]

Neither Lapouge nor his contemporaries arrived at their social attitudes as a result of the sort of syllogistic inference indicated by the "therefore" in the passage just quoted. But the Darwinian view of man had nevertheless contributed to the undermining of traditional humanistic and religious values. While Lapouge was not typical in a statistical sense, he was representative of the harsh sensibility that was so pervasive in pre-1914 Europe. He savored the reversal of values: "All men are brothers, all animals are brothers, but being brothers doesn't prevent one from being eaten. . . . Life is maintained only by death. In order to live it is necessary to eat, and in order to eat it is necessary to kill." As Sternhell puts it, this "luminous text" is a remarkable example of the new intellectual climate and the conception of man that it embodied. It illustrates a crisis of liberalism that had its roots in the contradiction between the traditional view of natural rights and "the new laws of existence which the generation of 1890 discovered in social Darwinism."[22]

Unlike Vacher de Lapouge, Friedrich Nietzsche is a commanding figure in modern European thought. He exemplifies certain distinctive aspects of the culture out of which fascism emerged. It is partly because Nietzsche was not a mere nihilist, not a German nationalist, not a proto-Nazi that his thought is so pertinent to an understanding of the cultural milieu that nurtured fascism. The crisis of late-nineteenth-century European culture is ominously symbolized in the fact that the most brilliant and original intellectual of his generation proposed to apply the knife of thought vivisectionally to the most cherished values of a liberal and Christian civilization.[23] He engaged in that morally ambiguous enterprise with a ruthless disregard for the consequences: "Man must have the strength to break up the past, and apply it, too, in order to live. He must bring the past to the bar of judgment, interrogate it remorselessly and finally condemn it."[24] This was the role that Nietzsche himself adopted with great zeal—destroying those remnants of the past that could not stand up to criticism: "Should the injustice of something ever become obvious—a monopoly, a caste, a dynasty, for example, the thing deserves to fall. Its past is critically examined, the knife put to its roots, and all the 'pieties' are grimly trodden under foot" (p. 21). Yet he was acutely aware of the risks of what he was doing. In the next breath he noted that "the process is always dangerous, even for life; and the men or the times that serve life in this way, by judging and annihilating the past, are always dangerous to themselves and others" (pp. 21–22).

Nietzsche had nothing but scorn for nationalist and racist demagogues. As Walter Kaufmann has emphasized, Nietzsche cannot be classified as a protofascist. He was first and foremost a moralist, determined to confront unflinchingly the weaknesses and inconsistencies of the conventional values of his day. He carried out that task with stunning brilliance. Karl Jaspers and Martin Buber, among others, have expressed their debt to him. Yet precisely because of his intellectual eminence and political independence, Nietzsche's assault on liberal values is all the more noteworthy, since it reflected a profound malaise within Western culture. A contemporary, Wilhelm Dilthey, was anxious about the practical implications of the new spirit of which Nietzsche was a symptom. Certainly he exemplified Western thought at its most corrosive, as Jaspers pointed out from a later vantage point.[25] The temper of his attack was ominous. He reviled the "glib-tongued and scribe-fingered slaves of the democratic taste and its 'modern ideas.' " With savage contempt he dismissed the liberal aspirations of the Enlightenment and the nineteenth century: "What they would like to strive for with all their power is the universal green-pasture happiness of the herd: security, lack of danger, comfort and alleviation of life for everyone. Their most frequently repeated songs and doctrines are 'equal rights' and 'compassion for all that suffers.' Suffering is taken to be something that must be *abolished*." In opposition, he exalted a rather different cluster of values: "We imagine that hardness, violence, slavery, peril in the street and in the heart, concealment, Stoicism, temptation, and deviltry of every sort, everything evil, frightful, tyrannical, brutal, and snake-like in man, serves as well for the advancement of the species 'man' as their opposite."[26] Thus Nietzsche ended up depicting well-established vices as means to the elevation of mankind.

Denouncing preachers of equality as secretly vengeful tarantulas,

Nietzsche attacked the whole humanitarian tradition as nothing but the expression of *ressentiment*. As a moralist he hoped to persuade his contemporaries to overcome this weakness: "That man be delivered from revenge, that is for me the bridge to the highest hope, and a rainbow after long storms."[27] Yet the deliverance that Nietzsche promised offered little grounds for hope. He could not overcome the implications of the thesis that the claim of human equality was, in Kaufmann's phrase, an expression of "the *ressentiment* of the sub-equal." That conviction moved Nietzsche to an almost physical revulsion from the aspirations of the left: "Whom do I hate most among the rabble of today? The socialist rabble, the chandala apostles," who make the worker envious, "who teach him revenge." For Nietzsche, what is bad is "all that is born of weakness, of envy, of *revenge*. The anarchist and the Christian have the same origin." He blamed Christianity for having spread the poisonous doctrine of "equal rights for all." In a familiar vein, he argues that out of the *ressentiment* of the masses Christianity "forged its chief weapons against *us*, against all that is noble, gay, high-minded on earth, against our happiness on earth. . . . The aristocratic outlook was undermined from the deepest underworld through the lie of the equality of souls."[28]

Nietzsche also anticipated another theme that was becoming increasingly common in the late nineteenth century: the tendency to equate humanitarianism with softness and effeminacy, as opposed to strength and virility. His denunciation of the triumph of Christianity fits into this pattern: "This cowardly, effeminate, and saccharine pack alienated 'souls' step by step from that tremendous structure—those valuable, those virile, noble natures who found their own cause, their own seriousness, their own pride in the cause of Rome."[29]

As a result of a number of disparate but interrelated developments, educated Europeans found themselves favorably disposed to a cluster of countervalues that may be loosely grouped under the headings of activism and social Darwinism.[30] In the wake of the unification of Germany and Italy, during the last third of the nineteenth century there ensued a period of intensified national rivalry and imperial expansion, accompanied by a new pride in national strength and the material virtues. Imperial expansion in Africa and Asia generated a more favorable view of force and violence, along with attitudes of racial superiority. Thus, the facts of international politics, together with the internal dialectic of reaction against the legacy of the Enlightenment, tended to cast the European mind in a harsher mold. The process was intensified by the presence of Darwinism, a body of thought that was the result of intellectual and scientific developments with a history of their own. Struggle between groups, defined in racial and biological terms, came to be perceived as a necessary contribution to progress. The categories of social Darwinism were ubiquitous. Thus, during the generation before the First World War the European mind went though a tough phase, unparalleled before or since. All of the "soft" values of Western culture came under attack. Sometimes they were openly repudiated or derided. Often their opposites were exalted. Such ingredients as these created the possibility of fascism.

The activist mentality of pre-1914 Europe was very much in evidence in England, albeit without the protofascist overtones characteristic of the Continent.[31] Here the new activism found expression even among men whose commitment to liberalism and democracy was beyond question and who were untouched by the revolt against reason or against positivism. Karl Pearson was such an Englishman. It was social Darwinism of a very doctrinaire variety that led him to reject humanitarian values that had held sway for so long. But Pearson's temper of mind was not merely the product of the dogmatic application of Darwin's categories to the social world; it reflects other pervasive currents moving in the same direction. He redefined the idea of progress in terms that in fact broke with the liberal tradition to which he still gave his allegiance in other respects. While Pearson's political attitudes remained fundamentally liberal, they were overlaid with other doctrines with which they were incompatible.

Pearson's view of the redeeming value of war had much the same content as that of the more shrill militarists on the Continent. His metaphors were by no means limited to biological categories. "This dependence of progress on the survival of the fitter race, terribly black as it may seem to some of you, gives the struggle for existence its redeeming features; it is the fiery crucible out of which comes the finer metal." He did not look forward to the day when "the sword shall be turned into the plough-share," or when the white man and the black shall share the soil between them, for that would mark the end of progress. Thus, he casually dismissed the passage from Isaiah that for so long had expressed the pacific ideals of the Judaeo-Christian tradition. Natural selection "renders the inexorable law of heredity a source of progress, which produces the good through suffering, an infinitely greater good which far out-balances the very obvious pain and evil." His view of the nation is not merely an expression of social Darwinism, but echoes new attitudes that had other sources as well: "I have asked you to look upon the nation as an organized whole in continual struggle with other nations, whether by force of arms or by force of trade and economic processes. I have asked you to look upon this struggle of either kind as a not wholly bad thing; it is the source of human progress throughout the world's history."[32] The war with inferior races must be pressed hard.

Theodore Roosevelt acclaimed American imperialism in the same language that was so common in England and Europe in the 1890s: "When great nations fear to expand, shrink from expansion, it is because their greatness is coming to an end. Are we still in the prime of our lusty youth, still at the beginning of our glorious manhood, to sit down among the outworn people, to take our place with the weak and craven? A thousand times no!" The passage expresses a number of familiar themes: the fear of decline and weakness along with an emphasis on virility, youth, and action. Of the same temper is his denunciation of "the futile sentimentalists of the international arbitration type": their softness and effeminacy threatened to create "a flabby, timid type of character which eats away the great fighting qualities of our race." In the same vein he wrote in a letter in 1895 that "this country needs a war." He announced that "no triumph of peace is quite so great as the supreme triumphs of war." His lyrical praise of warfare is in the European mode: "Every man who has in him any real power of joy in battle knows that he feels it when the wolf begins to rise in his heart." He also used the social Darwinist categories so pervasive in the 1890s, as for example, in his praise for Europe's imperial expansion: "In every instance the expansion has taken place because the race was a great race. It was a sign and proof of greatness in the expanding nation." Like so many of his European counterparts he dismissed traditional humanitarian objections to war as "false sentimentality," the expression of a "warped, perverse, and silly morality."[33]

While these activist and antihumanitarian attitudes were prevalent among Europeans of all political persuasions, they were expressed with special force on the right, which had originated in opposition to the principles of 1789 and to the institutions built on that ideological base. One of the traits that distinguished the new right of the late nineteenth century was the presence of such attitudes in intense form. Another new trait was a resurgent nationalism, which had been so alien to the conservatives of the early nineteenth century. The immediate ideological origins of fascism are to be found in the new right—nationalist, authoritarian, activist, and antidemocratic. But the far left also was relentless in its attack on "bourgeois liberalism," rationalism, and parliamentary government. Moreover, it too embraced nationalism. Thus, the far left displayed a number of affinities with the new right. The interplay between them, in the cultural milieu of pre-1914 Europe, was central to the genesis of fascism. This aspect of the process can be seen in France. While France cannot be said to have been "typical"—the word can be used in this instance only in the most general sense—it illustrates the new combinations and permutations that were present in Europe before the First World War.[34]

Charles Maurras exemplifies, in brilliant and extreme form, characteristics of the new right in France in the years before the outbreak of the First World War. In his thought, nationalism is fused with a number of ideas that had long been familiar on the right—opposition to liberalism, democracy, and the ideology of progress and emancipation expressed in the principles of 1789. But there is also in Maurras, as in so many others of his generation, a new harshness and absoluteness in his revulsion from what was perceived as the contamination and disease of humanitarian values that had been so prized from the very beginning of Western culture. It is the combination of nationalism and antiliberalism in the framework of a broader attack on established values that marks Maurras as an exemplar of the new right. And the fact that he was in the positivist tradition, unlike so many for whom the revolt against positivism was part of their protofascism, underlines how disparate were the elements that went into the genesis of fascism. In fact, the perverse and obsessive elements in his thought—his delight in the irrational—are all the more noteworthy because of the formally positivist cast of his mind.[35]

Maurras counterposed his nationalism to both humanitarianism and pacifism. Thus, he rejected the liberal nationalism of Hervé, whom he rebuked for believing that "there are greater interests than national interests and that above the fatherland exists the human race." Whereas the older Jacobin nationalism perceived the French nation as an instrument of the progress of all mankind, Maurras drew a sharp line between France and humanity as a whole. If one had to choose between them there was no doubt in his mind about what the choice should be: "Those who say . . . 'France first' are patriots, those who say: 'France, but . . .' are humanitarians." The use of "humanitarian" as a pejorative symbolizes a cluster of attitudes on the new right. Not only was the nation treated as an absolute, but nationalist values were contrasted with the ideas of Western culture.

Like so many others, Maurras exalted war and violence. He acclaimed war as "this beautiful crossfire of hatred and love." In addition to external enemies, the nation was threatened by enemies at home, "the barbarians from the depths." Under this heading came liberals, democrats, socialists, and all the champions of "egalitarian barbarism." Maurras attacked them with unrelenting savagery. "Democracy is evil, democracy is death," and the only way to improve it is to destroy it. He proclaimed a fundamental law of political existence: "Thus those peoples who are governed by their men of action and their military leaders win out over those peoples who are governed by their lawyers and their professors."[36] Maurras' metaphors reflect the sensibility of his age. Democracy is a disease that threatens to contaminate France. In the idiom characteristic of his day, he also equates democracy with effeminacy, softness, and decadence: the republic is like a woman, for it lacks "the male principle of initiative and action." Nolte contrasts Maurras' images—miasmas, leprosy, microbes—with the relatively benign metaphors of light and dark characteristic of the liberal tradition that was under attack.[37]

In France before the First World War the extreme left displayed a number of affinities with the new right. The collaboration between followers of Maurras and Sorel in the Cercle Proudhon represents an important aspect of the genesis of French fascism. There was a great deal of overlapping in ideology and in personnel between the two extremes. Nowhere can the affinities between the far left and the far right be seen more vividly than in Georges Sorel. First of all, he combined a commitment to the proletarian revolution, conceived as an apocalyptic transformation, with a total rejection of liberalism, rationalism, and democracy. Sorel was a man of the left who had retained the revolutionary impulse in negative and destructive form, while rejecting the moral, ideological, and intellectual presuppositions of the left in the nineteenth century. Second, he was an apostle of the attack on rationalism and the exaltation of violence, and he identified established values with decadence and decay. Moreover, his involvement with nationalism and the Action Française illustrates the sort of ideological recombination that entered into the making of fascism.

Since Sorel illustrates so directly the prehistory of fascism, we have to be careful not to see him primarily as a protofascist who prefigures satanic ideas to come. A revulsion against fascism should not lead us into a manichean view of its genesis. On the contrary, we have to recognize that we are dealing with an ironic and ambiguous process, which embraced not only destructive forces of resentment and hatred, but also a perversion of authentic efforts to actualize the ideals of Western culture. The forces of darkness alone—activism, racism, anti-Semitism, militarism—could not have produced so pervasive a movement. In the case of Sorel, he had in mind a radical view of human emancipation that represented an authentic expression of utopian aspirations generated by European culture. Sir Isaiah Berlin has described the *idée maîtresse* that dominated Sorel: "that man is a creator, fulfilled only when he creates, and not when he passively receives or drifts unresistingly with the current. . . . Man, at his best, that is, at his most human, seeks in the first place to fulfil himself, individually and with those close to him, in spontaneous, unhindered creative activity, in work that consists of the imposition of his personality on a recalcitrant environment."[38] It was in pursuit of that utopian vision that Sorel developed ideas and attitudes that were part of the protofascist currents that developed before the First World War.

In the early 1890s, Sorel absorbed Marxist ideas that remained at the heart of his thought: above all, a vision of the proletarian revolution and the destruction of bourgeois society as the source of a new order. Class conflict was the key to history. Established liberal and rationalist values were nothing but "bourgeois doctrine," imposed by the bourgeoisie in its rise to power, to be interpreted in the light of Marx's dictum that in every epoch the ruling ideas have been the ideas of the ruling class. Characteristically, however, Sorel sought to define the proletarian socialist alternative in terms of high moral principle. "Socialism is a moral issue in that it provides a new way of judging all human acts."[39] The proletariat was above all the carrier of higher moral values. In 1899 Sorel acclaimed the "admirable ardor" with which the workers were marching for "truth, justice, morality." In this context he hoped that the proletariat would emancipate itself. "Socialism is not a doctrine, not a sect, not a political system; it is the emancipation of the working classes who organise themselves, instruct themselves and create new institutions."[40]

But Sorel defined the role and values of the proletariat in terms that combined an especially harsh version of the class struggle with the new activist sensibility. Above all, he exalted violence and the heroic virtues that he associated with it. As he put it in the last sentence of the *Reflections*, "It is to violence that Socialism owes these high ethical values by means of which it brings salvation to the modern world."[41] With such words, so characteristic of the period, we are in a new thought world, to which no one was more sensitive than Sorel. In the name of high ethical values he celebrated the "sublimity" of "acts of violence grouping themselves around the idea of the general strike" (p. 251). In an explicitly Nietzschean passage, he saw the proletariat embracing the heroic values of the warrior classes of history. "People who have devoted their lives to a cause which they identify with the regeneration of the world could not hesitate to make use of any weapon which might serve to develop to a greater degree the spirit of class war" (p. 278).

Sorel's attack on the bourgeoisie and bourgeois values reflected a new sensibility that embodied a physical revulsion at what was felt to be decadent, corrupt, contaminated, sick, soft, effeminate, weak. The bourgeois values that Sorel found most contemptible were humanitarianism, liberalism, and rationalism. "Proletarian violence . . . seems to be the only means by which the European nations—at present stupefied by humanitarianism—can recover their former energy." The workers must have the energy "to bar the road to the middle-class corrupters, answering their advances with the plainest brutality." In order to show the middle class that they must "mind their own business and only that," the workers must "repay with black ingratitude the benevolence of those who would protect the workers, to meet with insults the homilies of the defenders of human fraternity, and to reply by blows to the advances of the propagators of social peace." He thought that it would be useful "to thrash the orators of democracy and the representatives of the government, for in this way you insure that none shall retain any illusions about the character of acts of violence" (p. 88–90).

By 1909 Sorel's revulsion against liberalism, rationalism, and democracy, along with his exaltation of violence and the warrior virtues, constituted a substantial body of common ground with the outlook of the Action Française and the far right. Sorel joined Maurras on a new journal, *Cahiers du Cercle Proudhon*, which expressed the views of both Sorelian syndicalism and the nationalism of the right.[42] The declaration of the Cercle Proudhon singled out democracy as the common enemy: "Democracy is the greatest enemy of the past century . . . in economics and politics it permitted the establishment of the capitalist regime, which destroys in the state that which democratic ideas dissolve in the spirit, namely, the nation, the family, morals, by substituting the law of gold for the laws of blood."[43] The institutions of democracy had to be destroyed in order to conserve and increase "the moral, intellectual and material capital of civilization." George Valois, who was to become a leader of left fascism after the war, hailed the cercle as a meeting place of two French traditions that had been opposed during the nineteenth century: "nationalism and the authentic socialism, uncorrupted by democracy, represented by syndicalism." It was argued that "nationalism like syndicalism can triumph only by the total eviction of democracy and democratic ideology." The "double revolt" of syndicalism and nationalism would lead to the "complete expulsion of the regime of gold and to the triumph of the heroic values over the ignoble bourgeois materialism in which Europe is suffocating." In other words, there had to be "a revival of Force and Blood against Gold."[44] This resurgence of national energy would overcome plutocracy and wage war against decomposition and decadence.

The emergence of protofascism in pre-1914 France, as embodied in the crosscurrents of nationalism, socialism, antiparliamentarianism, and antihumanitarianism in the Action Française and Sorelian syndicalism, does not yield a model that can be applied to Germany, Italy, or any other country. But France does illustrate, in a particular national setting, possibilities, combinations, and recombinations characteristic of pre-1914 Europe out of which emerged specific fascist movements. In some respects, in the presence of anti-Semitism and racism, for example, French fascism displays affinities with German National Socialism. In other respects, such as the role of genuinely left-wing elements, the resemblance to Italy is more pronounced.[45]

In Germany, as in France, a mixture of nationalism and socialism was also central to the genesis of fascism, but in a significantly different form. Both before and after the war the dominant ideological tradition in Germany, in contrast to France, was conservative and authoritarian. The Germanic ideology, in its various forms, pervaded the middle and upper classes, the bureaucracy and the army. *Völkisch* expressions of the dominant ideology were widespread in the *Mittelstand* in pre-1914 Germany. The new right in Germany was more pervasive and much less new than in France or in Italy. Wilhelmine Germany was rife with illiberalism, authoritarianism, militarism, anti-Semitism, racism, and social Darwinism. The nationalist and authoritarian "socialism" that developed in this milieu before the war, and which found fullest expression in the Strasser brothers after 1918, lacked the organic connection with the traditions of the left that characterized French and Italian syndicalism. It was primarily anticapitalist and asserted the power of the nation and of new elites against established ruling classes. The NSDAP started out as a "petty bourgeois, semi-socialist *ressentiment* movement." And it was impregnated with *völkisch* ideology.[46]

Because of the enormous national variations in fascist movements, it has been argued, with some plausibility, that the notion of a "generic fascism" be abandoned altogether. With good reason, Dietrich Bracher's *The German Dictatorship* keeps the concept of fascism well in the background in order to underline the distinctively German characteristics of National Socialism. In his study of fascist ideology, Zeev Sternhell is unequivocal: "This paper deals with fascism: it is confined to fascism and it deliberately omits nazism." He rejects the notion that National Socialism can be treated as a "mere variant of fascism."[47] Up to a point, this makes good sense. A degree of radical nominalism, so essential to historical understanding, is especially necessary in this case. It can be said that fascism is no more than a convenient label for a variety of movements in interwar Europe. It embraces not only Mussolini, Balbo, Rocco, Farinacci, and their followers, but also Hitler, Goebbels, the Strassers, and their followers. The conspicuous diversity is a warning to steer clear of reification of analytical constructs. National Socialism is certainly not to be explained primarily as a variant of an identifiable entity that may be said to have assumed a different form in the various nations of Europe. Neither National Socialism nor Italian fascism is to be understood as a species of an Aristotelian genus.

But we have to stop well short of accepting a totally nominalist view of fascism. In order to describe and explain the fascist movements of the interwar period it is necessary to operate with an ideal type construct, which makes possible both the description and comparison of phenomena that share important traits and the kind of historical explanation that locates the particular in a framework of unity and diversity. Thus Bracher begins his book by putting National Socialism in a European context. And Sternhell's analysis of protofascism in France and Italy casts light on the genesis of National Socialism, although he prefers to characterize the latter as sui generis. On the other hand, the specifically German components in the NSDAP—*völkisch* racism and the Germanic ideology—tend to overwhelm the European elements with which they were intermixed. Anti-Semitism was European, but the Holocaust was German. While National Socialism has to be understood in the context of the history of fascism in Europe, its German aspects command our attention. Although fascism in Italy was unmistakably Italian, it retained European ideas—and, to a degree, ideals—which in Germany were crushed by the tragic history that culminated in the German catastrophe.

ITALY

Even more than in France the genesis of fascism in Italy was characterized by the conspicuous presence of the new right and the extreme left, in an ambivalent relationship of conflict and collaboration.[48] As in Europe as a whole protofascism emerged in the context of resurgent nationalism and cultural crisis. What was noteworthy in Italy was the active role played by a segment of the far left. This was manifested not only in Mussolini's development from a revolutionary socialist into a fascist but also in the evolution of revolutionary syndicalism into the left fascism that embodied the most militant and fanatic elements in the movement that emerged after the war. In contrast to Germany, where an anticapitalist, authoritarian socialism developed in a right wing, *völkisch* setting, left fascism in Italy had authentic roots in the socialist traditions of the nineteenth century. There was an element of vestigial nineteenth-century idealism in Italian syndicalism, together with a conscious attempt to transform, improve, and even purify inherited revolutionary principles. Theoreticians like Sergio Panunzio took pride in their idealism, rationality, and moderation while firmly rejecting the cult of violence and irrationalism which they saw on the far left in France. Yet there is the most direct continuity from the revolutionary syndicalism of the early twentieth century to young fascists like Italo Balbo and Dino Grandi, who led the *squadristi* in violent assaults on the socialist movement in 1920 and 1921.

The striking thing about the genesis of fascism in Italy, then, is the extent to which it was shaped not only by new right activism and a cultural revolt against established values, but also by attitudes and principles within the left. In Italy the fascist assault on the progressive traditions and institutions of the nineteenth century was mediated— and masked—by an idealism rooted in those traditions. Whereas in Germany, racism and anti-Semitism constituted nihilistic elements at the core of protofascism from the very outset, in Italy more positive ideals entered into the process. Italian fascism embodied not only a repudiation of established values but the perversion of revolutionary ideals. It had its origins, in part, in contradictions within the far left, which made it vulnerable to the intrusion of activist and authoritarian ideas that were also found in the new right. Before turning to the paradoxical developments that transformed revolutionary syndicalism into "left fascism" we shall consider first the ways in which the authoritarian nationalism of the new right spawned protofascist ideas and attitudes that entered into disparate "fascisms" that fused in postwar Italy.

The Nationalism of Enrico Corradini combined a number of elements characteristic of the traditional European right—a rejection of the principles of the French Revolution and the ideological and institutional forms derived from it—with a novel impulse to radical change, remote from conservative defense of the status quo, expressed in the new activist temper of the turn of the century. In the first issue of *Il Regno* in 1903 he announced that a new voice was being raised, "first and foremost against the foul degradation of socialism," which embodied "the basest of angry instincts of cupidity and destruction." In socialism, "all the other classes were outlawed in favour of one class alone and the manual labourers' wages became the be-all and end-all of human society. Every value came under furious attack from the masses." Socialism was nothing but a "looting expedition," conducted in the name of justice. In 1909 he denounced the egalitarianism of the principles of 1789 and proclaimed inequality as fundamental to the Nationalist creed. Even in 1913 he was still denouncing the "contamination of democracy by socialism" and describing a "double antithesis" between nationalism and socialism. The whole cluster of enemies reviled by the European right were conspicuously present throughout his career: liberalism, parliamentarism, "base democracy," and "the doctrines of freedom and internationalism."[49] But Corradini's attack on those traditional enemies was made in a new temper and juxtaposed with other ideas and values that were a vivid expression of the new right.

The basis of Corradini's attack on socialism had little in common with the traditional right or with laissez faire liberalism. In the spirit of the new right, he perceived socialism as the symptom of a more fundamental cultural decay and corruption. Socialism is but one of many signs of "the loathsome decrepitude of degenerate people." Among these foul signs are "outmoded respect for transient human life, outmoded pity for the weak and humble." In this vein he traced the origins of socialism to the Bible: "The first socialism is in the Bible. The first justice of the lowest is in the Bible. The first violence of the meek against the violent, the first arrogance of the humble against the arrogant, are in the Bible. . . . The prophet is the revolution." Moreover, the bourgeoisie too have been "deeply infected by the contagion of the sociologies, the philosophies, the policies, the atheistic, secular, cosmopolitan mysticism which are the well-manured soil in which the seeds of socialism have grown and prosper." Corradini's attack on democracy also had a distinctive pre-1914 resonance. The greater had been driven out by the less—"driven out of teaching, literature, art, the theater, philosophy, science, history, wherever the materialistic democracy of tiny little men could drive out an *idea* and replace it by *matter*—replace it by the less, by those deficient in spirit and intelligence and ambition, by worthless ability, lifeless senility, incompetent honesty or dishonesty whose only competence lies in evil-doing."

In a speech in 1913 Corradini denounced pacifism as the expression of a decadent and cowardly bourgeoisie. He announced that the essence of Italian nationalism consisted in fighting pacifism in all its forms. The first type that he singled out was "the idealistic pacifism of the cultivated and cosmopolitan middle classes of contemporary Europe." This idealistic pacifism, he argued, was supported by "pious humanitarianism" and by "the principle that human life is sacred." In the idiom of Pareto he noted that at the bottom of such principles lies "a residue of atavistic cowardice." Thus the middle classes were "turning their backs on reality and wallowing in decadence." He even depicted socialism as contaminated by such soft middle-class doctrines: "The socialist international, founded on the solid community of interests of the proletariat, has been succeeded by the democratic international, fluid, sentimental and rhetorical in nature, an age-old humanitarian and pacifist secretion of decadent peoples, now secreted by the glands of the cultivated cosmopolitan classes of Europe."[50]

Another theme in Corradini, echoed in many of his European contemporaries, is the claim that he is asserting higher values and true moral principles and striving for a regeneration of national life on this basis. "Winning our war is not a simple-minded poetic or prophetic statement but a moral imperative. In a word, we propose a 'means of national redemption.' " Since the "higher values of mankind and the nation have been cast down," there is a need for a "change of system in order to find a better one, both human and material." Rejecting "all that is basely material in life," nationalism proclaimed "higher human and national values so that they may be seen by those who are resurrecting to new life."[51] Along with a revulsion against established values went a desire for an apocalyptic transformation. Thus, Corradini's nationalism is remote indeed from a conservative defense of established interests against challenge from the left. The bourgeoisie has been equally contaminated by the vices that threaten "the higher values" that Corradini acclaimed. His approach is not conservative but profoundly radical, not only in the call for a "change of system" but in the whole temper of his outlook. He recognized his kinship with the radicalism of the left.

Even in 1903 Corradini referred to "those of us who believe in socialism when it is not ignoble." Socialism was "ignoble" to the extent that it embodied liberal, internationalist, and humanitarian values. As revolutionary syndicalism developed a harsher version of socialism, Corradini found himself in sympathy with much of it and in 1910 emphasized the common ground between them. In a speech of December 3, 1910, in which he described Italy as a proletarian nation, he praised socialism for having developed the fighting spirit of the proletariat. Socialism "urged them to fight and, through that fight, forged their unity, their awareness, their strength, their very weapons, their new rights, their will to win." He concluded: "Well, my friends, nationalism must do something similar for the Italian nation. It must become, to use a rather strained comparison, our national socialism." Writing in the syndicalist journal, *La Lupa*, Corradini argued that nationalism and syndicalism shared the same "virtuous substance," specific to each. "The only morality of syndicalism is struggle. The only morality of nationalism is . . . war." Both shared a common adversary—the timid ruling bourgeoisie. They were both opposed to bourgeois commercialism and socialist economism: "Nationalism and syndicalism are the school of great aristocratic works which are pursued and accomplished in the course of centuries and millennia. The ultimate end of nations is, for nationalism, to create a new civilization and to give it to the history of the human race."[52]

The rhetorical excesses of Corradini and the intellectuals of *Il Regno* have a significance that goes beyond style. Their diction expresses not only a new form but a new substance. Giovanni Papini, one of Corradini's collaborators on *Il Regno*, expressed in characteristically extravagant form the contempt for humanitarianism—stigmatized as soft, decadent, and sentimental—that was so conspicuous in the outlook of the new right. In a speech in February 1904, he described democratic ideology as nothing but the rational expression of "democratic sentimentality." "Anti-war theories are not produced by reason but reasons are found to excuse the reluctance to accept bloodshed, the fear of conflict and other similar sentimental weaknesses." He derided the sentimentality underlying "the irrational respect for human life." He quoted his earlier comments on this subject in the first number of *Il Regno*, in 1903. There he had denounced the vicious principle—that every man has a right to live and everyone must live—which lay at the root of "all the claims of the proletariat, every anti-war protest or sentimental excess." What is noteworthy is the absoluteness of his rejection of Western values, including the notion that "a man has the right to live, that he possesses within himself that sacred and intangible something that is normally considered the mysterious attribute of divinity." Papini deplored the fact that ordinary morality which had become so much inflated by "squeamish and wordy philanthropy," was based on such sentimental and irrational notions. He even invoked hatred as a matter of high principle: "And in order to love something deeply you need to hate something else. No perfect Christian can love God without loathing the Devil." And of all the things that an Italian nationalist ought to hate, the "democratic mentality" was at the head of the list: "This mentality we despise and oppose and hate and guard against with every means in our power." Papini's characterization of the phenomenon made plain why he found it so loathsome. He described a "confused medley of debased feelings, empty thoughts, defeatist phrases and brutish ideals." Under this rubric he included a whole range of *bêtes noires* "from comfortable established radicalism to the snivelling anti-militarism of Tolstoy, from bogus positivism with its facile belief in progress and superficial anti-clericalism to the resounding *blagues* of the French Revolution—Justice, Fraternity, Liberty, and Equality."[53]

In pre-1914 Italy as in Europe as a whole, protofascist attitudes had the glitter of novelty for a substantial segment of the literary and artistic avant-garde. Men like Filippo Marinetti delighted in the shock value of activism and anti-intellectualism. Art, ideology, and politics mingled in his Manifesto of Futurism: "It is in Italy that we are issuing this manifesto of ruinous and incendiary violence, by which we today are founding Futurism, because we want to deliver Italy from its gangrene of professors, archeologists, tourist guides and antiquaries." He worked rather hard at achieving a shocking effect and succeeded, as for example his ninth point: "We want to glorify war—the only cure for the world—militarism, patriotism, the destructive gesture of anarchists, the beautiful ideas which kill, and contempt for woman." While the tenth thesis of the Manifesto is hardly "typical" of the culture of pre-1914 Europe, it could have been produced—and taken seriously—only at this time: "We want to demolish museums and libraries, fight morality, feminism and all opportunism and utilitarian cowardice."[54]

With his wonted excess, Marinetti acclaimed "the young strong and living Futurists" and called on "the good incendiaries with charred fingers" to burn the libraries. The oldest among them are not yet thirty; in ten years they will have done their work. "When we are forty let younger and stronger men than we throw us in the wastepaper-basket like useless manuscripts! . . . They will crowd around us, [and] . . . hurl themselves forward to kill us, with all the more hatred as their hearts will be drunk with love and admiration for us. And strong healthy injustice will shine radiantly from their eyes." He concluded with a line that sums up much of the pre-1914 sensibility that he was expressing with such gusto: "For art can only be violence, cruelty, and injustice."[55]

There is a surreal quality to the Futurist Manifesto, and in fact Marinetti described how it originated in all-night sessions with his friends, "discussing right up to the limits of logic and scrawling the paper with demented writing." He set out to "leave good sense behind like a hideous husk" and he succeeded. There is little "good sense" in his view of art, but there is a great deal of pre-1914 mentality. "We want to sing the love of danger, the habit of energy and rashness. The essential elements of our poetry will be courage, audacity and revolt." In literature he would "exalt movements of aggression, feverish sleeplessness, the double march, the perilous leap, the slap and the blow with the fist." In his activist esthetics "beauty exists only in a struggle. . . . There is no masterpiece that has not an aggressive character. Poetry must be a violent assault on the forces of the unknown, to force them to bow before man."[56]

After a detailed description of the many aspects of the "democratic mentality," Papini added that it was not only this that was so loathsome but "the whole mentality of our times. You can feel its hostile and dominating presence in everything at every moment."[57] The sense of profound alienation from "the whole mentality of our times" was by no means confined to Papini, Marinetti, and a coterie of literary men. To a significant degree, some such attitude was widespread among intellectuals and academics of the pre-1914 generation in Europe. The revolt against liberalism, rationalism, and humanitarianism was deeply rooted in this phase in the history of European culture; it was not merely an expression of the resurgence of the right. The far left also was affected.

It was a "left fascism" spawned by neosyndicalism that provided the dynamic element in the fascist movements in Italy in the early 1920s.[58] What brought about the transformation of syndicalism, committed to proletarian socialist revolution at the turn of the century, into a form of fascism that collaborated with the right in an assault on socialist workers and trade unions? At the heart of the process was the interplay between antirevisionist Marxism and a complex of ideas and attitudes derived from Pareto and the intellectual climate of pre-1914 Europe. The antiliberal and antiparliamentary strain in left-wing Marxism was accentuated by the infusion of activist and antirational elements in the context of a resurgent nationalism. In addition, there was an idealistic element in the genesis of left fascism in Italy, which stands out in contrast to the cult of violence in Sorelian syndicalism in France and to the harsh racism of the *völkisch* movements in Central Europe. Men like Panunzio and Lanzillo prided themselves on their idealism, rationality, and moderation, often taking issue with the hotheads in France. Their ties to the progressive left of the nineteenth century, above all to Mazzini, were strong. They drifted into fascism, persuading themselves at each stage that they were devising the policies that were necessary to solve Italy's problems and to actualize her ideals.

At the heart of revolutionary syndicalism in Italy lay the ambiguous legacy of Marxism. On the one hand, the syndicalists embraced the utopian ideal of a proletarian revolution that would transform capitalism into socialism, end the domination of the bourgeoisie, abolish exploitation and alienation, and actualize the freedom that is the true essence of man. As Marxists they envisaged a liberating revolution, grounded in social and economic forces that determined the course of history. On the other hand, the Italian syndicalists also accepted the Marxist attack on bourgeois values and institutions. As the ruling class in capitalist society, the bourgeoisie had imposed its ideology. The revolution would destroy the ideological and institutional domination of the bourgeoisie. Like other antireformist Marxists at the turn of the century, including Mussolini, the syndicalists became preoccupied with the parliamentary system and liberal democratic gradualism as obstacles to the proletarian revolution. In their conflict with reformist socialists they denounced as bourgeois the ideological and institutional structures of liberal democracy. Inevitably, the bourgeois taint was extended to the fundamental values of Western culture. This process of ideological corrosion was intensified as syndicalism assimilated elitist and activist ideas.

Arturo Labriola, the leading figure in the genesis of Italian syndicalism, combined Marxism with the ideas of Pareto, Sorel, and Francesco Merlino. Born in 1873 the son of an artisan, he was active in the republican cause while still in his teens. But Marxism soon claimed his allegiance and at the age of twenty he joined the newly formed Italian socialist party. From Marx he absorbed the vision of a proletarian revolution inherent in the historical development of capitalism. Like other socialists at the turn of the century, however, Labriola shifted the focus to the syndicates in which the proletariat was being organized. Rejecting Bakunist notions of a spontaneous insurrection by the people, he stressed the necessity for the gradual maturation of the proletariat through industrialization. He shared A. O. Olivetti's confidence in the growth of the syndicalist mentality under the stimulus of "large industry and the intense vibration of capitalist life" among the segment of the working class capable of feeling "the unique revolutionary impulse that is syndicalism pulsating in its veins and stimulating its will." That idiom, so characteristic of the pre-1914 intellectual climate was also present in Labriola's thought. As an antireformist Marxist, he rejected determinist gradualism in favor of voluntarist action by proletarian syndicates. The improvement of working conditions was not their aim: "The syndicalists are preoccupied above all with the *transformation* of society."[59] The task of the proletariat was to create something totally new.

From Sorel and Merlino came the notion that the proletarian syndicates would create new values for socialist society. The key question for socialists, Sorel wrote in 1898 in a work translated by Labriola in 1903, was "to determine whether there exists *a mechanism capable of guaranteeing the development of morality.*" Merlino conceived of socialism as fundamentally an ethical matter, a major theme in his writings. It was in a preface to a French translation of a work by Merlino that Sorel had written: "Socialism is a moral issue in that it provides a new way of judging all human acts, or, in Nietzsche's famous phrase, a revaluation of all values."[60] The cult of violence preached in the *Reflections* did not take hold, but as Labriola and the syndicalists took up the ideas of Pareto and others, they defined their new values in morally ambiguous terms.

Labriola's conception of the proletariat and its task was profoundly affected by a cluster of ideas derived from the elitist sociology of Pareto. First and foremost, the bourgeoisie was identified as a decadent elite, which had to be replaced by a dynamic new elite, the proletariat, which would create new values and take the necessary action, including the use of force, to displace the bourgeoisie and its corrupt beliefs. Labriola, who had worked as Pareto's research assistant in Switzerland, had the most direct access to these ideas. He defined socialism in terms of the development of anti- and postbourgeois values and institutions by a new proletarian elite. Through the syndicates the proletariat was developing a moral and legal alternative to the corrupt system dominated by the bourgeoisie. Pareto himself, writing in *Il devenire sociale* in 1905, lent his support to such a view of the proletariat as a new elite.[61]

From the very outset revolutionary syndicalism in Italy expressed itself in a grandiloquent rhetoric that echoed the Mazzinian idealism of the nineteenth century. This served to mask the intrusion of activist, elitist, and authoritarian ideas alien to the progressive traditions on which they were being grafted. Sergio Panunzio, an academic intellectual whose ideological development moved in a straight line from syndicalism to neosyndicalism and left fascism, exemplifies this pattern. In 1906 he expressed the syndicalist faith in the proletariat in the high-flown rhetoric that was to be the hallmark of his career as an ideologue: "Thanks to today's syndical organizations, the brute and disorganized labor forces, which have exerted so many vain efforts throughout history to redeem themselves from slavery, become intelligent, aware, organic forces; the static masses are converted into distinct and stable combinations and associations. So the syndicate marks a high degree of perfection, or elevation, in the mental, psychological, moral, and social evolution of the proletariat." In May 1914, writing in *Utopia*, a journal edited by Mussolini, Panunzio praised the utopianism and the demand for justice that lay at the base of Marxism, but argued that socialism as an inspiration ought to be realized as a matter of idealism rather than materialism.[62]

Preoccupied with moral goals and high ideals, Panunzio and the syndicalists moved steadily toward a reversal of the principles of the nineteenth-century left. As the shortcomings of the proletariat as a revolutionary force became increasingly apparent, a more elitist version of the new creed emerged: the revolution would be the work of an elite within the proletariat. At the same time the syndicalists' antipathy to the parliamentary system and its values deepened. In this situation, the activist, antiliberal, antihumanitarian, antidemocratic elements in their outlook were strengthened.

Within the proletariat, an elite uncorrupted by the parliamentary system and bourgeois values would create a new and purer system. Panunzio envisaged a purifying revolution made by a "new social aristocracy." In an article in 1909 on "Syndicalists and the Elite," Olivetti explained that the "special revolutionary call that is syndicalism, . . . more a state of mind than a doctrine," arises out of "a sensitivity that not all can share." Syndicalism required a "concentration of energy that the very historic and physiological conditions of the working class impedes from becoming common, still less universal. It would be excellent if all workers were conscious of their condition and wished to change it. But who does not recognize that this is an unattainable dream?" Olivetti pinned his hopes on a revolutionary minority within the proletariat who were concerned with "ideal aspirations." This "supremely human elite, composed of those possessed, in heart and mind, of greater humanity," was a true aristocracy of blood and nerve open to all the strong."[63]

In their frustration, the syndicalists came to see the parliamentary system and the political class that dominated it as the immediate en-

emy that had to be dealt with before turning to the economic and social structure of capitalism. The corruption of the proletariat as a whole
was attributed in part to participation in electoral politics. Filippo
Corridoni, for example, drawing on Mosca, argued that "the state is
always controlled . . . by a 'political class' composed of a handful of
people who make politics an unscrupulous profession." Prefiguring
ideological changes that lay ahead, Corridoni even saw the need for
some sort of preliminary revolution in which the proletariat would play
no part. Paolo Mantica went even further in identifying the parliamentary system as the immediate enemy that had to be dealt with first.
The introduction of universal suffrage would only compound existing
corruption. As Alceste De Ambris put it, "certain political conquests are indispensable to create the atmosphere necessary for syndicalism to live and develop."[64] Such conquests involved the destruction of the parliamentary system and the creation of a syndicalist
alternative. At a syndicalist conference in France in 1908 Labriola denounced the official socialist movement for accepting the rules of the
parliamentary game and substituting class cooperation for class struggle. "Socialism is not a derivation of democracy," he emphasized. With
democracy discredited, the road to authoritarian syndicalism was open.

An infusion of nationalist sentiment in the years before the 1914 war
moved syndicalism another step in the direction that led to fascism.
The first major development occurred during the Libyan war of 1911–
12, which was opposed by the vast majority of syndicalists, who remained faithful to the internationalist traditions of socialism. Three
dissidents who supported the war—Labriola, Olivetti, and Paolo Orano—foreshadowed the massive ideological shift to come. Of the three,
Labriola's support for the war is especially interesting, since he did
not follow the other two into neosyndicalism and fascism. His position
illustrates the appeal of nationalism and activism to a revolutionary
syndicalist concerned about the apathy of the proletariat. Like Olivetti
and Orano, Labriola supported the Libyan war because of the salutary
effect that he hoped it would have on the proletariat and on Italian
society as a whole: "O my comrades, do you know why the Italian
proletariat is not fit to make a revolution? For precisely the same reason it is not fit to wage war. Let the proletariat get used to fighting
seriously, and then you will see that it will learn to strike the bour-

geoisie itself!" The war would overcome the decadence of the proletariat and of Italian society: "It will be a tremendous and painful experience, but under that pedagogy we will remake ourselves."[65]

Although Panunzio did not support the Libyan war, his orientation was compatible with the militant interventionism of 1914–15 that led directly to neosyndicalism and left fascism. As early as 1904 he had argued that while peace is conservative and stabilizing, wars can exercise a progressive and revolutionary influence. A few years later he characterized pacifism as typical of a decadent bourgeois elite and implied that a war might contribute to the emergence of a new elite. After the outbreak of war in 1914 Panunzio formed an interventionist *Fascio* in Ferrara and enlisted Dino Grandi, Italo Balbo, and other idealistic young men. In 1916, in a book entitled *The Concept of the Just War*, Panunzio argued that socialism had a stake in a just war directed against German militarism. He depicted a "just war" as offensive in character, intended to create a new and more just order of things, to be contrasted with a merely defensive war to preserve the status quo. Here Panunzio was playing his usual role: putting a veneer of idealism—enthusiastically and passionately embraced—on protofascist principles and policies. A just war would bring about the "rectification of juridical experience in light of the Idea and the preparation of the final triumph of Justice, which is the implicit end of history." Characteristically, he set out to have the best in both worlds. He took pride in the fact that he did not celebrate war and violence for their own sake as did various "litterateurs and false poets."[66] He praised war only for the ideal ends to which it would contribute.

The ideological development that led from intervention to neosyndicalism and left fascism can be seen clearly in Agostino Lanzillo. During the interventionist debates, he remained firmly committed to the proletarian socialist revolution. He justified Italian intervention in the war primarily on the grounds that the defeat of Germany was necessary for the advance of socialism. In an article in Mussolini's *Il popolo d'Italia*, Lanzillo described the "war of redemption" as a prerequisite for socialism. "Our war" would help the proletariat to bring about the socialist revolution on the syndicalist model. When he wrote *The Socialist Defeat* in 1917, however, Lanzillo was no longer concerned with the proletariat, which had remained aloof from interventionism.

Rather he was transfixed by the "bloody and legendary regeneration" that was being brought about by the war. He saw mysterious forces, long smoldering within society, now burst to the surface, "to assume tragic forms, purifying and transforming society." Itself the product of the decadence of European society, the war was bringing new growth. It was a revolution, a "savage hecatomb" that was "giving birth to a prodigious renewal." [67]

One of the beneficent consequences of war envisaged by Lanzillo was the triumph of syndicalism, which he defined in terms that reflected the pre-1914 intellectual climate and the ideological development that he and other syndicalists had experienced since the turn of the century. "The truth of syndicalism," he wrote, "lies precisely in its long-standing opposition to democratic optimism and socialist materialism, and in its tireless advocacy of the importance of developing a proletarian consciousness which despises the sickly and corrupt democratic mentality of the bourgeoisie." Like other neosyndicalists, Lanzillo retained the nihilistic and destructive element in Marxism, the impulse to destroy values and institutions deemed to be "bourgeois," while taking for granted the impulse to emancipation. Among the "sickly and corrupt" elements in a decadent bourgeois society were democracy, humanitarianism, pacifism, and rationalism. Lanzillo welcomed the fact that the war upset "the whole scale of values, all the calculations of the socialist pedagogues and all the hopes of the humanitarians." The downfall of democratic ideology in the war was paving the way for regeneration and the creation of a new ideology. He acclaimed "the truth of the syndicalists' ideas on violence." The "most glorious manifestation of syndicalist activity" was the antiparliamentary struggle waged in France and Italy and he looked forward to "further major developments in the immediate postwar future." He praised the syndicalists' "refusal to recognize any legitimacy, usefulness or even reality in the strictly electoral attitude of the bourgeoisie and the socialists, as a party." [68] A decade and more of denunciation of both the bourgeoisie and reformist socialism had led Lanzillo and the syndicalists to a protofascist elitism and authoritarianism—directed against decadence, pacifism, liberalism, and parliamentarism.

What is especially noteworthy is the cluster of enemies that Lanzillo denounces. It is not capitalist exploitation of the proletariat that concerns him; nor is it the domination exercised by the bourgeoisie. Rather, it is "bourgeois" values and institutions that are stigmatized as decadent and corrupt. Thus, he deplores the "optimistic, pacifistic and reformist democratic processes" that were so far advanced in Europe. It is in this context that he welcomes the simultaneous appearance—"not purely by chance"—of nationalist and syndicalist movements at the turn of the century. There was some hope that these two "trends toward reform" might succeed in arresting the reformist democratic processes that were so far advanced. Although "the decadence of society had gone too deep and had become too complex and organic to be stopped by ordinary means and by minority movements," the war created new possibilities by bringing to the surface mysterious forces that might purify and transform society. When it seemed that "the forces of rationalism and intellectualism" were about to prevail, the war fortunately intervened.[69]

As a result of the war and the socialists' neutralism, Lanzillo and the syndicalists concentrated their fire on pacifism and on the humanitarian traditions in which it was rooted. He denounced pacifism as "one of the most eloquent and characteristic symptoms" of a decadent, enervated capitalist society. "Pacifism is the most authentic manifestation of society's lack of revolutionary spirit." It was to be understood in part as "the sentimental Utopian attitude that preaches the need for peace as it might preach happiness or goodness, with a similar likelihood of success." Lanzillo also depicted pacifism in broader pre-1914 terms "as something more comprehensive, a general reluctance of modern nationalities to settle the major conflicts of interests between peoples by recourse to tragic means."[70] The rhetorical sentimentality of the nineteenth century was being transferred, by Lanzillo and others, to an exaltation of rather different objects. The softness, fuzziness, and muddle remains—but in pernicious and dangerous form.

The most striking aspect of the evolution of neosyndicalism during the war was the abandonment of the notion that the proletariat would make a revolution. Now the neosyndicalists envisaged a new nonproletarian elite, created by the war, which would embody all the virtues hitherto imputed to the proletariat. Lanzillo referred specifically to Pareto in his account of the emergence of a new ruling elite that "must assume the leadership of the nation." Like other neosyndicalists, Lanzillo was disappointed that the proletariat showed so little enthusiasm for the "war of redemption." He no longer expected the development of a mature "proletarian consciousness" to bring about a revolution. Early in 1918 he was deploring the workers' "frenzy for enjoyment" and denouncing the "frigid and ignoble egotism" of the Turin metal workers, who rejected all sacrifice and forgot family and country. Like De Ambris he saw the Bolshevik revolution as a perversion of revolution and denounced the workers' occupation of the factories in 1919 and 1920 as the result of a misguided infatuation with bolshevism. Some neosyndicalists hoped that the remnants of a revolutionary elite within the proletariat might join with the new revolutionary force created by the war. In 1919 De Ambris advocated a coalition of war veterans in revolutionary action against the government. Inevitably, however, the main emphasis came to be put on the failure of the proletariat and on the corresponding strength of the new elite. Massimo Rocca put this point bluntly in an article, "Sorel's Error," which appeared in a fascist journal in July 1922. According to Rocca, both Sorel and the Italian syndicalists had been wrong in putting their faith in the proletariat as a source of "moral renewal."[71]

The syndicalists transferred to the nonproletarian elite their hopes for the destruction of corrupt beliefs and the creation of new moral values. Not content with merely reforming the bureaucracy, they saw "habits to be inverted, a new ethic to be constituted." Cheap parliamentary competitions must be eliminated and "our ethical foundations must be completely rebuilt."[72] Looking back on the syndicalist tradition, Panunzio accurately pointed out that it was the moral possibilities of organization that had attracted the syndicalists from the very beginning. Untainted by vulgar materialism, they had embraced the purest idealism. But the inner content of the syndicalist ideals of Merlino and Labriola at the turn of the century had been totally transformed in the intervening two decades.

An intensely idealistic neosyndicalism was the chief element in the "new radical fascism" of 1921. It was "young idealists" like Dino Grandi and Italo Balbo who led the *squadristi* in violent attacks on the socialists. They were the ones who saw fascism as a movement of revolutionary change destined to transform corrupt values and institutions. They were the exponents of what has been called "totalitarian super-democracy." Balbo, for example, perceived himself as the exponent of new and higher ideals, derived from syndicalism and adapted to the needs of Italy after the war. He had worked closely with Panunzio in the interventionist *Fascio* in Ferrara in 1915. An admirer of Mazzini, he wrote a university thesis on his social thought. When Balbo became a fascist in 1921, he complained of the lack of ideals in public life in Italy and on this basis opposed the moderate tactics then being pursued by Mussolini. It was in behalf of his ideals that he led the *squadristi.*[73]

Dino Grandi, who has been described as "the most coherent spokesman for the new radical fascism of 1921," turned to syndicalism before the war while still a high school student. He read Sorel and Olivetti's *Pagine libere*. In 1915 he joined Panunzio's interventionist *Fascio* in Ferrara and participated in a student strike at the University in support of intervention. Even before the war he saw the need to define syndicalism in broad terms that went beyond an exclusive link with the proletariat. After the war he developed a national syndicalism that envisaged an alliance of war veterans with the economically productive elements of the nation. They would seize the initiative from the socialists and take over the trade unions in order to make "the right kind of revolution." The new order would be based on a fusion of nationalism and syndicalism, which Grandi depicted as aspects of an Italian spiritual renewal that had begun before 1914. He drew on nationalists like Rocco in formulating his national syndicalism, a fuzzy and abstract collage of activist-idealist attitudes: "The syndicate as person, as will, as an autonomous, dynamic, organic nucleus, is by now such a vital and living force that to deny it means to place oneself in absurdity, outside reality, outside the revolution, outside history. . . . In the syndicate is the *true* revolution, and in it can be found already constructed the framework of the new state of tomorrow."[74]

Kurt Suckert (Curzio Malaparte) was another of the "young fascist idealists" of the early 1920s who saw fascism as a movement of revolutionary change. Like so many of the others, he was an admirer of Panunzio. In the early years of Mussolini's regime, he was a leading exponent of a second dose of *squadristi* violence. He illustrates the extent to which the inner content of the left had been transformed in neosyndicalism until only the impulse to revolution remained. He also illustrates the manner in which the assimilation of nationalist and activist ideas contributed to that transformation. "We are Italians, not philanthropists; and as Fascists and syndicalists, that is to say, deeply revolutionary, we are anti-democratic because we are anti-humanitarian."[75]

With Suckert we have come full circle. We are back in the pre-1914 world of activism, nationalism, and the revolt against Western values in their totality. He throws them all into the mix, helter-skelter. Mussolini is praised as the defender of Italy against "the skeptical, critical, nationalistic and enlightened spirit of Western and Northern Europe" and against "those ultimate political forms of the Reformation, liberalism, democracy and socialism." Mussolini will rescue present-day Italy, "debased by her acceptance and assimilation of European ideas." If he is to be successful in this revolt against the modern Western Nordic spirit, Mussolini must be "anti-bourgeois, anti-proletarian, anti-liberal, anti-European, anti-modern." His historic mission has been to give back to the nation "the physical sense of heroism." While the fantasies in the following passage were hardly typical in a statistical sense, they embody an aspect of the sensibility that nurtured fascism: "Our people must suffer, we must suffer; only deep and atrocious suffering, experienced by all, like that caused by famine, plague, or civil war, can transform us from being parochial and gluttonous into a magnificent imperial people."[76]

Mussolini's ideological development is central to an understanding of the genesis of Italian fascism, but the relationship between them is problematical. On the one hand, he exemplifies a line of development from revolutionary Marxism, embodying a number of characteristics of the activist culture of the turn of the century, into protofascism. Unlike the neosyndicalists, however, he did not take up a clearly defined ideological position. He was neither a left fascist nor a right fascist. Between 1919 and 1922 his "fascism" was protean and eclectic, linked to a flexible and opportunistic politics. But his commitment to the fundamentals of the fascist outlook—nationalist, authoritarian, antiliberal, inclined to some sort of radical change—enabled him to bring together into a single movement disparate elements of left and right.

At the turn of the century Mussolini was an antirevisionist Marxist whose socialism was suffused with the activist and antiliberal attitudes of the pre-1914 intellectual climate. His version of the doctrine of class struggle, for example, put violence at the very center. He even described Marx as the "magnificent philosopher of working class violence." From this standpoint he denounced the "socialism of the lawyers." With his usual gusto Mussolini made plain that the proletarian revolution would have to be a rather bloody affair: "Instead of deluding the proletariat as to the possibility of eradicating all causes of bloodbaths, we wish to prepare it and accustom it to war for the day of the 'greatest bloodbath of all,' when the two hostile classes will clash in the supreme trial." Mussolini was quite aware of the new ideas that he was drawing on in defining his socialist ideology and in attacking the revisionists: "The classic conception of revolution finds in today's trend of philosophic thought an element of vitality. Our conception rejuvenates. Reformism, on the other hand, the wide and duly evolutionary, positivist, and pacifist reformism, is henceforth condemned to decrepitude and decay." Hence it was necessary to purge socialism of the "idyllic, arcadian, pacifist conception" of the reformists. In this spirit, Mussolini clothed the doctrine of class struggle in the antipacifist, antihumanitarian language that was so conspicuous in the pre-1914 generation: "He who says fecundation says laceration. No life without shedding blood."[77]

Thus, Mussolini embodied a number of traits characteristic of the far left in pre-1914 Europe, notably an extreme hostility to the values of parliamentary democracy, which he expressed in the activist sensibility so characteristic of the period. At a number of points his outlook displayed affinities with the new right. "The undeniable decadence of Italian parliamentarism," he told a socialist congress in 1912, "is the reason why all the parliamentary groups . . . voted in favor of a broader suffrage; it is the oxygen that prolongs the life of the dying."[78] The metaphor of decadence and dying—viewed in conjunction with the exaltation of violence and the condemnation of humanitarianism—is not mere rhetoric, but an expression of values and attitudes that were to be constitutive of fascism.

In 1934 Joseph Goebbels acclaimed Mussolini and the triumph of fascism in Italy as a repudiation of the principles of 1789: "The march on Rome was a signal, a sign of storm for liberal democracy. It is the first attempt to destroy the . . . world which started in 1789 with the storm on the Bastille and conquered one country after the other in violent revolutionary upheavals, to let the nations go under in Marxism, democracy, anarchy and class warefare."[79] That is an apt characterization of the relationship between fascism and the French Revolution. As we have seen, however, the ideological consequences of 1789 were also involved more directly in the genesis of fascism. The French Revolution, Marxism, and fascism were linked in an intricate and ambiguous historical relationship. Each of these disparate phenomena was the product of processes embracing intellectual and ideological forces that had developed within Western culture.

PART TWO

CHAPTER FIVE

Heuristic Assumptions

Underlying every work of history is a conception of the human world and of the ways in which it may be understood and explained. This chapter is intended to make explicit the substantive and methodological assumptions on which the interpretation presented in part I is grounded. It is argued that these assumptions make possible an empirical inquiry into the role of ideas in particular events and developments, whereas the paradigms and theories discussed in chapters 6 and 7 tend to prejudge the answers to the questions they pose.

In considering the role of ideas in the genesis of a particular event, the historian brings into play a conception of the nature and interrelationship between cultural and social phenomena and of the ways in which they affect human actions. These generic characteristics of the human world have been analyzed systematically by social scientists and philosophers and the opening section draws on some of their work. But the historian deals with the interplay between cultural and social phenomena in specifically *historical* processes. The next section outlines the historical character of the human world and the role of intellectual forces shaping and constituting it. Along with such substantive assumptions, every historical interpretation presupposes a conception of how to go about understanding and explaining the past. Drawing on work in analytical philosophy, I sketch the distinctive sort of explanation, characterized variously as hermeneutic and teleological, required for the study of man, contrasted with modes of explanation appropriate to the study of physical phenomena. The chapter concludes with an account of specifically historical modes of understanding and explanation, especially in relation to the problem of the role of ideas.

CULTURE, SOCIETY, AND THE PROBLEM OF CAUSATION

Historical analysis of the interplay between intellectual and social forces presupposes the familiar distinction between the cultural and social aspects of the human world. In ordinary language we distinguish between culture and society, meaning and action, beliefs and behavior. The social realm embraces joint activity of one sort or another, ranging from institutions and social systems to structured relations of power, domination and status. The range of cultural phenomena encompasses ideas, beliefs, values, traditions, meanings, symbols, ideology, knowledge, and so on. (The word *society*, of course, is often used to denote a totality of which cultural and social phenomena form a part. But context usually makes clear the meaning.) There are many ways of describing these two interconnected aspects of the human world. Clifford Geertz's definition is precise and succinct: "Culture is the fabric of meaning in terms of which human beings interpret their experience and guide their action; social structure is the form that action takes, the actually existing network of social relations."[1]

We also can take as given the truism that cultural and social phenomena are indissolubly interfused in reality and can be separated only analytically. Their interpenetration makes very difficult a description of the dialectical interplay between them, apart from the question of primacy or relative importance. Here too Geertz has aptly characterized the problem of dealing with symbol systems that are at once "a product and a determinant of social interaction." He has emphasized the need "to distinguish analytically between the cultural and social aspects of human life, and to treat them as independently variable yet mutually interdependent factors." We have to regard ideas, concepts, and values as "independent but not self-sufficient forces—as acting and having their impact only within specific social contexts to which they adapt, by which they are stimulated, but upon which they have, to a greater or lesser degree, a determining influence."[2]

In establishing the distinctive characteristics of cultural phenomena, in their complex relationship of mutual interdependence with other aspects of the human world, we can draw on work that reflects the linguistic turn in social thought since the Second World War. Parallel and overlapping developments in diverse fields have explored "the centrality of language in the lived in world." There has emerged a view of man as a "signifying being," a language-using, symbol-making creature who inhabits a world of intersubjective meanings that he has created.[3] Of particular interest to the historian is the analysis of the interconnections between language and society by philosophers working in the mode of the later Wittgenstein. He argued that language is rooted in "forms of life," and therefore has to be understood as a social product, the result of interaction and communication between men. Peter Winch and others have contended that since language is grounded in society, the former can tell us a great deal about the latter. Critics of the logical empiricist theory of explanation have had to define the distinctive characteristics of the human world as an object of knowledge. In the process, analytical philosophers have shed a good deal of light on "the nature of human society and of social relations between men."[4]

Peter Winch was one of the first to explore the conceptual basis of human activity and social relations. Taking the notion of "following a rule," which Wittgenstein used chiefly to elucidate the nature of language, Winch applied it to "other forms of human interaction besides speech." He showed that analogous categories are applicable both to speech and to forms of human activity which have "a meaning, a symbolic character." From this perspective he argued that "social relations between men exist only in and through their ideas." He put the point without equivocation: "A man's social relations with his fellows are permeated with his ideas about reality. Indeed, 'permeated' is hardly a strong enough word: social relations are expressions of ideas about reality." Seeking to show the conceptual basis of human activities, Winch made much of the fact that "the use of language is so intimately, so inseparably bound up with the other, nonlinguistic activities which men perform."[5] It follows that in examining forms of human behavior it is essential to get at the concepts which "belong" to the activities under investigation. Moreover, the conceptual element in human actions sets them apart from natural events. While the behavior of a falling apple exists quite independently of the concept of gravity, acts of command and obedience are inseparable from the concepts embodied in them. Finally, underlying every society is a particular conceptual structure. Hence one can speak of the logic of a social system and of the conceptual links between actions in a society. Patterns of behavior in a society rest on a common conceptual scheme.

The thesis that language is constitutive of social reality, prefigured in the work of Winch, has been developed by Charles Taylor, in a synthesis of recent work in analytical philosophy, phenomenology, and hermeneutics. Taylor rejects as artificial the distinction between social reality and the language in which it is described: "The language is constitutive of the reality, is essential to its being the kind of reality it is. To separate the two and distinguish them as we quite rightly distinguish the heavens from our theories about them is forever to miss the point." He draws an analogy between language and the rules of chess: "Just as there are constitutive rules, i.e., rules such that the behavior they govern could not exist without them, and which are in this sense inseparable from that behavior, so I am suggesting that there are constitutive distinctions, constitutive ranges of language which are similarly inseparable, in that certain practices are not without them." Hence it can be said that "all the institutions and practices by which we live are constituted by certain distinctions and hence a certain language which is thus essential to them."[6]

Taylor's argument is directed against the misleading notion that "there is a social reality which can be discovered in each society and which might exist quite independently of the vocabulary of that society, or indeed of any vocabulary, as the heavens could exist whether one theorized about them or not." On the contrary, in the human world the reality of particular practices cannot be identified "in abstraction from the language we use to describe them, or invoke them, or carry them out." He cites as an example the inhabitants of a traditional Japanese village. The heavens exist despite the fact that the villagers lack the vocabulary to understand them. But the practice of bargaining negotiations, as carried out in modern industrial societies, cannot exist without an appropriate vocabulary. Implicit in such practices is "a certain vision of the agent and his relation to others and to society."[7] That picture, in turn, embodies norms and ideas that are constitutive of negotiations themselves. Moreover, the practice of negotiation—like other practices in society—also presupposes a host of distinctions built into the language of that society. These distinctions are inseparable from the practices, and the latter cannot exist without the former.

What is the significance of Taylor's analysis for the problem of the role of ideas in history? While it certainly does not establish any sort of primacy for language or culture in relation to behavior and practice, it does have implications that need to be kept in mind. First of all, since language is constitutive of every aspect of human reality, our *description* of the historical phenomena that we are interested in explaining—whether events or institutions or social and cultural structures—must include the symbolic conceptual aspect. That is, a description in narrowly behavioral terms, concentrating on "brute data" that exclude intersubjective reality, will yield a partial and truncated view of the explanandum. Second, in view of the intimate connection between language and the human world, in seeking to understand and explain an event, it is all the more essential to examine its relationship to the cultural matrix in which it occurs. Third, given the interfusing of cultural and social phenomena, it is necessary to recognize the possibility that a change in the former will have an effect on events and patterns of behavior.

Two themes that emerge from the linguistic turn in social thought are pertinent to the problem of the role of ideas in history: the relative autonomy of the symbolic aspects of the human world, which are more than mere epiphenomena; and their interpenetration with the social. Both these points are expressed in Paul Ricoeur's comment that since "language is just as much infrastructure as superstructure," we ought to "reject once and for all every behaviorist and, *a fortiori*, epiphenomenalist interpretation of the so-called cultural superstructures of society."[8] He reminds us that we are dealing with "a strictly circular phenomenon in which the two terms in turn implicate each other and transcend each other." But Ricoeur's dictum cuts two ways. Implicated in a circular relationship with social phenomena, language is thereby subject to the continuous pressure of social and institutional structures. As Taylor has emphasized, while social practices cannot exist without an appropriate vocabulary it is also the case that "the vocabulary of a given social dimension is grounded in the shape of social practice in this dimension."[9] In the case of language and practice we are dealing with a relationship between mutually interdependent phenomena. The special strength of social and institutional forces in that relationship has to be kept clearly in mind.

Critics of Winch's dictum that "our language and our social relations are just two different sides of the same coin" have rightly emphasized the irreducible strength and pervasiveness of structured relationships of power, status, and domination. There can be no doubt that while social structure is "partly a consequence of the way people *perceive* social relations, it is clearly more than this." Anthony Giddens has argued that analytical philosophy and phenomenology, notably in the work of Winch and Schutz, have failed to recognize "the centrality of power in social life." [10] Other critics of Winch's thesis have also emphasized the strength and independence of power and status relations. Noting the importance of *gesellschaftliche Gewaltverhältnisse*, Habermas argues that the social system as a whole "is also constituted by the constraints of reality," which, however they are mediated symbolically, are not to be derived from the linguistic infrastructure of the society. He warns against "the idealist premise that linguistically articulated consciousness determines the material being of life-activity." Power relations are independent of their linguistic forms. [11] Finally, there are cases in which the social structure may be said to "generate" particular attitudes and values in the most direct way, so that language provides no more than the form for a content that is socially determined. Thus, the interfusion of social and cultural phenomena permits the former to exert a good deal of influence on the latter. This brings us back to our starting point: the dialectical interplay between cultural and social phenomena.

The historian confronts the problem of the interrelationship between cultural and social phenomena when he looks into the "causes" or origins of particular events or developments. Whatever terminology he employs, his account presupposes a conception of causation and of the nature of the relationship between ideas and their effects. The primary question at issue is the extent to which human events are characterized by the same kind of causation that is found in the world of nature. Positivist social science affirms the "universality of cause and effect," the uniformity of causation affecting all events. Firmly lodged in mainstream social science and logical empiricism is the view given classic form by David Hume: causal relations in the human world are essentially the same as those in the world of nature. This view of causation, in turn, entails a corresponding conception of explanation.

The Humean view of causation and explanation has been subjected to searching criticism by analytical philosophers since the Second World War. We shall argue that the position they have developed provides a sound basis for an inquiry into the role of ideas in history, whereas the Humean view is inappropriate. Their analysis of the logical and conceptual character of the connection between intentions and actions has demonstrated that human action is not determined by causal processes of the Humean type.

The crux of Hume's theory of causation is constant conjunction—the regular connection between events or phenomena of a certain kind. When an event of type A occurs, then event B invariably follows as an effect. In Alan Ryan's phrase, "where there is regular sequence there is causation." Hume described "the relation of cause and effect" in a familiar passage of exemplary clarity. We gain knowledge of that relation, not "by reasonings *a priori*," but by finding through experience that "particular objects are constantly conjoined with one another."[12] Constant conjuncture is the prime indicator of a causal connection. A bite by an infected mosquito is a cause of malaria. An injection of penicillin will, in the case of certain diseases, bring about a cure. Thus, the Humean cause can be described as "a factor of a type temporally antecedent to and regularly associated with a type of effect." Hume's position is often referred to as the "regularity" view, because, as Mandelbaum has said, "it takes the cause-effect relation to be equivalent to an empirically established regularity between two types of events, one invariably following the other."[13]

A second aspect of the Humean view of causation is a sharp separation between cause and effect. The two are linked by a merely contingent connection. Causes are no more than antecedent conditions which are universally linked to their effects. Hume cited as an example one billiard ball communicating motion to another: "The mind can never possibly find the effect in the supposed cause, by the most accurate scrutiny and examination. For the effect is totally different from the cause, and consequently can never be discovered in it. Motion in the second billiard ball is a quite distinct event from motion in the first; nor is there anything in the one to suggest the smallest hint of the other."[14] In emphasizing this aspect of the cause and effect relationship Hume was rejecting the sort of pseudoexplanation of sleep on the basis of the property of dormitiveness. He was warning against any tendency to posit a logical or noncontingent connection between cause and effect. As Charles Taylor put it, Hume was scornful of "the empty repetition of the *explicandum* as in the 'virtus dormitiva' type of account." That is, Hume objected to "the picking out of the cause by that property of it which is its being productive of the effect."[15] Hence he stressed the contingent character of the relation of cause and effect.

Critics have shown that the salient features of the Humean view of causality—constant conjuncture, universality, and contingency—are not characteristic of human action. An action results from a *particular* intention or desire. The relationship between intention and action is not characterized by universality or constant conjuncture. Similarly, the connection between intention and action is noncontingent, for there is a logical or conceptual link between them. In what has been called "the Logical Connection Argument," Georg von Wright and other analytical philosophers have argued that the connection between intention and action is not causal (in the Humean sense) but rather of a conceptual or logical nature. Unlike the extrinsic relationship between cause and effect, there is an "inner conceptual connection" between the goals and beliefs of an agent and his action, as he conceives it. In a metaphor reminiscent of Collingwood, von Wright distinguishes between the outside and the inside of an action: "Action, one could say, normally presents two aspects: an 'inner' and an 'outer.' The first is the intentionality of the action, the intention or will 'behind' its other manifestations." Unlike the causal or nomic connection between physical phenomena, the relation between intention and action is teleological, in the sense that the action is directed to the achievement of a particular end. Similarly, von Wright has pointed out that "the connection between an action and its result is intrinsic, logical and not causal (extrinsic). . . . The result is an essential 'part' of the action."[16]

An agent's beliefs and intentions provide the premises of a practical inference, on the basis of which he takes action. Those beliefs, in turn, are grounded in the society and culture of which he is a part. A given action is based on premises provided by what von Wright calls a "cognitive-volitative complex" which defines both ends and the means to achieve them. Von Wright also points out that the manner in which norms come to exert a pressure on agents is teleological, rather than causal, in character. People may conform to a norm, because they share the purposes that they express, and take the necessary action in order that these purposes may be fulfilled; or they may conform in order to avoid punishment or disapproval. Thus, there is a teleological mechanism at work, to be contrasted with causal processes of the physical world. The "normative pressure" behind action is teleological in that it exerts an influence by providing the purposes to whose achievement action is directed. Frederick Olafson also has shown the connection between "the teleological organization of human life" and historical events.[17]

Wilhelm Dilthey also emphasized the "immanent-teleological" character of the interactions and interrelationships of the human world, in contrast to the world of nature. What lends particular interest to Dilthey's position is that, in keeping with his determination to find a middle ground between idealism and positivism, he insisted throughout his life that some form of causal explanation is indispensable to the study of man and the study of nature. In grappling with the problem of causality, he came to distinguish between two different forms of it: "There is no natural scientific causality [naturwissenschaftliche Kausalität] in this historical world, because 'cause' in the natural scientific sense [Ursache im Sinne dieser Kausalität] necessarily entails the production of effects according to laws, whereas history knows only the relations of effecting and of being affected, of action and reaction." What is unique to the human world is the creation of values and ends. Hence, "the causality of history has an immanent-teleological character." Men take action in pursuit of goals that they have created. The historical form of causality "works teleologically." In other words, "history does not cause, it creates." ["Die Geschichte verursacht nicht, sie schafft."] The fundamental characteristic of historical life is that it is constantly creating values, ends, and purposes. From this follows the "immanent-teleological" character of the "causal" processes in history, so different from those in nature. Although Dilthey used causal language to characterize both natural and historical processes, he also found it necessary to distinguish between a *Wirkungszusammenhang,* which produces values and realizes ends in the human world, and the *Kausalzusammenhang* in nature. "This system of interactions is distinguished from the causal order of nature by the fact that it produces *values* and realizes *ends*. . . . I call this the immanent-teleological character of human *[geistigen]* systems of interaction."[18]

What is the significance for the historian of the immanent-teleological character of relationships in the human world, of the conceptual connections between beliefs and action, and the constitutive relations between language and social reality? First of all, it can be said that ideas and beliefs do not function as causes that are separate and distinct from their effects. Rather, they exert their influence as constituents of the events and developments that they are affecting. Hence the impact of cultural forces is all the more intense and pervasive since they are constitutive of the phenomena that they are influencing or shaping. Secondly, the conceptual character of the constitutive relationship distinguishes it from relationships in the world of nature— such as that between an atom of oxygen and a molecule of water— which can be described in similar language. The part-whole relationship between the Enlightenment and the French Revolution, embracing meanings, values, and intentions on the one hand and a complex of actions on the other, is ontologically different. Similarly, the Enlightenment played a part in a process involving conceptual connections different from the reactions in a process comprising oxygen and hydrogen. That intimate historical interplay is conceptual and involves intrinsic, rather than extrinsic relations. Underlying the endless change characteristic of the human world are immanent-teleological processes that create new social and cultural forms that affect the course of events.

While a recognition of the conceptual and constitutive aspect of the connection between ideas and events provides a basis for dealing with the difficult problem of assessing the influence of mutually interdependent forces, it clearly does not entail the primacy of intellectual forces in history. A given action is affected not only by cognitive and normative patterns but also by the pressure of the social and institutional structure in which it occurs. Anthony Giddens has rightly criticized the tendency to treat action primarily as meaning and to neglect the involvement of actors with "the practical realization of interest." He points out that "even a transient conversation between two persons is a relation of power, to which the participants may bring unequal resources."[19] Norms and meanings are susceptible of differential interpretations, affected by variations in power and status. Moreover, a given "cognitive-volitative complex" will have been shaped by social and institutional forces. Thus, whether the historian is dealing with the role of ideas in events or in the creation of conceptual and normative structures, he has to look into the nature of the interplay between cultural and social forces. In order to get at the nature of that interplay in a particular case, however, it is necessary to recognize the immanent-teleological character of the relationships and processes involved, significantly different from the causality of the world of nature.

When a historian considers the question of the interplay between cultural and social forces in a particular historical process, then, he brings to bear a conception of the distinctive characteristics of both, to which the generalizations of philosophers and social scientists are pertinent. But theoretical discussion of the nature of cultural and social phenomena and of the relationships of mutual interdependence between them can carry the historian only so far. Such generalizations cannot simply be applied to the past in order to produce knowledge of past events and developments. The phenomena that the historian deals with are characterized not only by the generic traits described by analytical philosophy and social science but also by specifically "historical" qualities.

HISTORICAL PROCESSES

Ideas exercise their influence in specifically *historical* processes, involving the interplay between unique phenomena, themselves the product of antecedent processes of continuity and change through time. Hence, the role of ideas in history has to be understood not only in terms of generic and ahistorical characteristics of cultural and social phenomena and the interrelationships between them, but also in terms of the historical aspects of the human world that are excluded from synchronic and nomological modes of analysis.

When we say that man is an historical creature, we mean, first of all, that what he is at any moment is the result of his past. The social and cultural forms that define his being in a particular society were created by historical processes, characterized by continuity and change

through time. The forces at work in the human world are not fixed
entities but endlessly changing forms, each the product of the interplay between other such forms in the past, and giving rise to new forms
in the future. The historical world comprises unique phenomena, linked
in a relationship of continuity and change. Elements created at different points in the past—and which may be said to embody aspects of
the past—persist as constituents of every present. In every situation,
thought and action are shaped by patterns and structures inherited from
the past and embodying the past.

The historicity of human life, then, embraces a number of interconnected aspects: diversity and multifariousness of phenomena in time
and place—social and cultural forms, events and institutions; the relationship of continuity and change linking the unique phenomena of
one period with those which preceded and followed; the interplay between such unique elements in historical processes that create new
forms.

The word "unique" is a convenient way of characterizing the particularity and singularity of historical phenomena, in contrast to the
uniformity and regularity of the world of nature. But it cannot be used
in a literal or absolute sense. "Unique" historical phenomena also embody uniformities that are susceptible to analysis by the generalizing
methods of the social sciences. This use of the term may be distinguished from the historicist conception of *Individualität*, as defined by
Friedrich Meinecke and others in the tradition of "pure historicism,"
and from the conception of uniqueness in Windelband's representation of history as an idiographic discipline.[20] That is, history embraces
a tension between the unique and the general. We have to take account of both aspects of this polar relationship. An exclusively idiographic preoccupation with the unique would be one-sided and in-
complete. Moreover, "uniqueness" is not a quality that is confined to
the human world. No earthquake is identical to any other; every set
of fingerprints is unique. Similarly, biological phenomena display a
seemingly endless diversity and variation in time and place. Beneath
the diversity of nature, however, is a uniformity and regularity unknown to the historical world. "Unique" geological events and configurations are the product of the interaction between uniform entities,
such as sandstone and limestone, themselves composed of chemical

elements. The multifariousness of organic phenomena is the product of the combination and recombination of units of DNA. The uniqueness of historical phenomena is of a qualitatively different order. There are no uniform entities or units that enter into different combinations and arrangements. Words that presuppose the uniformity of nature—process, structure, interaction—can be applied only metaphorically to a human world characterized by historical uniqueness.

The unique social and cultural forms found in a particular society are the product of processes of change and development in the past. It is the continuity between past and present that Dilthey singled out as the essential characteristic of the historicity of human life: "The present is filled with pasts," hence "history is not something separate from human life or divided from the present by distance in time." Thus, "the essence of the historical" lies in the persistence of the products of human activity: "Whatever characteristics of its own the mind *[Geist]* puts into expressions are, tomorrow, if they persist, history." Dilthey emphasized the range of social and cultural structures in which "the past is a permanently enduring present." Thus, human life is characterized by *Historizität* or *Zeitlichkeit:*[21] being-in-time. To be sure, there is continuity and change in the world of nature also. The geological structure of the earth is the product of developmental processes that can be so characterized. Similarly, biological forms are the end product of evolutionary processes in which change and continuity, together with the persistence of elements created in the past, are even more pronounced. Here also, however, we are dealing with persistence of uniform entities in changing combination and arrangements. The phenomena that persist and change in the course of history are "unique" products of human thought and action.

The historicity of human life is rooted in man's capacity to create out of the legacy of the past novel forms that persist into the future while undergoing further change. It is a consequence of human freedom. For Karl Rahner freedom is the essence of man; hence "we must understand historicity as belonging to man's basic nature."[22] Thus, "free activity is essentially historical activity," and there is history wherever there is free activity. But this is a one-sided formulation derived from Heidegger and the existentialist tradition.[23] It minimizes the extent to which human action is shaped and limited by circumstances. Men exercise their freedom only in social and cultural contexts created in the past. It has often been said that man is both the creature and the creator of history. Historical circumstances not only impose constraints but also offer possibilities for the exercise of freedom. However one-sided, the existentialist emphasis on freedom and the historicist-idealist emphasis on "spontaneity" underline an essential aspect of the historical world. Within the limits inherent in the situation in which they find themselves, men enjoy a significant degree of freedom, ontologically distinct from the determinism of nature, which is the basis of their ability to change their world and bring into being new historical forms.

Every society, then, comprises historically unique components, each the product of processes of continuity and change through time. The conjuncture of such processes at a particular point defines the character of the totality as a unique configuration of interrelated elements. If we take Europe in the twelfth century, for example, two aspects of that totality were of particular importance: feudalism and Christianity. There was no intrinsic relationship between them. Their development in the circumstances following the fall of Rome, in discrete but interrelated processes, shaped the character of medieval Europe. Neither feudalism nor Christianity was unique in an absolute sense. Both embody significant points of similarity and affinity with comparable social and religious forms. They were "historically unique" in the sense that they embodied distinctive characteristics found only in that time and place; they were the product of processes that involved the interplay between unique elements.

In such historical processes cultural phenomena play a distinctive and important role. First of all, they are constitutive of historical uniqueness and particularity. Christianity was the essential constituent of twelfth-century Europe as a unique historical entity. While feudal institutions were equally necessary to the existence of that totality, they provided only social and economic foundations which, however important, were nevertheless compatible with diverse forms of being. It was Christianity which was directly constitutive of "twelfth-century Europe," whereas feudalism exercised an influence of a more general sort. Marshall Sahlins' distinction between culture and praxis is illuminating in this connection: "The general determinations of praxis are subject to the specific formulations of culture; that is, of an order that enjoys, by its own properties as a symbolic system, a fundamental autonomy."[24] The symbolic and conceptual dimension of human life encompasses the specific, the concrete, and the particular. A given socioeconomic system can produce only "general determination." The concrete particularity of a society is shaped by historically created cultural forms, operating in a general framework set by social and institutional forces. Moreover, it is through inherited ideas, beliefs, and traditions that unique phenomena created in the past are brought into the present. In this respect also intellectual forces have a special importance in specifically historical processes.

Cultural phenomena are also central to historical processes, because they carry a potentiality for change that is qualitatively different from the sort of change that results from institutional activity. It is in the realm of culture that men find the greatest scope for the exercise of freedom and for the creation of novel forms. The social world is more constraining. Human creativity and spontaneity finds expression in symbolic and intellectual activity.

Medieval Christianity can serve as an example of an historically unique entity, comprising elements created in the past, and contributing to the creation of new forms in the future. It was "unique" not only in comparison to other religious phenomena but also to Christianity in the eighth century or the fifteenth. Fusing ideas and beliefs derived from Israel and Greece, it embodied in the most direct way cultural forms created in the past. Moreover, Judaism and Hellenism were themselves the product of two periods of extraordinary creativity and originality. Working with cultural and symbolic forms common to the ancient Near East, those two societies transmuted them into religious and philosophical traditions that have been active in Western culture ever since. Within medieval Europe, Christianity was the source of historical developments that went far beyond the possibilities inherent in the social and institutional structure. Above all, it was Christian culture, incorporating the learning of antiquity, that made possible the development of modern science in the seventeenth century. While social and economic changes provided a favorable institutional setting, they were quite incapable of creating the components essential to the scientific revolution. In all these familiar ways, then, Christianity was an active ingredient in the processes that created Europe and shaped its subsequent development.

Intellectual forces have also been actively involved in the historical processes underlying political events and movements, first of all in shaping the contexts in which such events occur, and secondly in creating their constituents. Ideas and beliefs inherited from the past constitute the intentions and goals that lie at the core of every action. Ideas do not "cause" events in the way that the moon causes tidal movements. The link between ideas and events is not "causal" but logical and conceptual in character. There was a constitutive relationship between Lutheranism and the Reformation. That connection may also be characterized as intrinsically "historical" in the sense that Lutheranism was the product of the history of Christianity, of which it was an embodiment. In the case of the Puritan rebellion in England in the 1640s, Puritanism also was not only a necessary cause but also a historically unique constituent of those events. Both Lutheranism and Puritanism were the end product of historical processes, largely religious in character, antedating the social and institutional structures of the period in which the events in question took place.

A judgment that certain ideas played an essential role in the historical process underlying the genesis of a particular event entails a number of claims: first, that the ideas themselves were the product of processes in which intellectual forces played a significant role, and were not generated by social forces or circumstances; second, that the specific content of the ideas was essential to the event, and that they were not merely performing a socially determined function; third, that the character of the event was shaped by the conjuncture of disparate lines of historical development at this time and place.

HISTORICAL UNDERSTANDING AND EXPLANATION

Ideas and beliefs are central not only to historical processes but also to the modes of analysis that they require. In this section we shall begin with an account of the teleological or hermeneutic character of the explanation of human behavior, that is, by reference to intentions, purposes, and meanings. Then we shall turn to specifically historical modes of understanding and explanation. This description of historical practice, in turn, should be counterposed to positivist theories of explanation based on the natural sciences which, it is argued, are inappropriate to the study of the human world and prejudge important substantive questions. (See chapter 6.)

We can begin with a point emphasized by post-Wittgensteinian philosophers in their critique of logical empiricist theories of explanation.[25] They have shown that the explanation of human action is significantly different in a number of respects from the explanation of events in nature. The crux of the matter is that actions have to be explained by reference to intentions, reasons, motives, aims, purposes, values, and meanings. An agent does something for a particular purpose. We explain his action at least partially in terms of what he was trying to do or what he had in mind as a purpose or aim. We do this in everyday life and in the more complex explanatory analyses of history and the social sciences. This kind of explanation has been characterized as teleological, since the ends envisaged by the agent are so central to it. As such it is radically different from causal explanation of the positivist type, in its various forms, including the covering law model.

Charles Taylor develops a similar theme in arguing the thesis that "men and their actions are amenable to explanation of a hermeneutical kind."[26] That is, "interpretation is essential to explanation in the sciences of man." Interpretation involves making sense of an object of study that is characterized by meaning. Since human reality is permeated by meaning, it requires modes of analysis that involve interpretation. Taylor points out that the language that we use to characterize human behavior makes extensive use of a certain notion of meaning. "This is the sense in which we speak of a situation, an action, a demand, a prospect having a certain meaning for a person." Whether we are talking about action or the situations in which actions occur we refer to what it "means" to the agent. That is, the concept of the meaning of a situation for an agent "has a place that is integral to our ordinary consciousness and hence speech about our actions. Our actions are ordinarily characterized by the purpose sought and explained by desires, feelings, emotions." We make sense of a given action by showing the connection—the coherence—between it and the meaning of the situation for the agent. Thus, when we are dealing with human behavior seen as action of "agents who desire and are moved, who have goals and aspirations" we have to describe that behavior in terms of meaning. Explaining it also involves making sense of it, that is, offering an interpretation.

Such accounts of the teleological or hermeneutic character of the explanation of human action incorporate the notion of "understanding." That is, the action to be explained first has to be "understood" in terms of the intentions that it embodies. There is a close connection between the question of what the action was and the question of why it occurred. In von Wright's formulation, "a teleological explanation of action is normally preceded by an act of intentionalist *understanding* of some behavioral data."[27] The meanings embodied in the action have to be "interpreted"; the logical and conceptual connection between intentions and action has to be "understood." This sort of formulation entails a rejection of what Paul Ricoeur has called "the dichotomy which assigns to the two terms 'explanation' and 'understanding' two distinct epistemological fields which refer, respectively, to two irreducible modes of being."[28] In other words, Dilthey's dictum that we understand man and explain nature does not express a dichotomous relationship. While firmly excluding the sort of explanation adapted to the world of nature, it encompasses explanation of a hermeneutical kind. Moreover, Dilthey's conception of *Verstehen*, like Max Weber's, involves the rational interpretation of meaning, rather than intuition or *Einfühlung*. In this sense, there is an indissoluble connection between understanding and explanation, which is grounded in the intentionalist or teleological character of human action.[29]

An explanation of an action, of course, entails a good deal more than the accurate interpretation of an agent's intentions. His purposes and values are not unique to him, but are rooted in his culture. Hence explanation requires that the agent's intentions be located in what von Wright calls a "cognitive-volitative complex. Explanation involves an account of the "normative pressure" underlying patterns of behavior in a society: "People do things because the law of the state or of God requires it, or because the customs of the society or the codes of honor and good manners thus prescribe."[30] In addition, explanation of a hermeneutical kind involves taking into account the conceptual and cognitive forms that define the agent's view of the world in which he intends to act, along with the concepts and modes of classification that define his conception of reality.[31] Thus, we explain an action or an event by describing the normative and conceptual context from which its purposes are derived.

But explanation also involves locating the action in a social and institutional context comprising relations of power and domination as well as patterns of behavior. Their reconstruction and the analysis of their operation involves something more than the interpretation of meaning. Hence, as Anthony Giddens has emphasized, the study of human activity cannot be "purely hermeneutic."[32] His comment reflects concern that methodology defined in narrowly hermeneutic terms may in practice accord a privileged status, perhaps even primacy, to cultural and symbolic forces which embody meanings that have to be "interpreted." This is the point of Habermas' observation that while language is the essential medium of intersubjectivity, it is also "a medium of domination and social power." Conceptual and normative structures have themselves been shaped by social patterns that are not susceptible to a "purely hermeneutic" treatment. On the other hand, it should also be noted that the use of the term "explanation"—even when characterized as "hermeneutic" or "teleological"—is intended to encompass the sort of analysis to which Giddens and Habermas are referring. Relations of power and status have to be "understood" and interpreted, even though the connections involved are not conceptual or logical in character. While characterized by affinities to the causal relations of nature, they also embody "meanings" that have to be interpreted.[33]

Historical analysis shares the generic characteristics of the explanation of human action that have just been outlined. The historian accounts for events by reference to agents' reasons and intentions, which he locates in conceptual and normative structures within a sociocultural totality. In addition, there are other characteristics of specifically historical understanding and explanation, which are the consequence of the need to deal with the historicity of human life. Von Wright notes that an object of historical explanation is the origin of the agents' aims, which are sometimes "the rather subtle products of cultural, political, religious, etc. traditions."[34] The historian concentrates his attention on the cultural and social configurations characteristic of a particular time and place and on the processes that created those historically unique forms. He seeks to explain and understand actions by setting them in such contexts and by showing how they result from the dynamic interaction between such forces. That is, historical understanding and explanation entails the analysis of unique and changing phenomena, so as to show their genesis (in processes involving other unique and changing forms) and their interaction in particular time-bound contexts. It also involves showing the presence of the past in a particular situation and in the forces at work in such processes. The distinctive traits of historical analysis may be contrasted to an exclusively synchronic and nomological approach, which identifies the operative elements in a society at a particular time and analyzes their interaction on the basis of knowledge of how those types of phenomena tend to behave. The components of a nomological explanation are homogeneous entities characterized by lawlike regularities. Diversity is accounted for in terms of combinations and arrangements of such entities. While such an analysis is an essential aspect of the study of human behavior, it can carry us only so far. To achieve an adequate understanding of historical events and patterns, it is also necessary to take into account the fact that the forces at work in the human world and the relations between "causes" and "effects," unlike natural phenomena, do not have a fixed character. Their precise nature has to be established in each instance. Having been created by unique historical processes, they have to be analyzed "historically."

In various ways, historical understanding and explanation requires close attention to intellectual forces. As noted above, the particularity of phenomena in a society is constituted, to a considerable degree, by ideas, beliefs and traditions inherited from the past; they bring the past directly into the present. An adequate description of a sociocultural totality in its uniqueness must embrace such specifically historical components. This sort of description, in turn, is prerequisite to explanation, since it establishes the nature of the event, the context in which it occurred, and the "factors" or "forces" involved. Moreover, ideas and beliefs also require close attention because of their centrality in the historical processes that create unique social and cultural forms.

But history is not an exclusively idiographic discipline. It is characterized by a tension between the particular and the general, which is especially manifest in the multifariousness of cultural phenomena. On the one hand, human phenomena, unlike those in nature, are infinitely variable and cannot be defined in terms of fixed entities that display identifiable regularities and uniformities. On the other hand, however, human behavior is characterized by a degree of regularity that makes possible understanding and explanation. The dual aspect of historical inquiry is expressed in Louis Mink's comment that "We could not understand Greek civilization without the concept of *moira*, which is not part of our conceptual system, nor without the concept of culture."[35] We have to invoke such concepts as *moira*, because they are necessarily involved in "the agents' understanding of what they were doing" and therefore were, in a sense, constitutive of past actions. By themselves, however, such concepts are insufficient to provide a basis for historical understanding. Generic concepts—in this instance, culture—are also necessary. A similar point has been made by Charles Taylor, emphasizing the changeability of human behavior, in contrast to the natural world. The sciences of man have to contend with "the fact of conceptual innovation which in turn alters human reality." Hence they lack the conceptual unity characteristic of the natural sciences. Thus, Puritanism has to be understood, in part, in terms of conceptual changes to which it has contributed. On the other hand, of course, as Taylor points out, Puritanism also has to be understood in terms of the general category of the sacred, which is derived in part from "the study of human religion in general."[36]

The problem of conceptualizing phenomena characterized by endless diversity and change through time is especially formidable in the case of intellectual forces. The historian has to construct concepts that are capable of capturing an elusive and protean reality before he can begin to assess the "causal" role or the influence of such historically unique forces and structures. But he cannot make sense of these particulars without bringing to bear general concepts and general knowledge. The historian has to take into account aspects of the phenomenon that reflect characteristics common to all men, for it is evident that society, culture, and language, among other things, embody regularities that are susceptible to generalization. General knowledge of various kinds and degrees has been a component of historical discourse since Herodotus and Thucydides, and has remained so, despite the individualizing emphasis of historicist theory. As a matter of course the historian makes use not only of the rough generalizations of common sense but of the body of knowledge developed by the social sciences. But the historian cannot permit the universal aspects of a given phenomenon to obscure the uniqueness of time and place.

Max Weber's methodological essays, written while he was working on *The Protestant Ethic and the Spirit of Capitalism,* offer a judicious treatment of the problem of the unique and the general in historical conceptualization, with particular reference to the causal role of ideas and beliefs. While preserving the historicist preoccupation with the unique, he showed that such individualizing aims cannot be achieved without the use of general knowledge and generic concepts. Weber took as given the historian's awareness of the uniqueness and individuality of human phenomena. "Our aim," he wrote in 1904, "is the understanding of the characteristic uniqueness *[Eigenart]* of the reality in which we move."[37] Cultural phenomena must be understood in their *Individualität.* The social scientist is interested in "the real, i.e., concrete, individually structured configuration of our cultural life." At the beginning of the second chapter of the *Protestant Ethic,* Weber noted the difficulty of defining a phenomenon "significant for its unique individuality," that is, "an historical individual."[38] But he rejected Windelband's characterization of history as an individualizing or idiographic discipline. In order to understand the "historical individual" in its uniqueness, it is necessary to bring nomological knowledge into play.

Weber's treatment of this theme, in his account of the construction of ideal types and in his discussion of historical explanation, is still valuable. Whereas analytical philosophy has necessarily tended to concentrate on the agent and his action, Weber deals with the much more complex entities—events, institutions, socioeconomic structures, ideological and cultural patterns—that figure so prominently in historical analysis. Ideal types represent the specifically "historical concepts" that are required to describe and understand such entities. Weber also showed the ways in which much of historical explanation is concerned with the problem of establishing the "causal relations" between such entities and with locating phenomena in contexts reconstructed through the use of ideal types.

Weber's account of ideal types is especially pertinent to the problem of describing the character of particular intellectual forces and assessing their historical influence. Such concepts enable the social scientist and the historian to analyze "historically unique configurations or their individual components." Confronted with an infinite diversity of phenomena that do not lend themselves to the sort of generalization characteristic of science or of traditional logic, we have to use constructs designed for this purpose. A construct such as Calvinism or medieval Christianity represents a synthesis of "a great many diffuse, discrete, more or less present and occasionally absent concrete individual phenomena." The result is very different indeed from the class concepts of Aristotelian logic: "The goal of ideal-typical concept-construction is always to make clearly explicit not the class or average character but rather the unique individual character of cultural phenomena." The ideal type "medieval Christianity," for example, accentuates and abridges ideals which, in their original state, constituted "a chaos of infinitely differentiated and highly contradictory complexes of ideas and feelings" and assumed "the most multifarious nuances of form and content." [39]

In the *Protestant Ethic* Weber confronted the methodological difficulties involved in conceptualizing so protean an entity as the spirit of capitalism:

If any object can be found to which this term can be applied with understandable meaning, it can only be an historical individual, i.e. a complex of elements associated in historical reality which we unite into a conceptual whole from the standpoint of their cultural significance. Such an historical concept, however, since it refers in its content to a phenomenon significant for its unique individuality, cannot be defined according to the formula *genus proximum, differentia specifica*, but it must be gradually put together out of the individual parts which are taken from historical reality to make it up.

Ideal type constructs of that sort are "a necessary result of the nature of historical concepts which attempt for their methodological purposes not to grasp historical reality in abstract general formulae, but in concrete genetic sets of relations which are inevitably of a *specifically unique and individual character*" (emphasis added).[40] At the same time, however, phenomena described by ideal types are also "partly recurrent in character." In order to construct the concepts that make possible the description of unique historical configurations, the historian has to make use of general knowledge. Rejecting narrowly idealist formulations, Weber emphasized the nomological basis of ideal type construction. The ideal type is built with generic concepts.

In his discussion of explanation also Weber took pains to show that the historian must take account of both the unique and the general. It was characteristic of his deeply historical orientation, however, that in the essay of 1904 he began by stressing the individualizing character of historical explanation. In addition to understanding "individual events in their contemporary manifestations," the social scientist also wishes to understand "the causes of their being historically *so* and not *otherwise*." ("Cause" is a translation of *Ursache*, which lacks the positivist connotation of its English equivalent; but Weber's usage, which includes the adjective *kausal*, does not embody the sharp distinction that Gadamer makes between *Ursächlichkeit* and *Kausalität*.)[41]

In explaining the causal relationships between such unique phenomena, the social scientist will not find it useful to engage in a quest for "recurrent sequences" of the sort that provide causal explanation in the natural sciences. Weber argued that a different procedure was required in the social sciences: "where the individuality of a phenomenon is concerned, the question of causality is not a question of *laws* but of concrete causal *relationships;* it is not a question of the subsumption of the event under some general rubric as a representative case but of its imputation as a consequence of some constellation." That is, "if we wish to 'explain' this individual configuration 'causally' we must invoke other equally individual configurations." Hence, to understand a particular phenomenon, what is called for is "the tracing as far into the past as possible of the individual features of these historically evolved configurations which are *contemporaneously* significant, and their historical explanation by antecedent and equally individual configurations."[42]

In treating the role of ideas in history, then, the historian has to establish the connection—which Weber characterizes as a "concrete causal relationship"—between "individual configurations." Ideal-typical constructs—those quintessentially "historical" concepts—are necessary means of reconstructing such configurations, which embrace both the objects of explanation and "the causes of their being so and not otherwise."

The ideal type is a means of "imputing an historical event to its real causes." Such constructs make possible the conceptualization of "those 'ideas' which govern the behavior of the population of a given epoch, i.e., which are concretely influential in determining their conduct."[43] Among these "causes" are such "historical individuals" as Calvinism or the Enlightenment. Moreover, implicit in Weber's account of the use of ideal types in the description of the explanandum—for example, the French Revolution or fascism or the German Social Democratic Party—is the need for close attention to the intellectual and symbolic aspects of the phenomenon in question. Tracing the connection between two such "historical individuals" as the Enlightenment and the French Revolution—thus "imputing an historical event to its real causes"—is explanation of a hermeneutical kind, involving the interpretation of meanings and an account of logical and conceptual connections. While this procedure has an affinity to the teleological explanation of an action by reference to the intentions that are part of it, such historical explanation is clearly a good deal more complex, for it involves tracing the relationship between "individual configurations" that comprise intricately interconnected cultural and social forms.

Both in the methodological essays of 1904–5 and in the *Protestant Ethic* Weber was actively concerned with the problem of the role of ideas in history. The latter was intended as a contribution to an understanding of "the manner in which ideas become effective forces in history;" he wished to define as precisely as possible "the sense in which any such effectiveness of purely ideal motives" can be claimed. The value of the book does not lie in the refutation of a "naive historical materialism;" there is no need to argue the point that religious ideas "cannot be deduced from economic circumstances." What remains pertinent, however, is the thesis that such ideas "contain a law of development and a compelling force entirely their own." That formulation poses an important problem that requires continuing discussion and debate; and it reaches well beyond a mere acceptance of the "relative autonomy" of ideas. In the *Protestant Ethic* Weber illustrates that general thesis in various ways, for example, in his analysis of the disparate practical implications of the theological doctrines of Lutheranism and Calvinism: "The religious believer can make himself sure of his state of grace either in that he feels himself to be the vessel of the Holy Spirit or the tool of the divine will. In the former case his religious life tends to mysticism and emotionalism, in the latter to ascetic action. Luther stood close to the former type, Calvinism definitely to the latter."[44]

While subsequent scholarship has shown that the details of Weber's interpretation of the development of the spirit of capitalism cannot be accepted without substantial modification, the form of his analysis remains exemplary.[45] The differences between a quietistic Lutheranism and an activist Calvinism are still of considerable historical importance. Moreover, the same kind of question, concerning the practical implications of a body of ideas—from Judaism to Marxism—and the sense in which they may be said to contain "a compelling force entirely their own" comes up repeatedly in the course of historical inquiry. Weber has not only emphasized the importance of that kind of question but he has also shown how to go about answering it.

Weber's theory and practice of 1904–5, then, exemplify a mode of understanding exquisitely adapted to the analyis of historical processes, in which ideas "contain a law of development and a compelling force entirely their own," resistant to treatment by "abstract general formulae." He demonstrated what is involved in describing historical forms in their concrete particularity and in assessing the practical implications of unique belief systems in particular socio-institutional contexts. Implicit in Weber's approach is a recognition of the need to grasp the long term developmental processes—in which ideas contain specific potentialities of development—that produce the "historical individuals" whose dynamic interaction at particular moments in time is of special interest. Thus, Protestantism has to be understood in relation to Christianity and the religion of Israel.

This aspect of historical methodology, which Weber could take as given without the need for elaboration, is illuminated in Paul Ricoeur's discussion of the problems of interpretation and explanation posed by the myths of the Old Testament. (The context of Ricoeur's article is a critique of the inability of structuralism to deal adequately with phenomena that require historical-hermeneutic analysis.) Ricoeur's commentary puts in the foreground processes of change that bring novel phenomena into existence. Examining the myths of the Creation and the Fall in the Old Testament, he points out that they contain a "surplus of meaning" subject to endless re-interpretation and change. The continuing reuse of biblical symbols in Western culture rests on "a semantic richness, on a surplus of what is signified, which opens toward new interpretations." The myths of the Old Testament embody a "reservoir of meaning ready to be used again in other structures."[46] The "surplus of meaning" embodied in the religion of Israel was a dynamic element in the development of Western culture.

From a perspective quite different from Weber's, Ricoeur has shown the centrality to historical understanding of the analysis of the novel forms that emerge from the creation of new meanings out of inherited traditions of belief. Such novel phenomena are constitutive of the unique "historical individuals" created by the conjuncture of diverse streams of development. In addition, Ricoeur has dealt with the recurring problem of the unique and the general in a manner somewhat different from Weber: "The richness of the symbolic substratum [of the myth of Adam] appears only in diachrony. The synchronic point of view reaches only the current social function of the myth." Ricoeur was concerned with preserving historical-hermeneutic modes of understanding against erosion by structuralism.

The problem of maintaining specifically historical modes of analysis in a culture dominated by social science is prefigured in the intellectual development of Weber himself. In the last decade of his life Weber moved away from the primarily historical orientation that had characterized his work early in the twentieth century and developed the sociological theory that has since been so influential. His conception of ideal types was adapted to the handling of generic phenomena and transhistorical regularities. His approach to the past became more sociological.[47] It has since been applied with interesting results, in various ways, by both historians and social scientists. A predominantly sociological approach to the past presents difficulties, however, especially for the study of the role of ideas.

CHAPTER SIX

Social Science Paradigms

As history makes increasingly effective use of the social sciences, their methodological and conceptual structure exercises a proportionately greater influence on historical interpretation. In a number of ways, however, social science paradigms interpose obstacles to an adequate assessment of the role of ideas. Precisely those aspects of social science that make it so valuable and indeed essential to the study of the past—a grasp of the generic and universal aspects of the human world and the deployment of nomological and synchronic forms of analysis—pose difficulties for the historian.

The nomological orientation of mainstream social science entails an explanatory model that requires uniform entities—both as "causes" and "effects"—that are susceptible of lawlike generalization. If particular ideas are to be assimilated into such a model, they have to be homogenized and emptied of their specific content, so that they can be treated as instances of a type, such as "generalized beliefs" or ideology or fanaticism, about which general knowledge is available. Thus, the role of the Enlightenment, as a historically specific body of ideas and beliefs, in the genesis of the French Revolution, is screened out at the very beginning, because it cannot count as an explanation. Similarly, when the object of explanation is defined in terms of "categories of events, processes or states of affairs," the problem of accounting for the French Revolution in its historical specificity is bypassed. There is no room in such a paradigm for the question of the relationship between the Enlightenment and the French Revolution as described in chapter 2. Not only the explanans but also the explanandum have been defined in such a way as to exclude the possibility of exploring the historically unique character of the phenomena and of the relationship between them. Even a paradigm that assigns a prominent explanatory role to "meanings" or cultural phenomena runs into the problem of handling ideas and events in their concreteness and particularity.

The nomological and synchronic methodologies of the social sciences also impose constraints on specifically historical modes of analysis that are required for a full assessment of the role of ideas in history. On the one hand, since synchronic modes of analysis are concerned with the interrelationship between elements in a totality at one moment in time, there is no need to identify elements inherited from the past or to reconstruct the processes that brought into being the totality and its components. On the other hand, since nomological modes of analysis are concerned with types of phenomena and recurring patterns and relationships, the unique characteristics of a time and place tend to be treated primarily in generic terms that transcend historical particularities. There is no reason to treat "historical individuals" in their own terms or to look into the unique processes of continuity and change that produced them. Hence, paradigms that embody an ahistorical perspective are bound to experience difficulty in dealing with the historically specific character of ideas and of the processes in which they are involved.

Theda Skocpol's excellent study in the comparative sociology of revolution illustrates both the strengths of a social science approach to the past and the limitations built into a paradigm in which the controlling assumptions make it difficult to examine the role of ideas in the genesis of particular revolutions. Her book has the additional merit, so characteristic of the best social science, of giving explicit attention to conceptual and methodological principles.[1]

Like many historians and social scientists, Skocpol operates with a model of "sociohistorical reality" that puts primary emphasis on "patterns of relationships among groups and societies." In order to analyze social revolutions in their complexity, it is necessary to adopt a "structural perspective" that focuses upon "the institutionally determined situations and relations of groups within society and upon the interrelations of societies within world-historically developing international structures." This commitment to the primacy of social and institutional structures, in turn, is reinforced by methodological and epistemological assumptions which the author describes with characteristic lucidity. Skocpol outlines

the method of comparative historical *analysis*—in which the overriding intent is to develop, test, and refine causal, explanatory hypotheses about events or structures integral to macro-units such as nation-states. Comparative historical analysis has a long and distinguished pedigree in social science. Its logic was explicitly laid out by John Stuart Mill in his *A System of Logic.* . . . Logically speaking, how does comparative historical analysis work? Basically one tries to establish valid associations of potential causes with the given phenomenon one is trying to explain.

Within this conceptual framework, Skocpol examines "three positive cases of successful revolution" in France, Russia, and China and concludes that they "reveal similar causal patterns despite their many other differences." One consequence of such a paradigm is to relegate the specific content of ideas to the periphery, as aspects of the "many other differences" between revolutions that are not considered analytically significant.

This chapter will first consider substantive assumptions of the sort presupposed by Skocpol's interpretation and then discuss ways in which positivist methodological and epistemological principles, laid down in classic form by Mill, not only reinforce the tendency to assign a heavier weight to social factors but also impose constraints on any inquiry—even one inclined to privilege cultural and symbolic forces—into the role of ideas in history. While it is clearly impossible to do justice to the diversity of social science theory and practice, it is possible to identify certain pervasive assumptions and examine their implications for historical analysis.

SOCIETY AND CULTURE

A good deal of social science theory and practice tends to accord a significant degree of primacy to social phenomena—patterns of behavior and structured relationships—in relation to ideas, beliefs, attitudes, and values. This tendency has assumed a variety of forms and no single theory is dominant. Moreover, it has come under heavy criticism, especially from symbolic anthropology. Nevertheless, it is possible to identify the contours of a position that is widely held and which is built into the conceptual and methodological structure of mainstream social science. In this section I shall concentrate on the tradition of Durkheimian sociology, with its emphasis on the totality of interconnected social patterns and structures. In that tradition the primary category has been society as a whole, conceived as a socially constituted totality in which culture is a subordinate component. This conception of the "social" may be counterposed to the Marxist view, which has become increasingly influential in social science and social history, of the significance of economically determined class structures within the society as a whole. On the question of the relationship between social and cultural phenomena, however, there is extensive common ground between Durkheimian and Marxist sociology, as Durkheim himself made clear.[2]

In a review of a book by Antonio Labriola, an Italian Marxist, Durkheim began by defining the area of agreement between them. His formulation remains a classic statement of the primacy of social phenomena in relation to consciousness or culture as a determinant of human behavior: "We regard as fruitful this idea that social life must be explained, not by the conception of it held by those who participate in it, but by profound causes which escape consciousness; and we also think that these causes must be sought chiefly in the way in which associated individuals are grouped." Within the totality of society Durkheim singled out the "substratum," composed of "the members of society as they are socially combined." Social beliefs and values, the *conscience collective*, exist in a relationship of dependence on the substratum:

In order that collective *représentations* should be intelligible, they must come from something and, since they cannot form a circle closed upon itself, the source whence they derive must be found outside them. Either the *conscience collective* floats in a void, like a sort of inconceivable absolute, or it is connected with the rest of the world through the intermediary of a substratum on which, in consequence, it depends.[3]

In this passage Durkheim is suggesting not only that a cultural explanation of the *conscience collective* would be tainted by circularity but also that the origins of such beliefs must be external to them, in the way in which individuals are grouped. He also made this point in *Sui-*

cide, published in the same year: "Given a people, consisting of a certain number of individuals arranged in a certain way, there results a determinate set of collective ideas and practices, that remain constant so long as the conditions on which they depend are themselves unchanged."[4] A few years before, in a critical comment on the thesis advanced by Fustel de Coulanges in *La Cité antique,* Durkheim argued that "it is [social arrangements] that explain the power and nature of the religious idea"; Fustel had "mistaken the cause for the effect" (p. 230). Even in 1914 Durkheim could characterize "intellectual and moral life" as being "social and nothing but an extension of society" (p. 235).

Durkheim distinguished his position from Marxism by rejecting the notion that class conflict is the source of collective ideas and by denying that the causes of social phenomena "come back, in the last analysis, to the state of industrial technique, and that the economic factor is the motive-force of progress."[5] He insisted that, on the contrary, economic activity, like other forms of collective activity, derives from the "substratum." While economic factors, once in existence, exercised an influence of their own, they are nevertheless "secondary and derivative." Similarly, in his explanation of the collective consciousness, and the "moral consciousness of societies," Durkheim put his emphasis on the formative influence of "society as a whole," and depreciated the importance of dominant classes. The Marxist view of ideology did not fit into his scheme.

As Steven Lukes has shown, in the subsequent development of his thought Durkheim moved beyond the position set forth in the review of Labriola and put more emphasis on the influence of cultural phenomena in history. His thought was characterized by "an ever-growing explanatory role for religion and an ever-growing autonomy for 'collective *représentations.*' " He depicted the relative autonomy of religious beliefs in relation to their social substratum. As early as 1898 he characterized collective representations as "partially autonomous realities which live their own life," which had "the power to attract and repel each other and to form among themselves various syntheses." Such representations were caused by others and not by "this or that characteristic of the social structure" (p. 233). He cited religion as the most striking example of this phenomenon. In Greece and Rome, "the luxuriant growth of myths and legends, theogonic and cosmological systems, etc., which grow out of religious thought, is not directly related to the particular features of the social structure" (p. 234). Thus, Durkheim was very much aware of the problem of defining the role of cultural forces, and their relative autonomy in relation to the social substratum.

Durkheim's social ontology (as defined in the Labriola review), however, was at odds with his insight into the relative autonomy of cultural forms. Hence he was unable to resolve the problem, which he had recognized and clarified. But the sociology and anthropology that developed on Durkheimian foundations ignored the problem, concentrated on the social substratum, and tended to take meaning as "the mere 'cultural content' of relationships whose formal structure is the true concern."[6]

In the best tradition of Durkheim, British social anthropology has shown in analytical detail the nature and influence of institutionalized social relationships. Mary Douglas has justly praised the "insight into socio-economic relationships" that has characterized the work of that school. In a series of essays she has warned against the tendency to exaggerate the causal efficacy of cultural phenomena in relation to what Durkheim referred to as the social stratum. On this view, "the symbolic system should always be presented with a scrutiny of the social system in which it is generated."[7] The word "generated" does not allow much room for the relative autonomy of symbolic systems in the process of cultural change. In fact, Douglas warns against endowing culture with "independent power of action."[8] Preoccupied with the danger of having "cultural forces unattached to identifiable social forces," she assigns a clear primacy to the latter. She identifies herself with a tradition that "takes for granted that human thought serves human interests and therefore carries in itself at any given moment the social configuration of that time and place."[9]

Parsonian sociology also rests on the assumption that the social dimension of the human world is of predominant importance. But this position is obscured by formal emphasis on the significance of cultural phenomena. Parsons has characterized himself as "a cultural determinist, rather than a social determinist." He has also expressed the belief that "within the social system, the normative elements are more important for social change than the 'material interests' of constitutive units."[10] What has been called a "normative functionalism" depicts norms and values as the forces that hold a society together, rather than coercive power structures. On closer inspection, however, it is clear that these norms and values are not autonomous, but represent a response to the needs of a "system of social action." This is not immediately apparent, for the theory is explicitly antireductive and formally committed to the independence of culture.

Parsons characterizes the "social system" as only one of three aspects of the structuring of a "completely concrete system of social action," the other two being "the personality systems of the individual actors and the cultural system which is built into their action." Each of the three is indispensable to the other two, and "must be considered to be an independent focus of the organization of the elements of the action system in the sense that no one of them is theoretically reducible to terms of one or a combination of the other two." There is interdependence and interpenetration but not reducibility. Within the overall "system of social action," however, the "social system"—defined as "a plurality of individual actors interacting with each other"—is clearly dominant. Thus, while the cultural system cannot be "derived" from the social system, its essential characteristics are defined by the function it performs in relation to individual actors and the interaction between them within the overall system of social action. The actors' "relationship to their situations, including each other, is defined and mediated in terms of culturally structured and shared symbols."[11]

In the Parsonian mode, Neil Smelser holds that every social system is "governed" by a value system. While that verb seems to affirm the primacy of cultural phenomena, in fact this version of normative functionalism also subordinates values to the social system whose functions they perform. The following passage appears in the context of a description of "latent pattern-maintenance and tension-management," one of the functional exigencies of social systems: "Every social system is governed by a value-system which specifies the nature of the system, its goals, and the means of attaining these goals. . . . A social system is governed by a value-system which defines and legitimizes the activities of the social system."[12] The controlling metaphor here is the "governor" of a machine.

EXPLANATION

Any tendency to privilege the social aspects of the human world at the expense of culture is magnified by the epistemological orientation of mainstream social science.[13] The various paradigms of a positivist temper embody a conception of explanation which holds that particular events can be explained by reference to general knowledge of uniform factors operating in regular processes. Ideas and beliefs, characterized by particularity and diversity, do not fit into an explanatory system that requires uniform entities. By the same token, since social and institutional phenomena lend themselves more readily to generalization, they fit in more readily and acquire greater explanatory power.

The epistemological principles underlying the theory of explanation characteristic of various forms of mainstream social science have been lucidly and coherently defined by logical empiricist philosophers such as Karl Popper, Carl Hempel, and Ernest Nagel. Their work provides a convenient summary of the logical structure of a positivist social science. We shall also draw on the theory of W. G. Runciman, a practicing sociologist who has expounded and defended the "unity of science" position on causal explanation. Although they differ on points of detail, their views are essentially "variants of the explanation theory espoused by the classics of positivism, in particular by Mill."[14] On this view, whether one is dealing with cell division or a revolution, the logic of explanation is the same.

For historians the best-known statement of the logical empiricist theory of explanation is Hempel's celebrated article, "The Function of General Laws in History." There he argued that empirical science is not concerned with "what is sometimes called individual events," but with kinds of events:

The object of description and explanation in every branch of empirical science is always the occurrence of an event of a certain *kind* (such as a drop in temperature by 14 degrees F, an eclipse of the moon, a cell-division, an earthquake, a political assassination) at a given place and time, or in a given empirical object (such as the radiator of a certain car, the planetary system, a specified historical personality, etc.) at a certain time.

In this respect history is not different from geology: "Historical explanation, too, aims at showing that the event in question was not 'a matter of chance,' but was to be expected in view of certain antecedent or simultaneous conditions. The expectation referred to is not prophecy or divination, but rational scientific anticipation which rests on the assumption of general laws." Those laws apply to *types* of events. Although no two earthquakes are identical, the occurrence of the San Francisco quake can be explained by reference to the general laws governing the type. It follows that "there is no difference in this respect between history and the natural sciences: both can give an account of their subject-matter only in terms of general concepts, and history can 'grasp the unique individuality' of its objects of study no more and no less than can physics or chemistry." Science deals with singular events of a certain kind, not with "unique individuality."[15]

The core of Hempel's account of explanation has been accepted by many social scientists and by a number of historians. It has been said that exponents of the new social history embraced "a full-blown Hempelian view of history," while treating older paradigms as pre-Copernican.[16] Frederick Olafson has pointed out that historians seeking a rapprochement with the social sciences have tended to share the Hempelian assumption that as history transforms itself into a social science "it will more and more visibly conform to the logical requirements which that new identity carries with it."[17] Central to those requirements is the axiom that the assassination of Julius Caesar has to be explained in much the same way as the San Francisco earthquake. Despite the surface differences between the two occurrences, the logic of explanation is the same in each case. The historian or social scientist, like the geologist, is dealing with types of events, which may be explained by reference to the general laws governing the behavior of the kinds of phenomena involved.

From the principle of "the unity of the scientific method," Karl Popper also argues that history must adopt the standpoint of "causal explanation" characteristic of the natural sciences. He firmly rejects the notion that " 'unique' events, which occur only once and have nothing 'general' about them, may be the cause of other events." On the contrary, "a singular event is the cause of another singular event—which is its effect—only relative to some universal laws." Like Hempel he argues that events to be explained must be treated as typical, "as belonging to kinds or classes of events. For only then is the deductive method of causal explanation applicable." Thus, insofar as the historian is interested in the explanation of "specific events," he must proceed in the manner of a natural scientist, such as "the practical chemist, for example, who wishes to analyze a certain given compound—a piece of rock, say."[18] The differences between chemical compounds and historical phenomena are irrelevant to the logic of causal explanation that is applicable in both cases.

W. G. Runciman develops his account of the "unity of science" conception of causal explanation in the context of a critique of Max Weber's theory of "historical individuals." While rejecting the view that historical or sociological explanation involves subsuming an event under covering laws, he argues that it "does and must rest on the tacit assumption that there are lawlike generalizations." Explanation as such presupposes "the universality of cause and effect." In asking why people have done what they have done, we are asking a causal question that requires a causal answer based on the axiom that "common causes yield common effects." From this standpoint, Runciman removes various "concessions" that Weber has made to idealism, and denies "historical individuals" the status of causes. On this view, there can be no causal relationship between Protestantism and the spirit of capitalism in early modern Europe, since causation involves common causes that yield common effects.[19] The point of Weber's analysis, however, was to establish the causal impact of Protestantism as a unique complex of ideas and beliefs; he used the term "causal" in a non-Humean sense that embraced the influence of just such historically specific phenomena.

Runciman's denial of a causal relationship between Protestantism and the spirit of capitalism is a good illustration of Peter Winch's point that the empiricist methodologies of the social sciences involve "minimizing the importance of ideas in human history, since ideas and theories are constantly developing and changing, and since each system of ideas, its component elements being interrelated internally, has to be understood in and for itself. . . ." The empiricist theory of explanation interposes constraints even when ideas are reconstructed in their full complexity and particularity, as in Morton White's fine study of the philosophy of the American Revolution.[20] More often, however, ideas are disposed of more casually.

If ideas are to be fitted into a social science model that requires uniformities and regularities, common causes and common effects, they have to be emptied of their specific content and treated as instances of a type. Thus, any attempt to develop "a theoretical formulation of the necessary and sufficient causes of a revolution,"[21] must deal with generic entities such as ideologies, generalized beliefs, or fanaticism, rather than the unique content of the Enlightenment or Bolshevism. In Smelser's model of the six stages in the development of a revolution,[22] for example, "generalized belief" plays a common role in a variety of revolutions; in each case the specific content of the belief is irrelevant to the function it performs. This substantive conclusion follows from the methodological requirement of common causes and common effects.

The epistemological axiom of the universality of cause and effect entails an inclination to attribute greater explanatory power to those aspects of the human world—institutions, structures, and relationships—which display regularities and uniformities. This tendency, usually implicit, is explicit in Pareto. While Pareto's reductionism, like vulgar Marxism, has few adherents, it is nonetheless of interest because it presents, in extreme form, the substantive implications of positivist epistemology. As Peter Winch has pointed out, in Pareto's theory "the claim that there are sociological uniformities goes hand in hand with the claim that human intelligence is much overrated as a real influence on social events."[23] The fundamental aspects of human reality, "residues" in Pareto's terminology, embrace social institutions and structures which are characterized by uniformities that recur in different times and places. Ideas and beliefs, however—the "derivations" that are derived from the more stable and invariant aspects of human life—are characterized by extreme variability. In fact, for Pareto the "derivations" are no more than *post hoc* rationalizations of practices and institutions (p. 104). It is partly because the former are so unstable and variable in comparison to the latter that they are relegated to a subordinate position in Pareto's positivist sociology.

In various ways, then, the positivist assumption that human events must be explained by the sort of causal explanation characteristic of the natural sciences, encourages a tendency to assign a significant degree of primacy to causes that approximate those that operate in the physical world. A case in point is Durkheim's dictum, quoted above, that social life must be explained by "profound causes which escape consciousness." The positivist resonance in that passage is pronounced: "We even think that it is on this condition, and on this condition alone, that history can become a science and sociology in consequence exist."[24] Here the quest for causes that escape consciousness—along with explanation of ideas and values by reference to those more "profound" causes—is presented as a prerequisite to the truly scientific study of history and society. To be sure, Durkheim himself transcended the limitations of this theory and confronted directly the problem of the influence of ideas. But the positivist pursuit of Humean causes independent of consciousness remains pervasive, in one form or another, in the paradigms of mainstream social science.

The Humean view of causation often provides the underpinning for attempts to explain ideas by reference to "circumstances," or even to derive the former from the latter. As W. H. Walsh has shown, in his critique of the widespread disposition to find the origin of ideas in "circumstances that are independent of men's thoughts," it is misleading to posit a dichotomy between ideas and circumstances, as if they were two discrete entities, akin to Humean causes and effects. He argues that "circumstances (a) can be said to cause ideas only through the medium of other ideas, and (b) more seriously, themselves involve ideas to a vital extent. It follows that any causal regularities there may be in this area will hold, not between features of the independent world and men's thoughts, but between the world as envisaged or experienced and what men think, the world as envisaged or experienced being itself not independent of thought." Just as it does not make sense to think of circumstances as existing in total independence of thought, so we cannot think of them "as exercising straightforward natural causality." The Humean view of causation is inappropriate here because this is not a relationship between two entities that are "separately describable and in which instances of the first sort are found in constant conjunction with instances of the second." Walsh also points out that "to move beyond attitudes to the circumstances in which they were formed is not to penetrate to causes in the Humean sense, if only because such circumstances affect different individuals in very different ways."[25] Thus, there are two reasons why the relationship between ideas and circumstances cannot be said to manifest causal connections of the Humean sort: first, the interdependence of cause and effect, and the logical and conceptual links between them; second, the absence of the regularities characteristic of the world of nature.

A preoccupation with Humean causes characterized by constant conjunction entails the exclusion of an inquiry into what Walsh calls "intelligible connections" between ideas and circumstances. Yet it is precisely connections of that sort that the historian must look into. Walsh points out that the manner in which historians analyze the relationship between circumstances and ideas is different from the sort of thing that is required in order to establish causal relations of the Humean type. Thus, we validate such connections "not by looking round for a plurality of similar cases, in order if possible to arrive at some constant conjunction which is not to be denied, but by thinking ourselves into the position as envisaged, reconstituting the background, and then looking at things through the eyes of the agents concerned, in order to represent the development of the idea as natural." That is, the historian has to look for "intelligible connections" rather than constant conjunction. Walsh counterposes his account to the views of logical empiricism and positivist social science:

Philosophers professing empiricism will naturally (the word itself is significant) be dissatisfied with this account, and will insist that intelligible connections of the kind just spoken of be replaced by objective causal linkages. Intelligible connections as they see them have a double disadvantage: they rest on unsubstantiated personal insight, and they vary from case to case, thus falling short of universality.

Logical empiricist theory, concentrating exclusively on "objective behavior" that can be classified into clearly identifiable types, has no room for "intelligible connections." Rather, it demands scientific inquiry to determine the laws governing types of behavior and to establish correlations between "separately identifiable social phenomena."[26] To the social sciences is assigned the task of providing such laws. Whatever the merits of such an approach—and it is of proven value in many areas—it entails the methodological exclusion of the search for "intelligible connections." And that methodological exclusion, in turn, entails a truncated view of the human world and of the "causal" processes at work in it.

In other ways also the methodological and conceptual structure of mainstream social science leads to a depreciation of the role of ideas and beliefs in the genesis of events. Thus, the distinction between objective and subjective aspects of the human world, between an action and the ideas embodied in it, between observable behavior and invisible meanings, presupposes an ontology in which the essential human reality is constituted independently of beliefs about it held by individuals. While ideas and beliefs are not banished from the human world, they are treated as a second order of reality—fleeting, variable, soft, derivative.

Runciman's methodological distinction between "reportage and explanation" on the one hand and "description" on the other presupposes an ontological distinction between observable behavior (including beliefs), which can be identified, classified, and reported in an objective and scientific manner, and the meaning of the behavior for the persons involved. The former is the realm of causal relations: "the observer moves on from identifying and reporting to categorising and explaining the behavior he has observed." Meanings, however, lie outside the realm of causal relations and are of no explanatory value. Runciman draws a sharp contrast between "answering the question why people have done what they have done and describing (or even 'depicting') what it meant to them." Description of meanings necessarily poses questions that cannot be settled by reference to empirical evidence. Runciman's distinctions have the effect of depreciating the significance of the specific content of ideas and beliefs, as opposed to their generic aspects that are susceptible to being identified and reported objectively through the use of scientific concepts. By virtue of their particularity—or uniqueness—beliefs cannot be precisely defined, do not function causally, and are not useful for purposes of explanation. In this vein, Runciman distinguished between "grasping and conveying the 'feel' or the 'flavour' or the 'spirit' of a social situation or an institution" and "merely reporting the facts of it." [27] "Facts" are what count, both analytically and substantively. As opposed to ineffable meanings, they can be objectively identified and reported. Such facts are the basis of empirical science.

Charles Taylor has shown how mainstream political science of the 1960s, defining its object of study in conformity with the requirements of empiricist epistemology, constructed a conception of "objective" social and political reality from which ideas and beliefs were excluded. In an attempt to develop a verifiable science of politics, the category "political behavior" was developed, comprising phenomena susceptible of objective identification and description, without the intrusion of subjective interpretations. Political scientists concentrated their attention on "brute data," which could be described behaviorally; meanings requiring interpretation were excluded. Such data comprised overt acts capable of being defined "physically or institutionally," along with "assent or dissent to verbal formulae, or the occurrence or not of verbal formulae in speech." The category "political behavior," so conceived, identified objective reality with that which can be described in behavioral terms. Not being susceptible of such description, ideas and beliefs were treated as a subjective epiphenomenon, expressing the meaning of the objective political reality for the individuals involved. From the standpoint of mainstream political science, then, "what is objectively (intersubjectively) real is brute data identifiable. This is what social reality *is*."[28] Other aspects of the political world were assigned no more than a subjective reality, embracing individuals' beliefs about and evaluations of the objective social reality.

Empiricist epistemology, then, is not ontologically neutral. On the contrary, as Taylor has pointed out, one of the salient characteristics of mainstream social science is that it "reconstructs reality" in line with its epistemological principles; in the case of political science the category is political behavior. That reconstruction entails the exclusion of intersubjective meanings as constituents of social and political reality:

These [categorial principles] allow for an intersubjective social reality which is made up of brute data, identifiable acts and structures, certain institutions, procedures, actions. It allows for beliefs, affective reactions, evaluations as the psychological properties of individuals. And it allows for correlations between these two orders of reality: e.g., that certain beliefs go along with certain acts, certain values with certain institutions, etc.[29]

In this ontology, an objective social reality is counterposed to a subjective reality which consists of beliefs and values held in relation to the former. Thus, the category "political behavior" presupposes the subordination of ideas and beliefs to a presumably objective social reality from which they have been excluded.

The numerous studies of revolution by social scientists in the 1950s and 1960s illustrate the manner in which empiricist epistemology and methodology entails a depreciation of the role of ideas in events. Sheldon Wolin has pointed out that those studies were flawed by the presence of an assumption central to the culture of American social science: "that action can be abstracted from ideology and analyzed under a separate category."[30] That assumption denies the constitutive relation between thought and action, a relationship in which an action is inseparable from the meaning that it has for the actors. Once the action has been analytically severed from ideas and beliefs, it can be characterized and explained by reference to such categories as frustration, alienation, strain, etc. Thus, Talcott Parsons explains the occurrence of revolution in part by "the sudden alteration in the major balance of equilibrium of the social system by the ascendancy of a 'revolutionary' movement which organizes a set of alienative motivational orientations relative to the main institutionalized order."[31] What is decisive is the strength of alienative motivations. The specific content of the ideology is not a significant factor in the process underlying the occurrence of a revolution. In fact, once the ideology has been "stripped of its symbiotic relation with action,"[32] it can be disposed of by means of a general category. The revolutionary ideas become a rationalization of needs or frustrations generated by disequilibrium in the social system.

The treatment of revolution in Neil Smelser's sociology illustrates the manner in which the methodological and epistemological principles of mainstream social science—concerned with describing and explaining human activity in terms of types of phenomena—impede an adequate assessment of the role of ideas and beliefs in the genesis of events. In an account of his assumptions, Smelser shows how revolution is to be explained as a type of "collective behavior." His theory presupposes the existence of identifiable entities, types of behavior whose characteristics can be established scientifically. Such entities enter the analysis both as events to be explained (e.g., revolutions) and as their "determinants" (e.g., generalized beliefs or social strain). He defines his object of study in briskly positivist terms: "The forms of collective behavior constitute a series ranging from the simple to the complex. The more complex forms, moreover, include *as components* the elements found in simpler forms, but not vice versa." Such entities, however diverse, can be described in terms of combinations and permutations of their components. Particular human phenomena and their components can be described in much the same way that a scientist describes geological phenomena. Similarly, in explaining historical events it is possible to identify the "determinants," which operate in regular ways. In explanation the important thing is to "systematize the determinants, and note the changes in the combination of determinants which produce different outcomes." In seeking to define the determinants of "collective behavior," Smelser assumes the existence of such types of behavior as a "panic." On that assumption he asks: "What determines whether an episode of collective behavior *of any sort* will occur? What determines whether one type *rather than another* will occur? Many of the existing answers to these questions are unsatisfactory scientifically." In considering the contributory role of the minor determinants in the genesis of panic, a mere list will not do: "We must organize the determinants precisely enough so that panic is the *only* possible outcome. . . . We need, then, a *unique* combination of determinants which yields a *unique* outcome, panic."[33] Thus, it is the combination of determinants that produces a particular panic. Historical particularities, including the specific content of beliefs, are eliminated. Both the "determinants" and the "outcome" are generic entities—types—that are susceptible to scientific analysis.

From this perspective, Smelser deals with revolutions. He treats political revolution as a subtype of "value-oriented movements" in a model that covers "collective behavior" as a whole. Political revolution (such as "the French and Russian revolutions, or the German and Italian fascist revolutions") is one of a number of disparate entities that qualify as value-oriented movements: "Our definition encompasses the phenomena designated by the labels 'nativistic movement,' 'sect formation,' 'religious revolution,' 'political revolution,' . . . and many others." He begins with a model that covers all types of collective behavior, including value-oriented movements, and describes six determinants. The first three determinants of collective behavior are structural conduciveness, structural strain, and "the growth and spread of generalized belief." Applying this scheme to value-oriented movements, he describes the sequential relationship between the first three

determinants: "Under the conditions of conduciveness and strain outlined above, value-oriented beliefs begin to crystallize. Such beliefs
'explain' the conditions of strain which give rise to it. . . . Value-oriented beliefs also focus attention on concrete situations, bring a number of grievances together under a single cause or myth."[34] Crystalli-
zation is an apt metaphor for it denotes a process independent of the
consciousness of an agent. The content of the beliefs is irrelevant. Sugar
is sugar, whether it comes from cane or beets or a laboratory.

In sum, Smelser's methodology entails the elimination of the specific content of ideas and beliefs by treating them as instances of generic entities—generalized beliefs, messianism, status tension—that can
be fitted into the methodological scheme. In addition, his functionalist
approach also eliminates the specificity of values by treating them primarily in terms of the function they perform for the fundamental reality, the social system. Every social system includes, as one of its parts,
a value system that "defines and legitimizes the activities" of the system. The specific content of the beliefs is of no more than peripheral
importance, since the same function could be performed with infinite
variations in content, as is the case in different social systems.

AHISTORICAL ASSUMPTIONS

The nomological orientation of mainstream social science, then, entails a tendency to depreciate the causal significance of particular ideas
and beliefs, since they do not fit into an explanatory model that requires uniform entities susceptible to lawlike generalization. In addition, the ahistorical perspective that is intrinsic to the nomological and
synchronic methodology of social science interposes other obstacles to
an adequate assessment. The exclusion of specifically historical phenomena and processes from the human world, along with the modes
of analysis that they require, makes it very difficult even to pose the
kind of questions that the historian asks, much less to answer them
adequately. Even a social scientist who is committed to the primacy of
the symbolic order will have difficulty escaping from the limitations
inherent in ahistorical assumptions.

The social science approach to particular events is unhistorical both
in description and explanation. An event such as a revolution is treated

primarily in relation to the type, to be described in terms of varying combinations of uniform elements that recur in different times and places. Such description encompasses invariant elements, rather than the unique; cast in synchronic terms, it does not identify elements inherited from the past. This sort of description, in turn, entails explanation in nomological and synchronic terms. The components of the phenomenon, having been identified generically, can be taken as given; there is no need to account for unique elements, since they do not appear in the description; a synchronic explanation, in terms of interrelations at one point in time, is sufficient. Thus, the social science model of explanation, closely linked to the model of description, encompasses the operation of generic factors, without reference to the historically specific, and is limited to synchronic analysis, without reference to elements inherited from the past or to the unique historical processes that produced them.

As a result of the sort of description and explanation built into social science paradigms, the specifically historical is screened out in two interconnected ways. The event to be explained is defined in generic terms, with its distinctive characteristics reduced in significance. Once the object of study has been simplified, it lends itself readily to the kind of explanation that also concentrates on uniform factors, to the exclusion of the historically unique. Both explanandum and explanans are defined ahistorically. The interconnected questions of what and why, together with the form that acceptable answers may take, are so formulated as to exclude the historical. In the description and explanation of the Puritan Revolution, the French Revolution, and the Bolshevik Revolution, therefore, differences and similarities are dealt with in terms of combinations of uniform elements characteristic of the revolutionary phenomenon.

Once the historically specific aspects of the French Revolution have been removed from the explanandum, the explanatory importance of the Enlightenment as a historically unique entity is correspondingly diminished, if not eliminated altogether. If a particular revolution is described in much the same way as a particular earthquake, then "generalized beliefs" in one form or another, without reference to the specific content of the beliefs, will function efficiently in the kind of explanation required for a phenomenon defined in those terms. More-

over, once the Enlightenment has been emptied of its historically specific content by nomological and synchronic analysis, it can be assimilated to a type of thought structure, such as ideology, and treated in
terms of its generic characteristics. Given these definitions of explanandum and explanans, it is virtually impossible to ask the historical
question of the role of the Enlightenment in the genesis of the French
Revolution.

The manner in which empiricist epistemology entails the exclusion
of specifically historical modes of analysis can be seen clearly in Karl
Popper's handling of the problem of uniqueness in history. While recognizing the existence in the human world of phenomena that may be
characterized as unique, in contrast to the entities found in the physical world, Popper dismisses such uniqueness as of merely esthetic interest, to be perceived and savored, but not to be included in scientific
description or explanation. He acknowledges the diversity, changeability, and "intrinsic newness" that characterize human events but not
natural events: "In the world described by physics nothing can happen that is truly and intrinsically new. A new engine may be invented,
but we can always analyze it as a rearrangement of elements which are
anything but new. Newness in physics is merely the newness of arrangements or combinations." In presenting his views on "the question of the *uniqueness* of historical events" Popper argues that the unique
aspects of an historical phenomenon are tangential to its essential
characteristics and are irrelevant to the "causal explanation" required
by empiricist methodology. "The distinction . . . between 'novelty of
arrangement' and 'intrinsic newness' corresponds to the present distinction between the standpoint of causal explanation and that of the
appreciation of the unique." [35]

Popper's distinction between "novelty of arrangement" in nature and
"intrinsic newness" in history is extremely useful, not only from the
point of view of the different modes of explanation required in each
case but also from the point of view of the different kinds of forces
and processes at work. His logical empiricist theory dissolves both
questions, however. He argues that "causal explanation," dealing with
uniform entities whose behavior follows regular patterns, is equally
applicable to physical and historical events. Novelty in history can be
explained, as in physics, in terms of "newness of arrangements or

combinations." The principle of the unity of science requires that the historian, like the physicist, explain particular events by reference to combinations and rearrangements of uniform elements. While recognizing that historians are interested in "the description of a specific event as such," he does not assign any scientific value to that activity. He dismisses such an interest as essentially antiquarian and esthetic, irrelevant to scientific explanation. Although "one of [history's] most important tasks is undoubtedly to describe interesting happenings in their peculiarity or uniqueness," such description does not contribute to explanation.[36]

Popper's methodological distinction between "causal explanation" and "the appreciation of the unique" presupposes a one-sided view of causation in the human world that excludes specifically historical forces. Neither Christianity nor the Enlightenment has functioned as a "cause" in Popper's sense of the term. Yet it is clear that Christianity has "influenced" or "shaped" the history of Europe from the very beginning. Moreover, Christianity—an historically unique phenomenon—has been an active ingredient in the processes that have produced multifarious forms characterized by "intrinsic newness." Neither the genesis of Christianity nor the developments to which it contributed can be explained in terms of "newness of arrangements or combinations." Rather, they require "historical" explanation that takes account of the creation of "intrinsic newness" by the interplay between unique phenomena over time. Such explanation is concerned precisely with the genesis of new forms at a particular point and their subsequent influence.

Like Popper, W. G. Runciman disposes of the problem of uniqueness by removing it from the realm of explanation and treating it solely in connection with description. This, in turn, is linked to a view of causation that has no place for unique phenomena. Runciman's position is of particular interest because it is developed in the context of a critique of Weber's account of "historical individuals" and their causal role. He concedes that "despite the unity of science there are conceptual problems in the sciences of human behavior of a kind from which the sciences of nature are spared."[37] Both the sociologist and the historian have the task of describing the unique aspects of human behavior. Like Popper, however, Runciman argues that such phenomena have to be explained in terms of the universality of cause and effect; causation does not encompass unique forces. That is, explanation necessarily involves *types* of behavior, to which lawlike generalizations apply. From this standpoint, Runciman rejects Weber's thesis that the historian has to take account of two disparate aspects of historical causation: on the one hand, unique causal configurations involving "historical individuals" and on the other, recurring patterns that lend themselves to the generalizations of "nomological knowledge." Runciman argues, on the contrary, that "historical individuals" are themselves susceptible to explanation on the basis of psychological laws. Hence "lawlike generalizations" are capable of providing a sufficient explanation of human behavior, and a consideration of unique causal configurations is unnecessary for sociological explanation.

In the logical empiricist mode, Runciman argues that Weber could have "conceded the dependence of sociology and history on the presumptive laws of psychology without thereby surrendering their autonomy." He cites the familiar analogy of the autonomy of geology, despite its dependence on physics; and the autonomy of biology despite its dependence on physiology and biochemistry. Runciman draws together the various elements of the unity of science position:

All the historical and therefore open-ended sciences, whether physical, biological, or social, share both the same inability to predict accurately in advance and the same lack of autonomous general laws by comparison with mechanics. But this does not mean they do not constitute legitimate specialisms or that they are incapable of explaining the "historical individuals," in Max Weber's phrase, with which they are concerned. It means only that their explanations require the implicit backing of one or more sciences which are unhistorical and "pure" relative to them.[38]

In sum, historically unique phenomena are not causally significant and can themselves be explained by bringing to bear general knowledge.

In a number of interconnected ways, then, social science paradigms based on empiricist epistemology exclude both historical modes of analysis and the specifically historical aspects of the human world that require such analysis. On this view, the question of the effect of Christianity on the history of Europe between the thirteenth century and the eighteenth century has to be answered primarily by reference to general knowledge of the behavior of religious, social, and political phenomena. Our explanation need not take account of the unique characteristics of Christianity or their unique historical antecedents. Nomological and synchronic methodology excludes as irrelevant both historical uniqueness and the role of the past in creating the unique constituents of particular "causes" and "effects." Thus, Runciman's conception of description and explanation, along with the rigid separation between them, precludes specifically historical understanding and explanation. In history, description and explanation are closely linked because the precise character of the entities being examined—as "causes" and "effects"—needs to be established in each instance; neither the nature of the phenomena involved nor the relationship between them can be taken as given, as instances of an identifiable type. An analysis of the origins of the phenomena is essential not only to an explanation of how they came into existence but also to an understanding of their specific characteristics, including components created in the past. Moreover, what appears to be a purely methodological distinction between description and explanation also embodies a substantive judgment that denies the causal efficacy of "historical individuals."

The structuralist anthropology of Claude Lévi-Strauss is explicitly antihistorical in orientation. The case against history is set forth coherently and unequivocally. Lévi-Strauss denies that historicity is a fundamental characteristic of human life. Hence, in order to understand a phenomenon it is necessary to eliminate those aspects of it that are derived from history and conscious thought. In place of diachronic inquiry, Lévi-Strauss calls for the synchronic analysis of the structural elements composing the object of study at a particular moment in time. An explanation of a phenomenon requires the analysis of its "internal determinants." In this way Lévi-Strauss proposes to move beyond "empirical diversity" to the structural "invariants" that lie beneath. His methodology, however, is not based on the natural sciences, but on Saussurean linguistics. His structural invariants are linguistic units, which function like genes, combining and recombining to produce endless diversity.

Lévi-Strauss' antihistorical position is of particular relevance to the problem of ideas in history because he emphasizes the importance of the symbolic aspects of the human world and rejects any tendency to claim primacy for the social: "Society cannot exist without symbolism, but instead of showing how the appearance of symbolic thought makes social life altogether possible and necessary, Durkheim tries the reverse, i.e. to make symbolism grow out of society." He criticized Durkheim for having considered language, law, and religion as "projections of the social."[39] But Lévi-Strauss treats symbolic forms unhistorically. The specific content of ideas and beliefs is explained—and disposed of—by reference to the invariant linguistic forms of which they are composed. While semiological methods and concepts are potentially useful in the study of the role of ideas in history, they first have to be removed from their unhistorical framework.

The primary weakness in the structuralism of Lévi-Strauss springs from his attempt to extend to the whole of the human world methods designed for the study of language. Saussure developed his ideas in reaction against the narrowly historical orientation of linguistics in the second half of the nineteenth century. Having mastered the historical approach and having applied it successfully in a study of the Indo-European vowel system, Saussure saw the need to move beyond the dominant "diachronic" methodology, which failed to take account of the systematic and "synchronic" character of linguistic phenomena: a structural and functional analysis of language was required. It was necessary to analyze linguistic forms and their interrelationships "synchronically," without reference to their historical origins. Saussure showed that diachronic information is irrelevant to the analysis of the system of a language. For example, the description of the modern English *you* does not require a knowledge of its evolution into its present form. In an earlier state of the language it was a plural, defined in opposition to *thee* and *thou;* and was an object pronoun, in opposition to the subject pronoun *ye*. As Jonathan Culler observes, "The description of modern English *you* would remain exactly the same if its historical evolution had been totally different, for *you* in modern English is defined by its role in the synchronic state of the language."[40] While Saussure's conception of language as a self-contained synchronic system has proved to be immensely fruitful, however, it cannot be applied with comparable success to every aspect of the human world.

Lévi-Strauss' account of the virtues of synchronic analysis is sufficiently general to encompass not only his own structuralism, based on Saussurean linguistics, but also the methodological objectives of the social sciences as a whole. Their aim is to examine the phenomenon—

whether it is a kinship system or a social system or a mythological structure—as it exists at a particular moment in time, without reference to its historical origins. Thus, he stresses the importance, first of all, of identifying the constituents of the phenomenon and establishing the interrelationships between them: "It is impossible to discuss an object, to reconstruct the process of its coming into being without knowing first *what it is;* in other words, without having exhausted the inventory of its internal determinants."[41] The social scientist can examine the "internal determinants," which are finite in number, and demonstrate the interrelations between them. That analytical procedure defines the phenomenon once and for all, without reference to the specific historical character or historical origins of the components. The first task of the social scientist is to identify and analyze the phenomena at hand and to find out "to what extent their interrelations suffice to explain them." In carrying out such synchronic analyses, the social scientist seeks to get at "invariants beyond the empirical diversity of human societies," to move beyond historical particularities to something more fundamental, something susceptible of treatment by "analytical reason." Thus, the "ultimate goal of the human sciences" is to "dissolve man." Lévi-Strauss explains that "the verb 'dissolve' does not in any way imply (but even excludes) the destruction of the constituents subjected to the action of another body. The solution of a solid into a liquid alters the disposition of its molecules. It also provides an efficacious method of putting them by so that they can be recovered in case of need and their properties be better studied." Applying the chemical metaphor rather literally, Lévi-Strauss' method entails the reduction of human phenomena to their constituents, which can be analyzed scientifically. "Scientific explanation consists not in moving from the complex to the simple but in the replacement of a less intelligible complexity by one which is more so." His purpose is "to abstract the structure which underlies the many manifestations and remains permanent throughout a succession of events."[42]

In pursuing the "ultimate goal of the human sciences," Lévi-Strauss concentrates on the linguistic forms that constitute the "structural elements" underlying the heterogeneity of cultural and social phenomena. These basic elements remain permanent and unchanged. Diversity can be accounted for in terms of varying combinations and permutations of these elements. Lévi-Strauss uses the analogy of the genes:

. . . it is certainly legitimate to speak of evolution in a historical and socio-logical sense, but the elements to be organized into an evolutionary process cannot be borrowed from the level of a cultural typology which consists of mechanical models. They should be sought at a sufficiently deep level to in-sure that these elements will remain unaffected by different cultural contexts (as, let us say, genes are identical elements combined into different patterns corresponding to the different racial [statistical] models) and can accordingly permit the drawing of long statistical runs.

By dealing with linguistic forms the anthropologist can build "models whose elements are independent of their combinations and which re-main identical through a sufficiently long period of time."[43]

Lévi-Strauss' quest for the structural elements underlying cultural diversity involves giving primary attention to linguistic form, to the exclusion of specific content. In a discussion of the diverse cultures of New Guinea, he describes the kind of synchronic analysis that is in-tended to transcend superficial differences: "And yet these units whose identity, number, and distribution are constantly varying, remain linked by relationships whose content is equally variable but whose formal character is maintained through the vicissitudes in their history." After giving a few examples of common structural elements, Lévi-Strauss describes vividly the methodological principles and procedures in-volved: "In every case, something is preserved which may be gradu-ally isolated through observation—by means of a kind of straining process which allows the 'lexicographical' content of institutions and customs to filter through—in order to retain only the structural ele-ments."[44] The specific content of the beliefs is filtered out. What is left becomes the object of scientific analysis.

Here is a good statement of the methodological premises underlying Lévi-Strauss' quest for invariant structures:

In anthropology as in linguistics, therefore, it is not comparison that supports generalization, but the other way around. If, as we believe to be the case, the unconscious activity of the mind consists in imposing forms upon content, and if these forms are fundamentally the same for all minds—ancient and modern, primitive and civilized (as the study of the symbolic function, expressed in language, so strikingly indicates)—it is necessary and sufficient to grasp the unconscious structure underlying each institution and each custom, in order to obtain a principle of interpretation valid for other institutions and other customs provided of course that the analysis is carried far enough.[45]

Lévi-Strauss describes with admirable precision the manner in which structuralist analysis proceeds by eliminating specifically historical elements—the actual content of beliefs and attitudes and values. While the anthropologist "cannot remain indifferent to historical processes and to the most highly conscious expressions of social phenomena," he strives to "eliminate, by a kind of backward course, all that they owe to the historical process and to conscious thought. His goal is to grasp, beyond the conscious and always shifting images which men hold, the complete range of unconscious possibilities."[46]

In the preceding passage, Lévi-Strauss is describing the procedures of an anthropologist studying primitive societies. In such a situation, in the absence of historical evidence, synchronic analysis is a matter of necessity. The value of such an approach has been fully demonstrated, even where historical material is available. But Lévi-Strauss and the structuralists are not content to leave the matter there. He not only depreciates the value of historical analysis (despite formally favorable references to it), but denies that historicity is an intrinsic characteristic of human life. Here, as elsewhere, Lévi-Strauss does not fudge the issues. He calls for a rejection of "the equivalence between the notion of history and the notion of humanity which some have tried to foist on us with the unavowed aim of making historicity the last refuge of a transcendental humanism." He also rejects the notion of continuity presupposed by historical analysis. According to Lévi-Strauss, it is

not only fallacious but contradictory to conceive of the historical process as a continuous development, beginning with prehistory coded in tens of hundreds of millennia, then adopting the scale of millennia when it gets to the fourth or third millennium, and continuing as history in centuries interlarded, at the pleasure of each author, with slices of annual history within the century, day to day history within the year or even hourly history within a day.[47]

Lévi-Strauss argues that Sartre and other contemporary philosophers have "valued history above the other human sciences and formed

an almost mystical conception of it." In their eyes, "some special privilege seems to attach to the temporal dimension, as if diachrony were
to establish a kind of intelligibility not merely superior to that provided by synchrony, but above all more specifically human." Determined to cut history down to size, he insists that "historical knowledge has no claim to be opposed to other forms of knowledge as a
supremely privileged one." [48] In rejecting that "claim," however, Lévi-
Strauss eliminates distinctively historical analysis.

Unlike Lévi-Strauss, Clifford Geertz takes a favorable view of history. He has criticized both structuralism and functionalism for their
preoccupation with "timeless structural pictures" and their neglect of
social change. On this and other issues also Geertz has developed a
subtle position that avoids extreme formulations and false dichoto-
mies; he has moved beyond the constricting assumptions of a narrowly
positivist and behaviorist social science. While he leaves no doubt that
the study of culture can be "a positive science like any other," he argues that it cannot be "an experimental science in search of law but
an interpretive one in search of meaning." From this vantage point,
he has emphasized the importance of close attention to cultural diversity and particularity. He points out that in their preoccupation with
empirical universals anthropologists "shied away from cultural particularities." At the same time, however, he has insisted that the study
of such particulars must be conducted in the manner of a positive science. Cultural diversity is intelligible because "certain sorts of patterns and certain sorts of relationships among patterns recur from society to society." As a result, the meanings which symbols embody are
"in principle, as capable of being discovered through systematic empirical investigation . . . as the atomic weight of hydrogen or the
function of the adrenal glands." [49]

Geertz has combined the analytical rigor of the natural sciences with
a respect for the distinctive characteristics of the human world. He has
confronted directly the intractable analytical problem of the relationship between the universal and the particular. On the one hand, he
rejects the assumption that "unless a cultural phenomenon is empirically universal it cannot reflect anything about the nature of man." On
the other hand, the analysis of cultural particulars ought to be conducted without giving oneself over too completely to " 'the thrill of

learning singular things.' " He concludes that "it is not whether phenomena are empirically common that is critical in science . . . but whether they can be made to reveal the enduring natural processes that underly them." From this vantage point he urges the social scientist "to look for systematic relationships among diverse phenomena, not for substantive identities among similar ones." (p. 44).

Geertz exemplifies the complementary relationship between social science and history. With good reason he has been called the historian's anthropologist. But there is also an inescapable tension between the two disciplines. The predominance of a social science orientation in the study of the past is incompatible with a full understanding of the historical world and its processes. Precisely because of the evident value of Geertzian anthropology for the study of man and his history, it illustrates the limitations inherent in exclusively generic and synchronic categories. Geertz's comments on the French Revolution, made in passing in the course of his well-known essay on ideology, emphasize generic aspects of the event and of the processes that produced it. He presents a systematic account of general features of a particular phenomenon that usually appear in historical narrative only implicitly and unsystematically. At the same time, however, any attempt to approach the French Revolution exclusively in these terms can yield only a partial understanding, since it excludes the specifically historical.

Geertz discusses the French Revolution in the context of an analysis of the kinds of events that generate "extremist ideologies" and of the processes underlying events of that sort. What he has to say illustrates the kind of general knowledge that is essential to historical understanding: "The reason why the French Revolution was, at least up to its time, the greatest incubator of extremist ideologies, 'progressive' and 'reactionary' alike, in human history was not that either personal insecurity or social disequilibrium were deeper and more pervasive than at many earlier periods—though they were deep and pervasive enough— but because the central organizing principle of political life, the divine right of kings, was destroyed." He describes the complex of factors that help to explain why the central organizing principle of political life in France was destroyed: "It is a confluence of sociopsychological strain and an absence of cultural resources by means of which to make sense of the strain, each exacerbating the other, that sets the stage for the rise of systematic (political, moral, or economic) ideologies" (pp. 219–220).

Such an analysis, however, gets at only one aspect of the French Revolution. The historian must also examine that event in its historical uniqueness, in a relationship of continuity and change, similarity and difference, with other revolutions that preceded and followed. He also has to look into the historically unique phenomena and processes that shaped its character. Nomological and synchronic description and explanation are not sufficient.

Geertz's sensitivity to cultural particularities encompasses both geographically separate cultures in the present and different periods in the history of a single culture. Aware of the diversity produced by change through time, he has criticized the failure of many social scientists to take this into account. He dismisses Lévi-Strauss' model of society on the grounds that it "reflects neither time, nor place, nor circumstance." That "infernal culture machine . . . annuls history, reduces sentiment to a shadow of the intellect, and replaces the particular minds of particular savages in particular jungles with the Savage Mind immanent in us all" (p. 355). Like the historian, Geertz is preoccupied with particularity in time and place. The sort of "thick description" that he recommends is a useful instrument for the study of man, past and present. His account of how to go about understanding the cathedral at Chartres exemplifies the special strength of an anthropological analysis of a segment of the past (pp. 50–51).

If this sort of synchronic analysis is to contribute to a full understanding of Chartres, however, it has to be complemented by historical modes of analysis that lie outside the boundaries of social science paradigms. The historian has to identify and describe elements created under particular circumstances in the past, to describe the totality of French culture in the thirteenth century as a unique configuration of such elements, and in its relationship of continuity and change to the twelfth century and preceding centuries. Moreover, synchronic analysis has to be accompanied by an account of the processes that created the culture of the thirteenth century and its components. Historical description and explanation of this sort does not have a place in social science methodology. Finally, the social scientist's conception of cultural variation in time and space has to be extended to include *histor-*

ical diversity, which embraces continuity and change through time within a particular society.

Geertz has commented frequently on the importance of social change. He has criticized the "static, ahistorical" orientation of functionalism and structuralism. While functionalism has increased our understanding of the "social and psychological 'functions' of religion in a wide variety of societies," it has been less successful in dealing with social change (p. 143).

But Geertz's conception of social change, firmly lodged within a social science paradigm, necessarily excludes certain essential characteristics of specifically historical processes. Historical development embraces more than processes of "social change" defined in essentially nomological terms. In his critique of the ahistorical character of the functionalist treatment of religion, for example, Geertz cites its neglect of "disruptive, disintegrative, and psychologically disturbing aspects" of religion and its failure to demonstrate the manner in which religion destroys and transforms social and psychological structures. As a social scientist, Geertz conceives of social change as a universal process involving the interaction between types of phenomena such as religion. While such a conception of social change is clearly pertinent to a study of the past, it does not have a place for the interplay between historically unique phenomena in the creation of historically unique events, institutions, and ideas. Thus, for the historian, knowledge of the role of religion in social change is preliminary to an inquiry into the role of Christianity in shaping attitudes toward slavery. Similarly, the processes of historical development that brought into being the French political culture of the 1780s cannot be understood exclusively within the framework of a social science theory of social change.

At the same time, of course, the value of Geertz's theory and practice to the study of any aspect of the past is obvious, as many historians have recognized. Keith Thomas has commented on the usefulness of that sort of anthropology: "The older functional anthropology which inspired much historical writing in the 1960s may have little more to teach. But the newer anthropology which places its emphasis on meaning rather than functions still offers a rich resource to the next generation of historians."[50] That resource has to be adapted, however, to the modes of analysis required for the study of historical processes.

CHAPTER SEVEN

Marxist Theories

Marxism represents the most cogent and coherent assertion of the primacy of material forces in history. As such it may be counterposed to the argument of this book. If the historian operates on the assumption that social being determines consciousness—the principle that lies at the core of the Marxist theory of history—he will find it very difficult indeed to arrive at an adequate account of the role played by ideas in particular historical processes. Marxism, therefore, provides an explicit statement of substantive assumptions that depreciate the influence of ideas and settle in advance important questions that ought to be dealt with empirically on the basis of the evidence in each case.

At the same time, however, it is also necessary to recognize and take advantage of the invaluable contributions made by Marxist historians, both in theory and practice, to the analysis of the role of ideas in history. Classic Marxism, even when asserting the primacy of social being in polemical and dogmatic form, kept the problem in the foreground. Beginning with Engels' letters of the 1890s, Marxists have looked carefully into the problem of the interplay between disparate forces in the historical process. Continuing Engels' critique of economistic and deterministic versions of historical materialism, neo-Marxist historians have abandoned the base-superstructure model and all forms of materialist reductionism. Rejecting any tendency to treat ideas as the mere reflection of social reality, they have depicted processes that involve dialectical interaction between various forces. Hence the neo-Marxists are in a position to make the claim that, having rejected simplistic versions of Marxism, their theory and practice adequately take account of cultural factors.

Yet neo-Marxist historians have remained committed, in varying degrees, to some form of the principle that social being determines consciousness. Despite emphasis on the importance and "relative autonomy" of intellectual and cultural forces, they continue to be assigned a relatively subordinate role in paradigms that presuppose a significant degree of primacy for the social aspects of the human world. While the phrase "relative autonomy" signals the rejection of reductionist or "reflective" materialism, it does no more than open the question of the nature and significance of the role of ideas that have been accorded a considerable degree of independence. There are two ways in which that question comes up: first, the role of ideas in shaping the consciousness of a social group or the traits of a culture; second, the manner in which cultural and symbolic forms, the product of historical processes in which ideas played a part, affect actions and events. In both areas, neo-Marxist thought has tended to stress the effect of ideas on form rather than content and to take a functionalist or instrumentalist view of their relationship to socially determined interests and actions. Such a position commands a good deal of support among non-Marxist historians and social scientists. Once the myth of the revolutionary proletariat has been excised—and Marxist historians have disposed of it quite effectively in one way or another—the core of the neo-Marxist theory of society and history does not differ radically from homologous paradigms in social history. The neo-Marxist historians, however, have approached the problem of the role of ideas more directly.

While recognizing the continuing fertility of Marxist thought, as exemplified, for example, by E. P. Thompson and Gareth Stedman Jones, the non-Marxist historian who wishes to appropriate the valuable work done within that tradition has to contend with materialist presuppositions embedded in the mode of discourse. The historian who wishes to draw on neo-Marxist theory and practice cannot be sure just which elements of that complex and various tradition he is being asked to accept.

MARX AND ENGELS

Marx's theory of history underwent development and change for more than a quarter of a century;[1] it contains tensions and even contradictions. Inevitably, divergent interpretations of the theory have developed, emphasizing different aspects of it. Recently, two schools of thought have emerged. On the one hand, what has been called the "hard" or "fundamentalist" view, stresses the materialist side of the theory, with its emphasis on the primacy of social and economic forces and its deterministic tendencies. On the other hand, a "soft" interpretation depicts a theory that envisages the interaction between forces within a complex totality and allows a good deal of scope for ideas.[2] In the account that follows, I shall begin with a description of the materialist, anti-idealist core that lies at the heart of the Marxist theory of history: the claim that social being determines consciousness. Then I shall turn to other aspects of his theory, which deal in a more flexible way with the "mutual interaction" between forces in history. I shall argue, however, that every aspect of Marx's theory assigns a significant degree of primacy to praxis.

Marx and Engels worked out the theory of historical materialism in the 1840s, expounding its principles in *The German Ideology*. The title expresses the theme of the book—a polemic against the "innocent and childlike fantasies" of the young Hegelians and other German ideologists. In the course of their assault on "the idealistic view of history," Marx and Engels developed their materialist counterthesis: the decisive causal factors in history are to be found in the social and economic structure. They define their position in a number of familiar passages. Dismissing the illusions of the idealists, they announce that their theory "remains constantly on the real ground of history; it does not explain practice from the idea but explains the formation of ideas from material practice."[3] They leave no doubt as to the primacy of the material basis of all history:

> Our conception of history depends on our ability to expound the real process of production, starting out from the simple material production of life, and to comprehend the form of intercourse connected with this and created by this (i.e., civil society in its various stages), as the basis of all history; further to show it in its action as State; and so, from this starting-point, to explain the whole mass of different theoretical products and forms of consciousness, religion, philosophy, ethics, etc., etc. (p. 28).

There can be no mistaking the materialist thrust of the argument. In fact, the explanatory claim made in the last sentence of the quoted passage expresses a position that comes very close to what Giddens calls "reflective materialism," in which "forms of consciousness" are depicted as a direct reflection of a more fundamental socioeconomic reality. That view is reiterated, with the help of a number of reductionist metaphors, in another unequivocal passage in *The German Ideology:*

> We set out from real, active men, and on the basis of their real life-process we demonstrate the development of the ideological reflexes and echoes of this life process. The phantoms formed in the human brain are also, necessarily, sublimates of their material life-process, which is empirically verifiable and bound to material premises. Morality, religion, metaphysics, all the rest of ideology and their corresponding forms of consciousness, thus no longer retain the semblance of independence. (p. 14)

Marx's vivid language—reflexes, echoes, phantoms, sublimates—need not be taken literally as a statement of the fundamental principle of his theory of history. It is clear from his writings as a whole that he does not take the simplistic position that consciousness can be explained as a "reflection" of the economic base. On the other hand, the whole point of his materialist theory is to demonstrate that ideas have been far less efficacious in history than historians and philosophers have thought and to describe in detail the manner in which social and economic forces have exercised a predominant influence. That is, "social being determines consciousness."

The *locus classicus* of Marx's theory of history, the preface to *A Contribution to the Critique of Political Economy* of 1859, provides a succinct and schematic formulation of the principles of historical materialism developed in the 1840s. Two oft-quoted sentences express the sum and substance of the theory: "The mode of production of material life conditions the social, political and intellectual life process in general. It is not the consciousness of men that determines their being, but, on the contrary, their social being that determines their consciousness." While the dictum that social being determines consciousness asserts unequivocally the primacy of the "mode of production of material life," it is not reductionist and does not affirm a direct causal connection between the economy and consciousness. The word "conditions" (*bedingt*) in the first sentence makes a more limited claim than "determines" (*bestimmt*) in the second. Social being embraces a broad range of human reality. Although Marx's position cannot be characterized as economic determinism, he assigns a distinctly subordinate position to ideas and beliefs. His remarks on the relation between social being and consciousness have to be understood in the light of the preceding passage on base and superstructure: "The sum total of these relations of production constitutes the economic structure of society, the real foundation (*Basis*), on which rises a legal and political superstructure (*Uberbau*) and to which correspond definite forms of social consciousness."[4]

Since the base-superstructure model has been virtually eliminated from neo-Marxist thought in the twentieth century, it is important to recognize that the metaphor expresses a tenet that is basic to Marxism in any form. E. J. Hobsbawm has argued persuasively that a fundamental principle of Marxism throughout its long history has been a belief in a "hierarchy of social phenomena (e.g. 'basis' and 'superstructure')."[5] To be sure, Hobsbawm emphasizes that this principle is not to be understood in terms of a "simple relation of dominance and dependence between the 'economic base' and the 'superstructure,' even if mediated by 'class interest and the class struggle.' " These qualifications, however, do not significantly modify "the model of *levels*, of which that of the social relations of production are primary." In the hierarchy of social phenomena, ideas and beliefs occupy a rather low position.

Immediately after his comment on social being and consciousness Marx brings his theory to bear on the explanation of revolution. He envisages only a limited role for ideas, which provide only the ideological forms in which men become conscious of socially determined conflict:

At a certain stage of their development, the material productive forces of society come in conflict with the existing relations of production, or—what is but a legal expression for the same thing—with the property relations within which they have been at work hitherto. From forms of development of the productive forces these relations turn into fetters. Then begins an epoch of social revolution. With the change of the economic foundation the entire immense superstructure is more or less rapidly transformed. In considering such transformations, a distinction should always be made between the material transformation of the economic conditions of production, which can be determined with the precision of natural science, and the legal, political, religious, aesthetic or philosophic—in short, ideological forms in which men become conscious of the conflict and fight it out.

The next sentence represents an extreme formulation of the subordination of consciousness to social being: "Just as our opinion of an individual is not based on what he thinks of himself, so can we not judge of such a period of transformation by its own consciousness; on the contrary, this consciousness must be explained rather from the contradictions of material life, from the existing conflict between the social productive forces and the relations of production."[6]

In the writings that preceded *The German Ideology*, Marx put a great deal of emphasis on man as a free and conscious being, creating himself through history. Although these ideas were submerged in the anti-idealist polemic that ensued, they were never totally eliminated. They represent an aspect of Marx's thought that contributed to the strength of Marxist theory and historiography in the twentieth century. In the first thesis on Feuerbach, for example, Marx explained what he considered still valid in the idealist tradition, which he had already subjected to a trenchant critique, and distinguished his own position from eighteenth-century materialism: "The chief defect of all hitherto existing materialism—that of Feuerbach included—is that the thing, reality, sensuousness, is conceived only in the form of the object or of *contemplation*, but not as *human sensuous activity, practice*, not subjectively. Hence it happened that the *active* side, in contradistinction to materialism, was developed by idealism—but only abstractly, since, of course, idealism does not know real, sensuous activity as such."[7] In the 1844 Manuscripts Marx stated unequivocally the centrality of consciousness as the salient characteristic of man. Taking life activity as the criterion for defining the character of a species, he identified "free, conscious activity" as the essential characteristic of the human species. Whereas the animal "is *its activity*," man "makes his life activity itself an object of his will and consciousness. He has a conscious life activity. . . . Conscious life activity distinguishes man from the life activity of animals."[8] These characteristics of man, in turn, are reflected in human history. Marx noted with approval Hegel's conception of "the self-creation of man as a process." In the third thesis on Feuerbach he

denied "the materialist doctrine that men are products of circumstances and upbringing, and that, therefore, changed men are products of other circumstances and changed upbringing."[9] Against such
materialist doctrines, he emphasized the "*active* side" of human reality
and the role of "free conscious activity" in history.

"Softer" interpretations of Marx's theory of history, by Melvin Rader
and Anthony Giddens, for example, emphasize its Hegelian aspects and
depict its treatment of ideas in terms of a dialectical interplay within
a totality rather than as a reflection of the social and economic base.
While demonstrating that Marxism was not committed to a "reflective
materialism," however, they make plain its acceptance of the primacy
of socioeconomic forces.

Melvin Rader argues that Marx's theory contains not only a base-
superstructure model of the historical process but also an "organic totality" model; both models are nonreductive in their treatment of ideas,
although the second is more effective. According to Rader, Marx pro-
pounded a dialectical version of the base-superstructure model. This
version, which Rader contrasts to the "fundamentalist," holds that the
economic base prevails only "in the last instance," while depicting "a
dialectical interaction of unequal forces in which the base is far more
powerful than the superstructure." Moreover, the organic totality model
is even more successful in counteracting the "reductionist interpretations" built into the base-superstructure model. The basic principle
underlying this model is expressed in the *Grundrisse:* "Mutual interaction takes place between the different moments. This is the case with
every organic whole." As Rader points out, however, in the same passage Marx states that "production predominates . . . over the other
moments." Rader acknowledges that in this instance, as in Marxist
theory as a whole, there is a "weighting of elements—production being
weighted most heavily."[10] Rader characterizes this differential weighting as an expression of "the principle of hierarchy." Thus, in Marxist
theory, political and cultural elements in a social order are "causally
less dominant" than the economic.

In showing how the two principles of "hierarchy and organic inter-
relatedness" go together in Marx's theory, Rader leaves no doubt about
the prepondernace of social and economic forces. He cites the analogy
of an organism in which some functions, such as the circulation of the

blood, contribute more than others to the maintenance of the whole. "Just as there are hierarchical relations in the human mind-body, so there are relations of dominance in the 'social organism.' " Thus, having demonstrated that "the simplistic concept of linear causality is replaced by the idea of dialectical interaction within a comprehensive field," Rader also makes it plain that the primacy of the "base" is firmly maintained, albeit with a change of metaphor: "The mode of production is the more efficacious, but all the other structural elements are involved in the 'organic' play of forces."[11] The elements involved in dialectical interaction are clearly not of equal weight or significance. Even in this "soft" version of classic Marxism, the subordinate position assigned to ideas is unmistakable.

Anthony Giddens also underlines the point that Marx did not treat ideas as mere epiphenomena that reflect a more fundamental social reality but rather in a relationship of "reciprocal interaction" with it. He emphasizes the broad areas of theoretical agreement between Marx and Weber. Giddens concludes that Marxism, properly understood, provides a sound standpoint from which to examine the role of ideas in history. The Marxist theory of history, as described by Giddens, assigns a significant degree of primacy to praxis in its relationship of "mutual interaction" with ideas.

Singling out the Hegelian aspects of Marx, Giddens contends that "the dialectical relationship between subject and object in the historical process" is the most essential element in his theory. He finds in the *Theses on Feuerbach* the clearest statement of Marx's rejection of the sort of materialism that regards ideas as no more than a reflection of material reality. There Marx depicted "a constant reciprocity" between consciousness and praxis. Central to Marx's thought is "this dialectic between the subject (man in society) and object (the material world) in which men progressively subordinate the material world to their purposes, and thereby transform those purposes and generate new needs."[12]

From this vantage point Giddens glosses the dictum that it is the social being of men that determines their consciousness: "Much calumny has been heaped upon Marx for this observation. But the operative term here is *social* being, and there can be little objection to the generalization that consciousness is governed by human activity in

society." Nor, according to Giddens, can there be any objection to the
Marxist thesis that "consciousness is rooted in human Praxis, which
is in turn social." Giddens does not elaborate on the nature of the relationship that the words "governed" and "rooted"—the former entailing a much stronger claim than the latter—are intended to denote.
Having demonstrated that Marx does not treat ideas as mere epiphenomena, Giddens has no difficulty in accepting Marx's conception of
the primacy of social or "material" forces. He defends a modified version of the base-superstructure model:

The "real foundation" of society, upon which the "superstructure" arises, is
always constituted of the relationships of active, willing individuals, and thus
always involves both the creation and application of ideas. The main point
about the "superstructure" is not that it embodies ideas, whereas the relations
of production do not, but that it is comprised of a system of social relationships (especially in the shape of politics, law and religion) which order and
sanction a system of class domination.

In breaking down the dividing line between base and superstructure, Giddens in fact extends the domination of social factors over cultural aspects of the human world. Similarly, class structure continues
to exercise a predominant influence in shaping ideas, although it is
characterized as a "mediating" factor. In defending Marx against the
charge of reductionism, he points out that "where Marx generalises
about the relationship between ideology and material 'substructure,'
this is in terms of the specification that the class structure is the main
mediating link between the two." Thus, "the decisive characteristic of
Marx's materialism is to be found in the links which are drawn between *class structure* and ideology."[13]

Giddens also argues that in applying his theory to European history
Marx recognized the role of ideas including "the influence of religious
beliefs upon the origins of the capitalist order." Hence he concludes
that there is a good deal of truth in Schumpeter's comment that "the
whole of Max Weber's facts and arguments (in his sociology of religion) fits perfectly into Marx's system." According to Giddens, Marx
shared Weber's view that "religious systems express the creation of
human values, which are not 'given' in the biological makeup of man,
but are the outcome of the historical process." Giddens' explication of
Marx's position, however, makes it clear that religion has a subordi-

nate role in relation to social forces. On the one hand, Giddens suggests that Marx took up Feuerbach's notion that religion is "the source of ideals toward which man should strive. God is man as he ought to be, and therefore the image of the deity holds out the hope of what man could *become*." Giddens adds that Marx mated this Feuerbachian conception "with the dialectical view that it is the reciprocal interaction of such ideas with the social organization of 'earthly men' which must form the core of an historical perspective."[14] The difficulty, however, is that the "reciprocal interaction," in this instance and in others, does not take place between forces of equivalent strength. Ideas tend to carry out functions determined by social processes. This is clear in the example that Giddens cites from the *Eighteenth Brumaire* to illustrate Marx's awareness of the influence of religious beliefs on the origins of the capitalist order:

Cromwell and the English people had borrowed speech, passions and illusions from the Old Testament for their bourgeois revolution. When the real aim had been achieved, when the bourgeois transformation of English society had been accomplished, Locke supplanted Habakkuk.[15]

In this well-known passage, Marx has assigned a very limited role to religious ideas. The predominant element in the historical dynamics is the socially determined "bourgeois transformation" and "bourgeois revolution." Puritanism provides no more than the rhetorical form and reinforcement. (The Enlightenment is assigned a similar function in the bourgeois revolution in eighteenth-century France.) The predominant social process bends to its purposes whatever ideas happen to be available. Their specific content is irrelevant to the essence of the event. While Marx does not treat Puritanism as a reflection of capitalism, he does not consider it to have affected the essence of England's "bourgeois revolution" or of the "bourgeoisie."

The flaws in Marx's conception of the bourgeoisie and the "bourgeois revolution," rooted in a materialist ontology, were magnified by anti-Kantian epistemological assumptions taken over from Hegel. As Lichtheim put it, "Marx's 'materialist' inversion of Hegel conserved the problematic enshrined in Hegel's earlier critique of Kant."[16] In accepting the "cognoscibility of being" Marx stands with Hegel against Kant. Although Marx rejected Hegel's notion of the identity of subject and object, he believed that thought might achieve a direct knowledge of being. That is, although Marx denies that being is identical with thought, he does not regard it as an "unknowable 'thing-in-itself.' "[17] Moreover Marx assumes the existence of entities, such as the proletariat, whose essence can be known directly through concepts formulated by the human mind. These are not Aristotelian essences, of course. Once they are historically created, however, their character is fixed. The "bourgeois revolution" occurred in England in the seventeenth century and in France in the eighteenth. Its essence was socially determined. Thus, Marx's historical and materialist version of "essentialism" compounds the difficulties inherent in the principle of the primacy of social being.[18] The notion of a "bourgeois revolution," which has heuristic value if conceptualized as an ideal type construct, becomes extremely rigid if it is treated as a concept that directly represents the essence of a socially determined entity.

In a series of justly famous letters written in the 1890s, Engels directly confronted the problem of the role of ideas from the standpoint of historical materialism. He dissociated Marxism from reductionist economism and emphasized the historical importance of various aspects of the "superstructure." The letters had two distinct targets in mind: on the one hand, simplistic versions of the Marxist theory of history; on the other hand, critics, such as Paul Barth, who had criticized Marxism for overlooking the role of noneconomic forces in history. In a positivist framework, Engels advanced a thesis that was to be revived in different form among the Hegelian Marxists of the interwar years: historical materialism, properly interpreted, takes fully into account the role of ideas. At the same time, however, he remained uncompromisingly materialist in assigning ideas a distinctly subordinate role, although the extent to which this is the case is concealed by pluralist language of reciprocal interaction.

Engels denounced the crude economic determinism that had come to be expounded in the name of Marxism or historical materialism. While conceding that he and Marx were themselves partly to blame for the fact that "the younger people sometimes lay more stress on the economic side than is due it," he rejected out of hand the position that was later to be labeled economism or "vulgar Marxism." He reproached "many of the more recent 'Marxists' " for having produced "the most amazing rubbish."[19] Against economic determinism he set forth a flexible and pluralistic version of historical materialism. He pointed out not only that various aspects of the "superstructure" could not simply be derived from the economic base, but also that they had played a part in history. Rejecting mechanistic causation, he stressed the interaction between multiple forces.

At the beginning of his letter to Joseph Bloch, Engels stated the theme that he was to develop in his correspondence in the 1890s: "According to the materialist conception of history, the *ultimately* determining element in history is the production and reproduction of real life. More than this neither Marx nor I could have ever asserted. Hence if somebody twists this into saying that the economic element is the *only* determining one, he transforms that proposition into a meaningless, abstract, senseless phrase." Engels pointed out that it would be silly, for example, to argue that the ascendancy of Brandenburg Prussia was "specifically determined by economic necessity." As for the origins of religious and philosophical beliefs, he noted that they have for the most part "only a negative economic element as their basis," and have to be understood in terms of a prehistoric stock of "bunk" inherited from the remote past. Hence "it would surely be pedantic to try and find economic causes for all this primitive nonsense."[20] In these and other passages Engels made clear that "reflective materialism" had no place in the Marxist theory of history.

Going beyond the rejection of economic determinism, Engels also pointed out that "the various elements of the superstructure," which cannot be derived from the economic base, also exercise an influence on the course of history. "Even the traditions which haunt human minds" have a part to play. Drawing his metaphor from physics, he emphasized the complex interaction between different forces in the historical process: "There are innumerable intersecting forces, an infinite series of parallelograms of forces which give rise to one resultant—the historical event" (p. 498). Each of these forces "contributes to the resultant and is to this extent included in it." He counterposed this view to "the common undialectical conception of cause and effect as rigidly opposite poles, the total disregarding of interaction" (p. 542).

But the interaction does not take place between equal forces. On the contrary, Engels saw at work in history, "very unequal forces, the economic movement being by far the strongest, most primeval, most decisive" (p. 507). Earlier in this letter to Conrad Schmidt he makes the same point in a comment on the relation between the economy and politics in history:

> It is the interaction of two unequal forces: on the one hand the economic movement, on the other the new political power, which strives for as much independence as possible, and which, having once been established, is also endowed with a movement of its own. On the whole, the economic movement gets its way, but it has also to suffer reactions from the political movement which it itself established and endowed with relative independence. (p. 503)

The last sentence is especially revealing. Engels takes it for granted that the economic movement "established" the political movement. And whatever "relative independence" the latter enjoyed it had been "endowed" with by the former. In such phrases as these the predominance imputed to material forces is clear.

Engels is trying to have it both ways. On the one hand, he accepts the point made by critics that "we deny an independent historical development to the various ideological spheres which play a part in history." They have only the "appearance of an independent history," for in fact they have been "brought into the world by other, ultimately economic causes." On the other hand, Engels refuses to accept the criticism that "we deny them [the various ideological spheres] any *effect upon history*" (p. 542). His point is valid, but only within limits. For the effects that he imputes to an ideological element are narrowly limited by the fact that the latter does no more than "react back" on "its environment and even on the causes that have given rise to it." Thus, in the act of claiming to recognize the influence of ideological forces, Engels includes a reductionist account of their relationship to economic causes that is hardly consistent with his critique of economism.

Even in the history of science and philosophy Engels asserts "the dominating influence of economic development." His account of philosophical development in France and Germany elaborates that thesis, which is mitigated only slightly by references to the indirect manner in which economic factors exert their influence:

In France as well as Germany philosophy and the general blossoming of literature at that time were the result of a rising economic development. I consider the ultimate supremacy of economic development established in these spheres too, but it comes to pass within the conditions imposed by the particular sphere itself: in philosophy, for instance, by the operation of economic influences (which again generally act only under political etc., disguises) upon the existing philosophical material handed down by predecessors. . . . It is the political, legal and moral reflexes which exercise the greatest direct influence upon philosophy (p. 506).

While Engels is well aware of the tendency of the "more recent 'Marxists' " to deal simplistically with intellectual forces in history, his materialism prevents him from resolving the problem. His continual insistence that economic forces are "ultimately decisive" is a symptom of his inability to move beyond the limits imposed by his theory. Although the precise meaning of that phrase is not clarified, it functions to preserve the primacy of the base against erosion by too enthusiastic an attention to the superstructure:

We make history ourselves, but, in the first place under very definite assumptions and conditions. Among these the economic ones are ultimately decisive. But the political ones, etc., and indeed even the traditions which haunt men's minds also play a part, although not the decisive one (p. 498).

Another formula that indicates these limits is the suggestion that superstructural elements, after all, determine only the "form" of events, while their content is ultimately determined by economic causes. In the first paragraph of Engels' letter to Bloch, where he emphasizes that the various elements of the superstructure "exercise their influence upon the course of the historical struggles," he comments that in many cases they "preponderate in determining their *form*" (p. 498). And in his letter to Mehring, the *mea culpa* that he issues in behalf of himself and Marx is confined to their having neglected "the formal side . . . for the sake of the content." But he insists that they were right "to lay the main emphasis, in the first place, on the *derivation* of political, juridical, and other ideological notions, and of actions arising through the medium of these notions, from basic economic facts" (p. 540). Engels' metaphors indicate the extent to which intellectual forces are subordinate to material factors. Along with "superstructure," the term "reflexes" imparts a distinctly materialist, if not reductionist, cast to his discussion. A case in point is his description of the various elements of the superstructure whose importance he wishes to stress, in the face of their neglect by economic determinists:

Political forms of the class struggle and its results, to wit: constitutions established by the victorious class after a successful battle, etc., juridical forms, and even the reflexes of all these actual struggles in the brains of the participants, political, juristic, philosophical theories, religious views and their further development into systems of dogmas, also exercise their influence upon the course of the historical struggles and in many cases preponderate in determining their *form* (p. 498).

Against those critics who have charged Marxism with a neglect of extraeconomic factors in history, he emphasizes that he and Marx were well aware of the "reaction of the political, etc., reflexes of the economic movement upon the movement itself" (p. 507). If extraeconomic factors are primarily "reflexes of the economic movements," however, they do not enjoy much independence.

Unlike Engels, the neo-Marxists who flourished in Central Europe between the two world wars formulated a Hegelianized Marxism that was antipositivist in orientation. Intent on excising every vestige of the base-superstructure model, they stressed the unity of the social totality and derided the notion that an economic base might "generate a corresponding superstructure." Like Engels, however, they preserved the primacy of the social and economic aspects of the human world.

NEO-MARXISM

Western Marxism in the twentieth century has echoed many of the themes of Engels' letters. Economic determinism has been exorcised. The epithet "vulgar Marxism" has been applied to various forms of economism and to mechanistic views of causation in which economic forces directly determine ideas and beliefs. The base-superstructure model has come under heavy fire. There has been a great deal of emphasis on the importance of culture. Some accounts of Western Marxism may give the impression that there has been an idealist resurgence: "It had been habitual among Marxists—indeed, it had once been thought to be a distinguishing methodological priority of Marxism— to stress the determining pressures of being upon consciousness; although in recent years much 'Western Marxism' has tilted the dialogue heavily back towards ideological domination."[21] In fact, however, most forms of Western Marxism in the twentieth century have remained faithful to the doctrine of the predominance of material forces in history, while defining it in more sophisticated ways.

A convenient summary of the neo-Marxist position in the 1970s is provided by the writings of Raymond Williams. Characteristically, he takes as his premise the "crudeness of the base/superstructure model," with its suggestion of a "definite and fixed spatial relationship," implying "the reflection, the imitation or the reproduction of the reality of the base in the superstructure in a more or less direct way." At the same time, however, Williams reaffirms the validity of Marx's emphasis on "productive activities, in particular structural relations, constituting the foundation of all other activities." He finds the word "base" still useful, provided that it is understood to refer to "the specific activities of real men, and provided that it is not conceived in mechanistic terms." In the neo-Marxist mode, Williams uses the concepts of "mediation" and "totality" to fashion a version of the principle that social being determines consciousness in a form that avoids mechanistic reductionism. Thus, "mediation" refers to a process in which "something more simple than reflection or reproduction" occurs, that is, in which the socioeconomic structure exercises its influence indirectly, through intermediate forms and structures. In his account of the development of Marxist thought in the twentieth century, Williams notes the importance of the concept of totality, in the work of Georg Lukacs and others, in displacing mechanistic models: "The totality of social practices was opposed to this layered notion of a base and a consequent superstructure. This totality of practices is compatible with the notion of social being determining consciousness, but it does not understand this process in terms of a base and superstructure."[22]

At the very beginning of an essay on Rosa Luxemburg in 1921, Lukacs struck a Hegelian note that was to recur in subsequent neo-Marxist writings: "It is not the primacy of economic motives in historical explanation that constitutes the decisive difference between Marxism and bourgeois thought, but the point of view of totality. The category of totality, the all-pervasive supremacy of the whole over the parts is the essence of the method which Marx took over from Hegel and brilliantly transformed into the foundation of a wholly new science." The concept of totality required "the subordination of every part to the whole unity of history and thought."[23] Having disposed of the mechanistic models of "vulgar Marxism," Lukacs used such concepts as totality and mediation to reformulate the fundamental principles of historical materialism. His book, *Toward the Ontology of Social Being*, is a systematic and coherent statement of one influential version of the neo-Marxist position.

Lukacs takes as his point of departure a critique of "vulgar Marxism." Commenting on the passage on consciousness and social being, he points out that Marx "does not reduce the world of consciousness with its forms and contents directly to the economic structure." Lukacs rejects any version of that passage which makes too much of the base-superstructure reference: "The determination of consciousness by social being is thus meant in a quite general sense. It is only vulgar materialism (from the period of the Second International through to the Stalin period and its consequences) that made this into a unilateral and direct causal relationship between the economy, or even particular aspects of it, and ideology." Over against the economistic position Lukacs emphasizes the importance of attending to the complexity of relationships within a complex totality. Dismissing the quest for direct causal relationships, he proposes to explore the "rich field of interactions and interrelations."[24]

While emphasizing the complexity of interrelationships within the totality, however, Lukacs preserved undiluted the principle that it is the social being of men that determines their consciousness. He points out that Marx "does not counterpose social being to social consciousness, but to any consciousness." That is, Marx was "asserting the ontological priority of social being over consciousness" (pp. 149-50). Lukacs reaffirms "the general Marxian doctrine that the essential development of man is determined by the way in which he produces." To underline the point, he adds that "even the most barbaric or most alienated mode of production forms men in a specific way, which plays the ultimate determining role in interrelations between human groups, no matter how 'extra-economic' these may appear." Marx's standpoint is that "of the primacy of man forming and transforming himself in production" (p. 66). Lukacs insists that "even the directly extra-economic transformations are in the last instance economically determined; the English form of the abolition of feudal relations of distribution . . . was determined by the fact that England was in transition from feudal agriculture to sheep-raising." Lukacs used this example to illustrate "the Marxian conception of reality: that the starting-point of all ideas is the actual expressions of social being" (pp. 67–68).

Having rejected the economistic conception of direct causal relationships, Lukacs restates in modified form the "commonplace" that "the Marxist ontology of social being assigns priority to production." Noting that this priority has been "overstretched in a vulgarizing way," he applies it through the concept of "the predominant moment in the field of complex interactions" (p. 59). Specifically, Lukacs urges us to examine "the way in which the real social production and reproduction of human life forms the predominant moment" in the complexities and "intersecting interactions" of the historical world (p. 68). He argues that Marx "does not reduce the world of consciousness . . . directly to the economic structure, but rather relates it to the totality of social existence." Within the "totality of social being" there is a "life-giving interaction between the properly economic and the extra-economic reality." Lukacs notes that each element in the totality "retains its ontological specificity, and reveals this in all its interactions with other categories." But he adds a second point that makes clear the extent to which the fundamental Marxist tenet has been preserved and presented in new form: "These interrelations are not of equal value, either pair by pair or as a whole, but they are rather all pervaded by the ontological priority of production as the predominant moment" (pp. 59–61). In Lukacs, as in other neo-Marxists, culture is subordinated to a "social being" that is assigned an ontological priority. The elements in the "complex interactions" of history are not of equivalent strength or importance.

Through the concept of mediation Lukacs is able to describe interrelationships in which "the real production and reproduction of human life" forms the predominant moment, while avoiding the taint of direct causal relations entailed by the base-superstructure model. Thus, he argues that although the economy is "the primary dynamic center of social being," its influence is exerted indirectly through mediating forces (p. 49). For example, "the economic category of value works so as to call into being its realization in relations of social mediation. . . . In these realms of mediation, the most varied systems of human values gradually arise" (p. 153). Lukacs' "mediations" comprise a broad range of phenomena, all of which are dependent on social being and the economy. Describing the "forces of mediation that have necessarily arisen historically in society (institutions, ideologies, etc.)," he concedes that they "acquire an internal independence." But this is merely a matter of "chance connections" that do not affect their "ultimate dependence . . . on economic laws" (p. 97). He explains that "scientific laws can only fulfill themselves in the real world as tendencies, and necessities only in the tangle of opposing forces, only in a mediation that takes place by way of endless accidents" (p. 103). In this way, the concept of "mediation" enables Lukacs to establish the indirect character of the influence exercised by "social being" and to avoid the discredited economism of crude versions of historical materialism. As in Marx, however, social being is assigned a clear primacy.

Lukacs' discussion of the relation between the economy and non-economic values illustrates concretely the extent to which the concepts of predominant moments, totality, and mediation define a relationship of dependence that leaves no significant autonomy for culture in the creation of values. He argues that "the concrete here and now of the present stage of economic development ultimately determines in an irrevocable way the social being of the content and form of value" (p. 155).

Karl Korsch, another distinguished Hegelian Marxist of the interwar period, also reaffirmed the fundamentals of historical materialism in the context of a repudiation of the errors and misconceptions of "vulgar Marxism." Foremost among those errors was a continuing adherence to the "abstract-scientific materialism" that Marx had repudiated in his theses on Feuerbach. Korsch had no patience with any tendency "in good Feuerbachian fashion to reduce all ideological representations to their material and earthly kernel." He scornfully dismissed the standpoint in which "all consciousness is approached with totally abstract and basically metaphysical dualism, and declared to be a reflection of the one really concrete and material developmental process, on which it is completely dependent (even if relatively independent, still dependent in the last instance)." Thus, Korsch forcefully repudiated the base-superstructure model and its metaphysical presuppositions. He also denounced the tendency inherent in this abstract materialism to "explain away the *intellectual (ideological) structures of society* as a mere *pseudo-reality* which exists only in the minds of ideologues—as error, imagination and illusion, devoid of a genuine object." [25]

The controlling principle of Korsch's Hegelianized Marxism was the "coincidence of consciousness and reality." Rejecting the dualism of mind and matter or base and superstructure, he asserted the indissoluble unity of thought and action. From this premise flowed the methodological principle that "intellectual life should be conceived in union with social and political life, and social being and becoming (in the widest sense, as economics, politics, or law) should be studied in union with social consciousness in its many different manifestations, as a real yet also ideal (or ideological) component of the historical process in general." Korsch stressed the totality of social life, of which consciousness was an integral component: It is a mistake to counterpose the various forms of consciousness against the "reality" of the social historical world. "They exist within this world as a real and objective component of it, if also an 'ideal' one." Korsch spelled out the implications of the coincidence of consciousness and reality: "Its consequence is that the material relations of production of the capitalist epoch only are what they are in combination with the forms in which they are reflected in the pre-scientific and bourgeois-scientific consciousness of the period; and they could not subsist in reality without these forms of consciousness." Thus, Korsch insisted that the various forms of social consciousness "are not mere chimeras, but 'highly objective and highly practical' social realities" (pp. 71–83).

Having firmly rejected the vulgar Marxist account of the relation between consciousness and society, Korsch nevertheless ends up effectively subordinating ideas to a social totality, albeit in a nonreductionist way. In fact, his critique of reductionist materialism tends to obscure the extent to which he continues to assign a significant degree of primacy to social being. Thus, he rejects the notion that economic ideas should be understood as a reflection of the socioeconomic base. "Economic ideas themselves *only appear* to be related to the material relations of production of bourgeois society in the way an image is related to the object it reflects." The actual relationship, Korsch argues, in keeping with his emphasis on the "totality" of society, is that between the parts of a unified whole. "Bourgeois economics belongs with the material relations of production to bourgeois society as a totality."

But Korsch defines "totality" in unequivocally materialist terms. Thus, the totality to which he refers in this passage is "bourgeois society." The terminology reflects the primacy that is in practice accorded to the social aspect of human reality in Korsch's theory. The language in which he describes the various components of bourgeois society conveys the same point. He writes that "this totality also contains political and legal representations" as well as "the higher ideologies of the art, religion and philosophy of bourgeois society." To be sure, he emphasizes, in his usual way, that economic, political and legal representations cannot be understood as reflections of objects existing independently of them. In properly materialist fashion, albeit in neo-Hegelian form, however, Korsch treats all such ideas as "expressions" of a totality that is defined in social terms: "They merely express bourgeois society as a totality in a particular way, just as do art, religion and philosophy." Moreover, in his next sentence, Korsch comes very close indeed to reinstating the base-superstructure model: "Their ensemble forms the *spiritual structure* of bourgeois society, which corresponds to this same basis."

What does "correspond" imply in this context? Clearly, it does not imply a relationship of "reflection" between an object and its ideological form. Yet the economic structure clearly is predominant over the spiritual structure that "corresponds" to it. Moreover, the "totality" itself is identified by reference to its socioeconomic structure in the phrase "bourgeois society." Thus, for all its Hegelian and dialectical character, Korsch's Marxism remains anchored in a view of reality that presupposes some sort of primacy for the "social" aspect of human life. There is no mystery about this. The whole point of the Marxist theory of history at the outset was to correct the one-sidedness of the various forms of idealism. But that fact tended to be lost in the Hegelian language of the critique of economic determinism.

In the 1930s the Frankfurt school continued the attack on reductionist Marxism while emphasizing mutual interaction between elements or "moments" in a totality, within which processes of "mediation," rather than mechanistic causation occurred. In the neo-Marxist mode, Horkheimer, Adorno, and others depicted a constant interaction between relatively autonomous factors, none of which could be derived from or reduced to any other. Culture is not a mere epiphenomenon, not a mere reflection of something more fundamental. At the same time, however, their critique of economism did not entail a weakening of the dominance of material forces.[26]

The point of view of the Frankfurt school is succinctly and precisely expressed in a letter written by Adorno to Walter Benjamin, in which he criticized the point of view in an article that had been submitted by the latter:

> I regard it as methodologically unfortunate to give conspicuous individual features from the realm of the superstructure a 'materialistic' turn by relating them immediately and perhaps ever casually [sic] to corresponding features of the infrastructure. Materialist determination of cultural traits is only possible if it is mediated through the *total social process*.

While the first sentence in that passage expresses the familiar critique of reductionist treatments of the "superstructure," the second is a reminder that the Frankfurt school was attempting to formulate a "true materialism," purged of the sort of reflectionist materialism implicit in the base-superstructure model. Thus, Adorno remains confident of the possibility of the "materialist determination of cultural traits," provided that "it is mediated through the *total social process*." Through the formulas of totality and mediation the essential claim of historical materialism was preserved and invested with plausibility.

E. P. Thompson's formulation of neo-Marxist theory is of particular interest and importance, since he writes not primarily as a theorist but as an historian whose masterly studies of English social history have been guided by Marxist principles. Provoked into a full statement of those principles by the structuralist Marxism of Louis Althusser, Thompson has expounded an attractive version of historical materialism. Rejecting Althusser's economistic structuralism, he emphasizes the "relative autonomy" of ideas in history. Against Althusserian determinism, he underlines the importance of human "agency." At the same time, however, Thompson reaffirms the Marxist principle of the primacy of social being. While rejecting any suggestion of a mechanistic causal connection between the socioeconomic structure and culture, he assigns greater weight to social and material factors: " 'Experience,' (we have found) has, in the last instance, been generated in 'material life', has been structured in class ways, and hence 'social being' has determined 'social consciousness.' "[27] In developing that thesis, Thompson imposes severe limits on the autonomy—and therefore the influence—of ideas in history.

Thompson argues that he and other Marxist historians have recognized the importance of ideas in history by applying the principle of "relative autonomy," which they acquired from Engels: " 'Relative autonomy' was where we started from, and we started with the aid of others who had started there before us. It would, after all, have been somewhat difficult for us to have examined the drama of Aeschylus, ancient Greek science, the origins of Buddhism, the city-state, Cistercian monasteries, utopian thought, Puritan doctrines, . . . without, somewhere along the line, stumbling upon a difficulty." Thompson describes the ways in which he and other historians dealt with difficulties that required them to enter into "the real silences of Marx" (p. 362). They were careful to steer clear of economism and reductionism:

If we are to employ the (difficult) notion that social being determines social consciousness, how are we to suppose that this is so? It will surely not be supposed that 'being' is here, as gross materiality from which all ideality has been abstracted, and that 'consciousness' (as abstract ideality) is there? For we cannot conceive of any form of social being independently of its organizing concepts and expectations, nor could social being reproduce itself for a day without thought (p. 200).

He reminds Althusser of the extraordinary complexity that historians encounter when they examine, in the course of their everyday research, the formation of social consciousness and the tensions within it. The historian's evidence "does not stand compliantly like a table for interrogation: it stirs, in the medium of time, before our eyes. These stirrings, these events, if they are within 'social being' seem often to impinge upon, thrust into, break against, existent social consciousness" (p. 199). Thompson emphasizes the need to attend to the interplay between consciousness and other aspects of the human world:

What Althusser overlooks is the *dialogue* between social being and social consciousness. Obviously, this dialogue goes in both directions. If social being is not an inert table which cannot refute a philosopher with its legs, then neither is social consciousness a passive recipient of "reflections" of that table. Obviously, consciousness, whether as unselfconscious culture, or as myth, or as science, or law, or articulated ideology, thrusts back into being in its turn: as being is thought so thought also is lived—people may, within limits, *live* the social or sexual expectations which are imposed upon them by dominant conceptual categories (p. 201).

In an effort to develop a more supple Marxism, capable of dealing with such difficulties, Thompson uses "experience" as a mediating concept between social being and social consciousness. He begins with a question posed by the categories of classic Marxism: "If a correspondence could be proposed—and in some part demonstrated—between a mode of production and historical process, how, and in what ways did this come about?" Thompson invokes "experience" in order to answer this question and resolve the problem of the manner in which social being determines consciousness: "What we have found out (in my view) lies within a missing term: 'human experience' " (p. 356). Through this concept Thompson seeks to overcome the flaws in the vulgar Marxist tendency to treat the superstructure as a reflection of the base: "Experience is a necessary middle term between social being and social consciousness: it is experience (often class experience) which gives a coloration to culture, to values, and to thought: it is by means of experience that the mode of production exerts a determining pressure upon other activities" (p. 290).

By interposing "experience" between social being and consciousness, Thompson avoids mechanistic causality while reaffirming a conception of the predominance of the mode of production and social being that fits comfortably into the framework of classic Marxism: "Changes take place within social being, which give rise to changed *experience:* and this experience is *determining*, in the sense that it exerts pressures upon existent social consciousness, proposes new questions, and affords much of the material which the more elaborated intellectual exercises are about." This formulation limits the scope of his comment that the dialogue between social being and social consciousness goes in both directions and that consciousness "thrusts back into being in its turn" (pp. 200–201). Throughout the book, it is clear that Thompson does not envisage the dialogue as taking place between equal partners. The dynamism of history is located in the socioeconomic system. Thompson rejects the notion that there are "other, and co-existent, *systems,* of equal status and coherence . . . exerting co-equal determining pressures" (p. 363). Although he has abandoned the base-superstructure metaphor, he envisages a hierarchy of levels in which the "social" and the "material" exercise a predominant influence.

Since Thompson's theory formally puts so much emphasis on the role of cultural factors in history, some Marxist critics have argued that he has gone too far in that direction. His position has been stigmatized as "culturalist." On closer inspection, however, it is clear that his theory assigns culture a distinctly subordinate role in relation to "material" phenomena. The point of Thompson's cultural *materialism* is that culture has to be explained in terms of the pressure exerted by productive activity and social relations connected with it. Culture functions in an intermediate—and distinctly subordinate—way, between the realm of material activity and the concrete particularities of individual actions on the one hand and values on the other. Culture is "another necessary middle term," a junction concept. It has to be understood in relation to "experience," which is defined in terms of productive activity and class relations. That is, socially structured experience is the decisive factor. Culture merely provides a means of "handling" it (p. 363).

The problem of the relationship between consciousness and social being comes up in a very direct way when the neo-Marxist historian examines the processes underlying the genesis of human values and their development and change. At that point he has to deal with the question of the degree of autonomy enjoyed by inherited ideas, beliefs, and traditions. Thompson emphasizes that "material life" is the matrix in which human values take shape. Without treating the socioeconomic structure as a direct causal factor, he assigns a distinct primacy to material forces in relation to cultural phenomena in the etiology of values. Thompson argues that "values are neither 'thought' nor 'hailed'; they are lived, and they arise within the same nexus of material life and material relations as do our ideas." While no one would deny that values need to be examined within the nexus of material life and material relations, there remains a question about the nature and extent of the influence exercised by "material life" in relation to inherited traditions of thought that cannot be explained by reference to material life, past or present. Very much in the Marxist tradition, Thompson's handling of that question reflects a preoccupation with refuting an "idealist" position whose evident one-sidedness serves to legitimate an antithesis that turns out to be correspondingly one-sided in the opposite direction: "A materialist examination of values must situate itself, not by idealist propositions, but in the face of culture's material abode: the people's way of life and, above all, their productive and familial relationships." Thompson's account of what is entailed by a materialist examination of values shows the extent to which the impact of "culture's material abode" is the decisive element in the process: "The affective and moral consciousness discloses itself within history, and within class struggles, sometimes as a scarcely-articulate inertia, . . . sometimes as a displaced, confused, but nonetheless 'real' and passionate encounter within religious forms" (pp. 367–368). The word "displaced" carries a great deal of weight here: it indicates clearly the secondary position of religious beliefs in consciousness and in history.

Closely connected with the problem of the role and "relative autonomy" of ideas in history is the question of the degree of freedom or independence or creativity exercised by individuals. In Thompson's discussion, there is an unresolved contradiction between his emphasis on human "agency" and on the determining pressure of social being. In the following passage Thompson is commenting on the missing term, human experience, which Althusser and his followers "wish to blackguard out of the club of thought." While emphasizing the importance of human beings as the active subjects of history, however, Thompson at the same time confines their autonomy within narrow, socially determined limits:

Men and women also return as subjects within this term—not as autonomous subjects, 'free individuals,' but as persons experiencing their determinate productive situations and relationships, as needs and interests and as antagonisms, and then 'handling' this experience within their *consciousness* and their *culture* . . . in the most complex (yes, 'relatively autonomous') ways, and then (often, but not always through the ensuing structures of class) acting upon their determinate situation in their turn (p. 356).

This passage illustrates the limited character of the "agency" attributed to individuals in Thompson's theory of the historical process. The decisive factor is "determinate productive situations and relationships," which men experience "as needs and interests and as antagonisms." Consciousness and culture merely influence the ways in which they "handle" their socially determined experience.

Whatever its limitations, Thompson's theory remains an invaluable treatment of the problem of the interplay between cultural and social forces in all its complexity. He compels attention to the critical questions of the nature and significance of the role of ideas. We have argued that, in the final analysis, Thompson assigns them a relatively subordinate role in relation to social being: ideas affect form rather than substance, and they stand in an instrumental and functional relationship to socioeconomic circumstances. While they are accorded a significant degree of "relative autonomy," in the sense that they are not derived directly from praxis, the range of influence open to them is circumscribed. Yet the role accorded ideas in Thompson's theory is by no means inconsiderable. His well-argued position, which is not susceptible to brief summary, is a cogent representation of views widely held by non-Marxist historians and social scientists.

Moreover, the quality of Thompson's historical writing, notably *The Making of the English Working Class*, demonstrates the heuristic value of his theory. In a later book, *Whigs and Hunters*, he linked his study of law in the eighteenth century with the reminder that "one must resist any slide into structural reductionism." He characterizes the rule of law as a cultural achievement of universal significance and emphasizes the extent of its impact: "The rhetoric and the rules of a society are something a great deal more than sham. In the same moment they may modify, in profound ways, the behavior of the powerful and mystify the powerless. . . . And it is often from within that very rhetoric that a radical critique of the practice of the society is developed." E. J. Hobsbawm, whose thought has been somewhat closer to classic Marxism, also has emphasized in his studies of English working-class politics that "a political or ideological tradition, especially if it sums up genuine patterns of practical activity in the past, or is embodied in stable institutions, has independent life and force, and must affect the behaviour of political movements." He rejects the notion that traditions may be regarded as "so many lumps of plasticene, to be moulded to fit the shape of their movements' mood and practical situation."[28] In their practice also, then, Marxist historians have given careful attention to the influence of cultural forces. The questions at issue concern the way in which the nature and extent of that influence may be characterized.

INTERPRETATIONS OF MODERN HISTORY

In conclusion, I shall consider a few examples of the complex connection between Marxist and neo-Marxist assumptions and the interpretation of the political and ideological history of modern Europe. On the one hand, neo-Marxist historians have produced valuable analyses of the influence of ideas on particular events and developments. On the other hand, such analyses are embedded in paradigms that impose constraints on a full assessment of the nature and significance of the role of ideas.

Marxist historiography dealing with the period since the middle of the eighteenth century has been dominated by the "bourgeois revolution" thesis, which is inadequate both as a description of the nature of the event and as an account of the process that produced it. Operating with that concept, Marxist historians have produced a great deal of valuable work, including suggestive treatments of the role of ideas. At first glance, Jaurès' comment on the French Revolution appears to assign equivalent weight to intellectual and social forces in the genesis of the event: "En un mot, la bourgeoisie parvenait à la conscience de classe, pendant que la pensée parvenait à la conscience de l'univers. Là sont les deux ressources ardentes, les deux sources de feu de la Révolution. C'est par là qu'elle fut possible et qu'elle fut éblouissante."[29] Even in this formulation, however, ideas do little more than affect the form of a phenomenon whose essence is determined by social forces. Similarly, Lefebvre's perceptive handling of the relationship between the Enlightenment and the French Revolution is constricted by the concept of the "bourgeois revolution" and the paradigm on which it rests.

E. J. Hobsbawm's account of the "dual revolution" that transformed Europe between 1789 and 1848 represents a succinct statement of a social interpretation of modern history which, in one form or another, commands a good deal of support among historians and social scientists of diverse methodological and ideological orientation. It may be counterposed to the theme of this book. Hobsbawm depicts a "dual revolution—the rather more political French and the industrial (British) revolution" as "the twin crater of a rather larger regional volcano." While the simultaneous eruptions that occurred in France and England differed somewhat, all such occurrences "are at this period almost inconceivable in any form other than the triumph of a bourgeois-liberal capitalism." He argues that "the revolution which broke out between 1789 and 1848 . . . forms the greatest transformation in human history since the remote times when men invented agriculture and metallurgy, writing, the city and the state. . . . The great revolution of 1789–1848 was the triumph not of 'industry' as such, but of *capitalist* industry; not of liberty and equality in general, but of *middle class* or '*bourgeois*' *liberal* society." He also notes the "historic force of the revolutionary socialist and communist ideology born out of reaction against this dual revolution, and which by 1848 had found its first classic formulation."[30] In this framework there is not much room for the role of ideas, which have no more than an instrumental function in relation to predominant social and economic forces.

When Marxist historians turned from the "bourgeois revolution" of 1789 to the political and ideological history of the working class in the nineteenth century, they had to come to terms with the myth of the revolutionary proletariat. Whereas the bourgeoisie had clearly engaged in a revolution in 1789, which had been duly recognized and celebrated by bourgeois historians, the proletariat proved to be quite nonrevolutionary. The intrinsically revolutionary character of the proletariat was a myth, in the Sorelian sense, a prophetic proclamation, which Marx justified by reference to the principles of historical materialism and by analogy to the "bourgeois revolution." In writing the history of the working class in the nineteenth century, Marxist historians have been successful in disposing of the myth of the revolutionary proletariat. They have produced some very good history, not only by Thompson and Hobsbawm, but also by a younger generation of historians who have drawn on the social sciences. But this work has not escaped the limits imposed by paradigms that presuppose the primacy of social being.

The myth of the revolutionary proletariat—whose being was determined by its social situation and whose historic task was to serve as the gravediggers of capitalism—was first demolished not by historians but by Marxist socialists who were compelled by practical exigencies to develop a realistic analysis of the nature and history of the working classes that they hoped to make the basis of a mass movement. At the turn of the century Marxists of every ideological hue—among them Bernstein, Kautsky, and Lenin—recognized that the capitalist forces of production clearly were not generating a revolutionary proletariat. In *What Is to be Done?* Lenin pointed out that the social and economic development of capitalist society was producing only "trade union consciousness," which was neither socialist nor revolutionary. Lenin concluded that socialist consciousness must be imposed from the outside. He argued that it was the task of socialist intellectuals "to divert the working-class movement from the path that is determined by the interaction of material elements and the material environment." Their task was to "combat spontaneity."[31]

But Lenin did not confine himself to a realistic description of the proletariat and a call for a vanguard of socialist intellectuals to bring revolutionary consciousness to the masses. He included a full theoretical analysis that makes clear the inability of classic Marxism to account for the history of working-class and revolutionary movements in the nineteenth century:

The history of all countries shows that the working class, exclusively by its own effort, is able to develop only trade union consciousness, i.e., the conviction that it is necessary to combine in unions, fight the employers and strive to compel the government to pass necessary labour legislation, etc. The theory of socialism, however, grew out of the philosophic, historical and economic theories that were elaborated by the educated representatives of the propertied classes, the intellectuals.

Lenin quoted Engels to good effect on the intellectual origins of Marxist socialism: "Without German philosophy which preceded it, particularly that of Hegel, German scientific Socialism—the only scientific Socialism that has ever existed—would never have come into being." In 1902 he was also able to quote Kautsky, to whom he was indebted for many of his views on trade union consciousness: "Socialist consciousness is something introduced into the proletarian class struggle from without and not something that arose within it spontaneously [*urwüchsig*]." He also quoted Kautsky on the intellectual origins of socialist consciousness: "Modern socialist consciousness can arise only on the basis of profound scientific knowledge. . . . The vehicle of science is not the proletariat, but the *bourgeois intelligentsia*."[32] This interpretation of the social and ideological history of the nineteenth century is at odds not only with the myth of the revolutionary proletariat but also with certain fundamental principles of historical materialism as elaborated in classic Marxism. Seliger has aptly summed up the implications of Lenin's analysis: "From the point of view of Marxist principles, the implicit paradox is that socialist consciousness had to be created for the working class by members of the bourgeois intelligentsia, in disregard both of the consciousness which their own class position ought to have induced in them and of the consciousness which the class position of the workers had actually produced in the workers."[33]

Implicit in *What Is to be Done?*, then, is a cogent demonstration of the inadequacy of the principles of historical materialism to account for the history of socialism and socialist movements in the nineteenth century, along with a rejection of the myth of the revolutionary proletariat. As such it is pertinent to any consideration of the capacity of Marxist paradigms to provide a satisfactory assessment of the role of ideas in history. This aspect of Lenin's thought had little impact on Marxist historiography, however. What proved to be influential was his notion of the "labor aristocracy," which he developed during the war, in the course of his struggle with the Second International for the allegiance of working-class groups that showed little disposition to embrace his version of revolutionary socialist consciousness.[34] In this situation, Lenin developed a new version of the old myth. He explained the incorrigibly revisionist tendencies of the European working class by reference to the emergence of a labor aristocracy of skilled workers, which diverted the proletariat from actualizing its revolutionary potentialities. It was the labor aristocracy thesis, not the trenchant critique of 1902, which shaped post-1945 Marxist accounts of the history of the Victorian working class.

Eric Hobsbawm took up the labor aristocracy concept—which Lenin had extracted from the English situation in the late nineteenth century as depicted by the Webbs—and applied it to Victorian England.[35] The depth of his research and the analytical power of his interpretation contributed to the impact of Hobsbawm's work. In the 1970s a new generation of social historians, working within the Marxist tradition, produced a number of important local studies, in which the labor aristocracy thesis is the key to the explanation of the reformist and non-revolutionary character of the Victorian working class. In the neo-Marxist mode, they also put a great deal of emphasis on their rejection of economic determinism, and stress the importance of cultural phenomena as "mediating" factors in historical processes. In fact, however, the socially determined characteristics of the labor aristocracy remain decisive, and cultural factors are assigned a distinctly subordinate role. Their work illustrates the difficulty of doing justice to the "relative autonomy" of ideas within a neo-Marxist paradigm.

Robert Gray begins his book by criticizing earlier versions of the labor aristocracy thesis which "appear to operate with implicit models in which cultural and ideological differences passively reflect the social structure." He characterizes that position as a "serious vulgarization, both of the 'labour aristocracy' thesis specifically and of the Marxist mode of historical analysis generally." Rejecting "mechanistic economic determinism," Gray argues that the "key question is that of cultural mediation of different economic experiences." In his interpretation, however, the mediating function of culture affects no more than the form of socially determined phenomena. What is decisive is the social being of the labor aristocracy. While minimizing the direct impact of economic factors in determining values and patterns of aspirations among skilled workers, Gray points to "the traditions, expectations, and value systems inculcated by particular occupational cultures."[36] The determining factor is the occupation and the values and attitudes that it inculcates. The phrase " 'labor aristocratic' forms of social consciousness" indicates a very direct link between "class situation" and consciousness. Similarly, Geoffrey Crossick combines a forceful rejection of "economic or structural determinism" with a firm commitment to the primacy of social factors in shaping the character of the labor aristocracy. While emphasizing the importance of "cultural mediation" and warning against any tendency to elevate "an economic basis for other structural and ideological developments into a sole determining cause," his account of the genesis of values and attitudes among skilled strata of the working class makes plain that the decisive factor is "the logic of stratification," which determines the essential content of the consciousness of a particular "social formation." Thus, it is difficult to accept without qualification the claim that his explanation of working-class political patterns is not an instance of "direct economic or structural determinism," on the grounds he has shown that these structures were "mediated through the experience of the local communities, and an ideology was developed to comprehend it."[37] Even in this formulation it is clear that social mechanisms have been accorded a privileged status. References to "mediation" cannot conceal the predominant role assigned to socially determined experience.

The labor aristocracy thesis has by no means won universal acceptance among Marxist historians. A major work by Patrick Joyce, addressing the problem of explaining "the more accommodative, quiescent popular attitudes seen after mid-century," not only refutes the thesis but also shows that an adequate explanation can be framed without attention to "cultural mediation." On the question of the nonrevolutionary character of the factory proletariat, Joyce demonstrates the explanatory power of the classic paradigm of historical materialism, especially when reinforced by sociological concepts and techniques. The reformist political behavior of the Victorian factory workers, along with their accommodative relationship with their employers, can be understood to a considerable degree by attending closely to the social relations of production, and to the behavioral and ideological implications of the system of power and domination. If the phenomenon to be explained is defined simply as reformist activity and ideology among the factory workers, there is no need to bring in cultural factors, especially if they are to be accorded only an illusory independence. Similarly, Joyce shows that there is no need to invoke the labor aristocracy as a causal factor deflecting the proletariat from carrying out its preordained mission. Joyce argues that the onset of reformism and stability in the post-Chartist decades was due to the fact that in the middle of the nineteenth century "a modern factory proletariat came into mature being." The transforming power of mechanization, which so often "is innocently seen in terms of the *de novo* creation of a radical class-conscious proletariat," in fact contributed to the "erosion of class feeling and the augmentation of class domination." Joyce concludes that the consolidation of mechanized factory industry was "the occasion of class harmony rather than of class conflict."[38]

Reversing Marx's formula, Joyce shows that the bourgeoisie produced not its own gravediggers, but rather faithful retainers in a system of industrial deference. Emphasizing the "social effect of the capitalist work-place," he provides a masterly analysis of the factory-dominated society of the industrial towns and cities of the North of England. At the heart of a complex social system was the power and influence exercised by the factory owners. Confronting a weak, vulnerable, and dependent work force, the paternalist employer was able to translate dependence into deference. Immersed in a "factory-dominated culture," the worker acquiesced in his subordination and internalized the experience of dependence. This acceptance of power relations together with the stability that accompanied it was rooted in the family, the neighborhood, and the community.

Precisely because of the evident value of Joyce's social interpretation, its limitations need to be recognized. For one thing, the phenomenon to be explained has been defined in rather narrow terms, the absence of instability or of the sort of militant agitation that characterized the preceding Chartist decades. That, in turn, leads to a blurring of the question of the nature and extent of working-class resistance to the hegemony of the employer class and the question of the challenge posed even by the "respectable" radicalism of the mid-Victorian period. Similarly, the question of the continuity between the indigenous radicalism of the West Riding and the subsequent emergence of the socialism of the Independent Labour Party (I.L.P.) is not confronted. This narrowness in the definition of the explanandum, in turn, reinforces the tendency, inherent in the paradigms of the new social history, to extend the reach of social explanation to areas where a more complex mode is required, such as the nature, origins, and development of working-class radicalism in the nineteenth century.

Having concluded that the consolidation of the factory system was the primary cause of mid-Victorian stability, Joyce depicts Chartism, the chief manifestation of the preceding instability, in narrowly social terms as "essentially the ideology of the artisanate." He refers to the "pre-mechanical ideology" of artisans threatened with loss of control over the labor process.[39] Thus, Chartism becomes "the most characteristic expression of the ferment preceding the consolidation of mechanization." To treat Chartism in this fashion as essentially "a political theory of the artisanate" is to come very close to reductionism. It does something less than justice to what E. P. Thompson has called the "intelligence and moral passion" of the Chartists, who organized the most powerful and sustained working-class mass movement of the nineteenth century. Such an approach excludes the question of the relation between Chartism and the complex traditions of radicalism on which it drew and which shaped its character.

Chartism, then, cannot be understood primarily as an "artisanal movement," but rather as the product of a history in which cultural, ideological, social, and political phenomena played a part. Thompson's masterwork, *The Making of the English Working Class*, is essential to an understanding of the prehistory of Chartism. It is a splendid reconstruction of the diverse strands that went into the development of popular radicalism, in their social context. But this superb historical analysis is set in an interpretive framework that constrains its analytical strength. The degree of "agency" or freedom exercised by radical workingmen is confined to a rather narrow area. Similarly, the role of cultural and ideological forces in the shaping of working-class radicalism is in fact confined to an effect on the form, while the essential content is determined by "class." Thus, the "relative autonomy" of cultural phenomena is not especially significant. On the one hand, for example, Thompson provides a characteristically fine account of Painite radicalism in the development of the political and social consciousness of English workingmen. On the other hand, however, the assumptions built into his paradigm tend to exclude serious attention to the problem of the significance and "relative autonomy" of inherited ideas and beliefs in the process that shaped Paine's thought.

The burden of Thompson's interpretation of Chartism is that it is to be understood primarily as the expression of a "working class" that had come into existence and had achieved full class consciousness by 1832. By then "the working-class presence" was "the most significant factor in British political life." As he looks ahead to Chartism at the end of the book, Thompson depicts imminent changes in class consciousness in response to industrialization: "These years reveal a passing beyond the characteristic outlook of the artisan, with his desire for an independent livelihood 'by the sweat of his brow,' to a newer outlook, more reconciled to the new means of production, but seeking to exert the collective power of the class to humanise the environment." He sets Chartism and its prehistory in a Marxist framework: "From 1830 onwards a more clearly defined class consciousness, in the customary Marxist sense, was maturing, in which working people were aware of continuing both old and new battles on their own."

Thompson's interpretation of Chartism and of the "making" of the English working class is developed within a paradigm that unequivocally asserts the primacy of social and economic forces: "The class experience is largely determined by the productive relations into which men are born—or enter involuntarily. Class-consciousness is the way in which these experiences are handled in cultural terms: embodied in traditions, value-systems, ideas, and institutional forms."[40] The predominant influence is socially determined experience. If Chartism and its prehistory are interpreted primarily in terms of the maturing of a "class consciousness" that is presumed to be inherent in the relations of production of industrial capitalism, much of the analytical power of Thompson's reconstruction of the multifarious forms of working-class radicalism is lost.

Gareth Stedman Jones, whose intellectual lineage is also Marxist, has developed a striking reinterpretation of Chartism and its prehistory set in a new paradigm: "In contrast to the prevalent social-historical approach to Chartism, whose starting-point is some conception of class or class consciousness, it argues that the ideology of Chartism cannot be constructed in abstraction from its linguistic form." In a brilliant essay Jones rejects the social interpretation of Chartism that for so long has been the reigning orthodoxy among historians of every methodological and ideological orientation. He questions the notion that the language of Chartism "can simply be analysed in terms of its expression of, or correspondence to, the putative consciousness of a particular class or social or occupational group." What Jones proposes instead is an approach that "attempts to identify and situate the place of language and form, and which resists the temptation to collapse questions posed by the form of Chartism into questions of its assumed sub-

stance." He argues that "if the interpretation of the language and politics is freed from *a priori* social inference, it then becomes possible to
establish a far closer and more precise relationship between ideology
and activity than is conveyed in the standard picture of the movement."[41]

Jones takes as his point of departure *The Making of the English
Working Class:* "The great achievement of Thompson's book is to have
freed the concept of class consciousness from any simple reduction to
the development of productive forces measured by the progress of large-
scale industry and to have linked it to the development of a political
movement which cannot be reduced to the terminology of incoherent
protest. To have established this connection is a vital advance." Jones
argues, however, that it is necessary to go beyond the position represented by Thompson's theory and practice: "Thompson's concept of
class consciousness still assumes a relatively direct relationship between 'social being' and 'social consciousness' which leaves little independent space for the ideological context within which the coherence of a particular language of class can be reconstituted. A simple
dialectic between consciousness and experience cannot explain the
precise form assumed by Chartist ideology."

Jones emphasizes that "the language of class was not simply a ver-
balization of perception or the rising to consciousness of an existential
fact, as Marxist and sociological traditions have assumed." On the
contrary, class consciousness as defined by Thompson "formed part of
a language whose systematic linkages were supplied by the assumptions of radicalism: a vision and analysis of social and political evils
which certainly long predated the advent of class consciousness, however defined." To be sure, Jones' argument

is not intended to imply that the analysis of language can provide an exhaus-
tive account of Chartism, or that the social conditions of existence of this language were arbitrary. It is not a question of replacing a social interpretation
by a linguistic interpretation, it is how the two relate, that must be rethought.
Abstractly the matter determines the possibility of the form, but the form
conditions the development of the matter.[42]

Jones has cleared the ground of a number of assumptions, implicit in
various forms of the "social" interpretation of history, that inhibit empirical inquiry into the question of the role of ideas in particular his-

torical processes. Put more positively, his paradigm invites that sort of inquiry, underlines its importance, and calls into question any social ontology that forecloses it a priori. It transcends factitious debates about the respective merits of "idealism" and "materialism." It makes possible a more effective handling of problems of "agency" and "relative autonomy" posed by Thompson's theory and practice. In the case of Chartism, Jones' emphasis on language and on the continuity with a radical discourse that developed under very different social and political circumstances opens the way to a broader set of historical questions concerning the nature and genesis of that radicalism, and the character of the forces that entered into the process that shaped it. And the English experience, of course, has to be understood in the context of the history of Europe and Western culture. This brings us back to the problem that we started out with: the role of cultural forces in the historical origins of radical and revolutionary politics in modern Europe. In taking a final look at that topic, I shall turn to a familiar passage from a Marxist historian of an earlier generation.

Epilogue

In the concluding chapter of *The Coming of the French Revolution*, Georges Lefebvre discusses the relationship between the Enlightenment, viewed as the end product of the history of Western culture, and the Declaration of the Rights of Man. His observations bring into view a number of the themes and problems that we have been considering throughout this book.

Lefebvre takes as his point of departure various attempts to explain the Declaration of 1789 primarily by reference to the influence of various bills of rights adopted by the American colonies, especially Virginia. While acknowledging the influence of America, Lefebvre stresses the fundamental importance of the Enlightenment in the genesis of the declaration: "The whole philosophic movement in France in the eighteenth century pointed to such an act; Montesquieu, Voltaire and Rousseau had collaborated in its making." The same movement of thought provided the "inspiration and content" of the Declarations of 1789 and 1776. "In reality, America and France, like England before them, were alike tributaries to a great stream of ideas, which, while expressing the ascendancy of the bourgeoisie, constituted a common ideal that summarized the evolution of Western civilization. Through the course of centuries our Western world, formed by Christianity yet inheriting ancient thought, has directed its effort through a thousand vicissitudes toward the liberation of the human person."[1]

That formulation poses the question of the role of intellectual and cultural forces in the genesis of the French Revolution and of the politics of modern Europe. In order to get at the question, however, it has to be removed from an interpretive framework that narrows its scope and restricts the range of possible answers. First of all, the analytical reach of the passage from Lefebvre has to be extended, so that it embraces the problem of explaining not only the Declaration of 1789 but also the Revolution itself. While the declaration was "the incarnation of the Revolution as a whole," the reverse was also the case. That is, the constitutive relationship between the Enlightenment and the Revolution has to be recognized. Secondly, the significance of Lefebvre's comments on the declaration can be grasped only if they are detached from the interpretation of 1789 as essentially a bourgeois revolution. By the same token, it is also necessary to put aside the notion that the *philosophes* "simply put into definite form" the new ideology of the bourgeoisie. In this way, we can accord a significant degree of independence (or "relative autonomy") to the Enlightenment and to the ideas of Western culture in which it had its origin. With these modifications, it becomes possible to consider the role of the traditions described by Lefebvre—derived from Christianity and antiquity—in the process underlying the French Revolution.

In order to appropriate the valuable core of Lefebvre's interpretation, however, it is also necessary to excise a remnant of idealist teleology. One cannot accept his picture of the Western world as having "directed its effort" over the centuries toward the liberation of the human person. The following passage expresses an important point in misleading form:

The Church upheld the freedom of the individual so that he might work in peace for his salvation and entrance into heaven. From the sixteenth to the eighteenth centuries philosophers proposed that man also throw off the fetters that held down his rise on earth; they urged him to become the master of nature and make his kind the true ruler of creation. Different though such doctrine seemed from that of the Church, the two were at one in recognizing the eminent dignity of the human person and commanding respect for it.

The Church may be said to have "upheld the freedom of the individual" only in a sense that requires extensive qualification. Similarly, we have come to be aware of the ambiguity of the movement to throw off the fetters and become the true rulers of creation. Clearly, it is necessary to take account of various social and institutional changes that were essential to the process that created the ideas and values embodied in the Declaration of 1789. But Lefebvre's use of the bourgeoisie as a causal factor—like later accounts of "modernization"—simply brings into play another kind of teleology, in which the being of the bourgeoisie is inherently liberal, so that it automatically embraces and puts to use ideas directed to the liberation of the person.

Once Lefebvre's interpretation has been divested of such teleological elements, along with the bourgeois revolution thesis and the social ontology that it presupposes, it underlines the intimate connection between the Enlightenment, the eighteenth-century phase in the history of Western culture, and the French Revolution. His reference to the beliefs of Christianity and of antiquity is a reminder of the free and spontaneous activity—thinking, dreaming, fantasizing, hoping, wishing—that entered into the creation of a culture that provided the matrix in which modern revolutionary politics developed. From that history came the constituents of revolution in its modern form. Cultural forces exercised this influence, of course, only in interaction with social and institutional structures that were the product of a separate history. At the heart of the historical process that made possible the French Revolution was the convergence in the mid-eighteenth century of separate cultural and social-institutional developments, each of which was relatively independent of the other, despite intertwining and intersection and mutual influence over the centuries.

The French Revolution transmuted what it took from the legacy of the past and created new ideological and symbolic forms that shaped the political history of the next two centuries. It exercised that influence not only in conjunction with urbanization and industrialization but also with socialism, especially in its Marxist form. Marx drew on the new revolutionary ideology and on the intellectual and religious traditions of Western culture in creating a socialist creed of remarkable power. He exemplifies in striking form the freedom and creativity that went into the development of that culture, as well as the ambiguous and ironic possibilities inherent in the fervent pursuit of its highest ideals. In a very different sequence of developments, the fascist assault on Western values also drew on the intellectual resources provided by European culture. The exercise of freedom had produced both creative and destructive forces, reflecting the view of man inscribed in the great myths of Israel and Greece. Throughout this history, of course, massive structures of power exercised an influence on cultural development and bent ideals to practical ends. Yet that history was also profoundly affected by intellectual activity that transcended the limits imposed by society and culture.

Notes

PREFACE

1. F. Gilbert, "Intellectual History: Its Aims and Methods," in F. Gilbert and S. R. Graubard, eds., *Historical Studies Today*, p. 148 (New York: Norton, 1972).

2. L. Veysey, "Intellectual History and the New Social History," in J. Higham and P. K. Conkin, eds., *New Directions in American Intellectual History*, p. 6 (Baltimore, Md.: Johns Hopkins University Press, 1979).

3. K. Baker, "On the Problem of the Ideological Origins of the French Revolution," in D. LaCapra and S. L. Kaplan, eds., *Modern European Intellectual History: Reappraisals and New Perspectives*, p. 198 (Ithaca, N.Y.: Cornell University Press, 1982).

4. M. Weber, *The Protestant Ethic and the Spirit of Capitalism* (New York: Scribner, 1930), p. 55.

5. Throughout this book a number of terms—ideas, beliefs, traditions, cultural and symbolic forms—are used loosely to embrace such phenomena as the Enlightenment, Marxism, and social Darwinism. The argument is based on a rough distinction, embedded in ordinary language, between cultural and social phenomena. For a subtle and systematic analysis of the problem of treating "sociological and cultural processes on equal terms," see C. Geertz, *The Interpretation of Cultures* (New York: Basic Books, 1973), pp. 143–145, 249–254, 360–364.

1. CONCEPTUAL PROBLEMS

1. P. Conkin, "Afterword," in J. Higham and P. K. Conkin, eds., *New Directions in American Intellectual History*, pp. 231–232 (Baltimore, Md.: Johns Hopkins Press, 1979).

2. J. Searle, *Intentionality: An Essay in the Philosophy of Mind* (Cambridge: Cambridge University Press, 1983), chapter 4. In practice historians have followed Patrick Atkinson's eclectic counsel with very good results: "There has often been a tendency to dismiss non-regularity, non-Humean uses of 'cause' as merely confused, but I believe that the implication of the more careful recent discussions is that historians and other 'ordinary' speakers have no reason

to allow themselves to be brow-beaten in this way. They should not be too ready to abide by restrictions, imposed in the name of Hume, philosophy, even science, on what they are otherwise inclined to say." P. Atkinson, *Knowledge and Explanation in History* (Ithaca, N.Y.: Cornell University Press, 1978), p. 145. See also the discussion of Max Weber's conception of "causes," chapter 5, note 41, below.

3. G. Wood, "Intellectual History and the Social Sciences," in Higham and Conkin, *New Directions*, p. 33. On similar grounds Dilthey rejected the notion that the Enlightenment could be said to have "brought about" the French Revolution. *Gesammelte Schriften*, vol. 2 (Stuttgart: B. G. Teubner, 1958), p. 71. Michael Ermarth has emphasized that Dilthey "rejected as preposterous the view that the ideas of the Enlightenment produced the French Revolution." *Wilhelm Dilthey: The Critique of Historical Reason* (Chicago: University of Chicago Press, 1979), p. 295.

4. B. Bailyn, *The Ideological Origins of the American Revolution* (Cambridge: Harvard University Press, 1967). In an earlier article, "Political Experience and Enlightenment Ideas in Eighteenth-Century America," *American Historical Review* (January 1962), 67:339–351, Bailyn pointed out that although Enlightenment ideas cannot be characterized as a cause of the American Revolution, they nevertheless played an important part in "lifting into consciousness and endowing with high moral purpose inchoate, confused elements of social and political change." The Enlightenment played a similar role in France in the summer of 1789, partly in response to developments in America. (See also chapter 6, note 20, below.)

5. K. Baker, "On the Problem of the Ideological Origins of the French Revolution," in D. LaCapra and S. L. Kaplan, eds., *Modern European Intellectual History: Reappraisals and New Perspectives*, pp. 206, 196 (Ithaca, N.Y.: Cornell University Press, 1982).

6. F. Gilbert, ed., *The Historical Essays of Otto Hintze* (New York: Oxford University Press, 1975), "Introduction: Otto Hintze, 1861–1940," pp. 3–30.

7. *Ibid.*, p. 23.

8. *Ibid.*, pp. 25, 364–365, 400.

9. J. P. Vernant, *The Origins of Greek Thought* (Ithaca, N.Y.: Cornell University Press, 1982), p. 10. In this elegant study, originally published in 1962, Vernant argues that "the origin of rational thought must be seen as bound up with the social and mental structures peculiar to the Greek city," p. 130.

10. M. Schofield, "From Polis to Philosophy," *Times Literary Supplement*, Oct. 29, 1982.

11. *Ibid.*

12. *Ibid.*

13. W. H. Walsh, "The Causation of Ideas," *History and Theory* (1975), p. 191.

14. See James Henretta, "Social History as Lived and Written," *American*

Historical Review (1979); G. Iggers, *New Directions in European Historiography* (Middletown, Conn.: Wesleyan University Press, 1975).

15. F. Gilbert, "Intellectual History: Its Aims and Methods," in F. Gilbert and S. R. Graubard, eds., *Historical Studies Today*, pp. 154–155 (New York: Norton, 1972).

16. R. Berkhofer, "Comments," *American Historical Review* (December 1979).

17. See T. Stoianovich, *The French Historical Method: The Annales' Paradigm* (Ithaca, N.Y.: Cornell University Press, 1976); P. Ricoeur, *The Contribution of French Historiography to Theory of History* (Oxford: Clarendon Press, 1980); M. Perrot, "The Strengths and Weaknesses of French Social History," *Journal of Social History*, 10:167–175.

18. F. Braudel, "History and the Social Sciences," in P. Burke, ed., *Economy and Society in Early Modern Europe*, (New York: Harper & Row, 1972), pp. 26–29. For another translation see Braudel, *On History* (Chicago: University of Chicago Press, 1980).

19. H. Trevor-Roper, "Fernand Braudel, the *Annales*, and the Mediterranean," *Journal of Modern History* (1972), pp. 469–470. See also J. H. Hexter, "Fernand Braudel and the *Monde Braudellien*," *ibid*.

20. R. Darnton, "The History of *Mentalités*: Recent Writings on Revolution, Criminality, and Death in France," in R. Brown and S. Lyman, eds., *Structure, Consciousness, and History*, (Cambridge: Cambridge University Press, 1978), p. 133; *New York Review of Books*, May 31, 1979.

21. M. Vovelle, "Le tournant des mentalités en France, 1750–1789," *Social History* (1977).

22. *Ibid*.

23. H. Trevor-Roper, in S. J. Woolf, ed., *European Fascism*, p. 24 (New York: Vintage Books, 1969).

24. L. B. Namier, *Personalities and Powers* (New York: Macmillan, 1955), p. 2.

25. P. Clarke, "Political History in the 1980s," *Journal of Interdisciplinary History* (1981), 12:45–47; "Expediency in High Places," *Times Literary Supplement*, May 20, 1977; M. Cowling, *1867: Disraeli, Gladstone, and Revolution: The Passing of the Second Reform Bill* (Cambridge: Cambridge University Press, 1967).

26. H. Butterfield, *George III and the Historians* (New York: Macmillan, 1959), pp. 193–210, 222–226.

27. Whereas the problem of ideas and interests is central to political and idcological history, the role of ideas, beliefs, and traditions takes a rather different form in the history of science, where the influence of social and institutional circumstances is necessarily tangential, albeit of considerable interest. By the same token, processes of a different sort are involved in the history of the family and sex. For a masterly study of the interplay between social and

cultural forces in that area see L. Stone, *The Family, Sex, and Marriage in England 1500–1800* (New York: Harper & Row, 1977).

28. F. Gilbert, in Gilbert and Graubard, pp. 148–155. Gilbert's position is based on an acceptance of the fact that by the end of the nineteenth century "the notion of history as a process reflecting ideas and controlled by them was abandoned." By then "the linkage between political and intellectual activities which the belief in the power of ideas over history had established was broken." *Ibid.*, pp. 149–150.

29. See Gilbert's introduction to *Hintze's Essays*, p. 24. The reaction against German historicism has now reached the point where, it has been suggested, the discussion of the issues needs to be *enttheoretisiert, entontologisiert*, and *entidealisiert:* see T. Nipperdey, "Historismus und Historismuskritik heute," in his *Gesellschaft, Kultur, Theorie* (Göttingen: Vandenhoeck & Ruprecht, 1976), pp. 59–73. The need to divest idealist historicism of its metaphysical husk is especially evident in Friedrich Meinecke's essay, "Values and Causalities in History," in F. Stern, ed., *Varieties of History* (New York: Meridian Books, 1956), pp. 268–288. The value of Meinecke's theory and practice remains considerable nevertheless.

30. F. Gilbert, ed., *Hintze's Essays*, pp. 314, 391, 397, 24.

31. *Ibid.*, pp. 94–95. Michael Ermarth has concluded that Dilthey's rejection of any "simple, unilateral historical idealism" led him to a rather similar position: "Ideas may provide the direction and legitimation of social and political action, but they do not often constitute the direct impetus." *Wilhelm Dilthey*, p. 295.

32. *Essays of Hintze*, p. 94.

33. The translation quoted here is from R. Bendix, *Max Weber: An Intellectual Portrait* (New York: Anchor Books, 1962), p. 46.

34. *Essays of Hintze*, pp. 94–95.

35. P. Ricoeur, *History and Truth* (Evanston, Ill.: Northwestern University Press, 1965), pp. 213, 126–127.

36. *Ibid.*, p. 128.

37. R. W. Southern, *The Making of the Middle Ages* (London: Hutchinson, 1953), p. 107.

38. H. Marcuse, "Remarks on a Redefinition of Culture," in G. Holton, ed., *Science and Culture*, p. 224 (Cambridge, Mass.: Houghton Mifflin, 1965).

39. I. Hartig and A. Soboul, *Pour une histoire de l'utopie en France au XVIIIᵉ siècle* (Paris: Société des études robespierristes, 1977).

40. Z. Bauman, *Socialism: The Active Utopia* (London: Allen & Unwin, 1976), p. 18.

41. R. Geuss, *The Idea of a Critical Theory: Habermas and the Frankfurt School* (Cambridge: Cambridge University Press, 1981), pp. 82–88.

42. J. Habermas, *Knowledge and Human Interests* (Boston: Beacon Press, 1971), p. 280. See also A. Wellmer, *Critical Theory of Society* (New York: Seabury Press, 1974).

43. K. Jaspers, *The Origin and Goal of History* (London: Routledge & Kegan Paul, 1953), part 1. See also, S. N. Eisenstadt, "The Axial Age: The Emergence of Transcendental Visions and the Rise of Clerics," *Archives européennes de sociologie* (1982), 23:294–314. See the Spring 1975 issue of *Daedalus*, "Wisdom, Revelation, and Doubt: Perspectives on the First Millennium B.C."

44. J. Habermas, *Communication and the Evolution of Society* (Boston: Beacon Press, 1978), ch. 3 and 4.

2. THE ENLIGHTENMENT AND THE FRENCH REVOLUTION

1. M. Robespierre, *Oeuvres* (1967), 10:544.

2. The quoted phrase is from H. Arendt, *On Revolution* (Harmondsworth: Penguin Books, 1973), ch. 1, which presents a suggestive but idiosyncratic interpretation. The best introduction to the problem in its complexity is F. Gilbert's article "Revolution" in P. Wiener, ed., *Dictionary of the History of Ideas* (New York: Scribner, 1968); see also Karl Griewank, *Der neuzeitliche Revolutionsbegriff* (Weimar: H. Bohlous Nachfolger, 1955) and K. M. Baker, "A Script for a French Revolution: The Political Consciousness of the Abbé Mably," *Eighteenth Century Studies* (1981), 14:249–253. See also J. Habermas, *Theory and Practice* (Boston: Beacon Press, 1974), pp. 82–91; M. Lassky, *Utopia and Revolution* (Chicago: University of Chicago Press, 1976), pp. 582–583 and passim; F. Furet, *Interpreting the French Revolution* (Cambridge: Cambridge University Press, 1971), pp. 22–23. For a rather different interpretation from the one presented here and at notes 13–17 and 69–75 below see the wide ranging study by J. Billington, *Fire in the Minds of Men: Origins of the Revolutionary Faith* (New York: Basic Books, 1980), ch. 1. From a social science perspective, Michael Walzer, *The Revolution of the Saints: A Study in the Origins of Radical Politics* (New York: Atheneum, 1973), locates the French Revolution in a different historical context that embodies a broad definition of modern radical politics, embracing both reform and revolution—"a politics of party organization and methodical activity, opposition and reform, radical ideology and revolution." In describing the origins of radical politics so defined he emphasizes the interaction between Puritanism and the process of modernization. Characterizing Puritanism as "the earliest form of political radicalism," Walzer treats "the history of reform and revolution" primarily in relation to the broader process of modernization: "In those years, Puritanism provided what may best be called an *ideology of transition*. It was functional to the process of modernization not because it served the purposes of some universal progress, but because it met the human needs that arise whenever traditional controls give way and hierarchical status and corporate privilege are called into question" (pp. vii, 312).

3. A definitive study of the ideological origins of the French Revolution is

being written by Keith Baker; see below at note 19. An important aspect of the problem has been suggestively examined by Norman Hampson in *Will & Circumstance: Montesquieu, Rousseau, and the French Revolution* (Norman: University of Oklahoma Press, 1983). As Patrice Higonnet has pointed out, "the historiographic climate has changed dramatically in the past twenty years, and the ideology of the Enlightenment is now thought to have been critical to the Revolution in various ways." *London Review of Books*, January 20–February 3, 1983, p. 4. Higonnet's *Class, Ideology, and the Rights of Nobles During the French Revolution* (Oxford: Clarendon Press, 1981) puts the ideology of "bourgeois universalism" at the center of his interpretation, and argues that "it is altogether impossible to understand the zeal of bourgeois Revolutionaries in 1789–99 if the genuineness of their ideological convictions is brought into question" (p. 33). Higonnet's account of the nature and origins of those convictions puts primary emphasis on the "exigencies of individualistic capitalism." (See note 20 below.) While stressing the importance of ideology, Higonnet at the same time assigns a significant degree of primacy to social and institutional forces. See N. Hampson, "Friend Robespierre," *London Review of Books*, August 5–18, 1982.

4. J. L. Talmon, *The Origins of Totalitarian Democracy* (New York: Praeger, 1960).

5. W. Doyle, *Origins of the French Revolution* (Oxford: Oxford University Press, 1980), part 1, "A Consensus and Its Collapse: Writings on Revolutionary Origins since 1939." See also D. Johnson, ed., *French Society and the Revolution* (Cambridge: Cambridge University Press, 1976); G. Ellis, "The 'Marxist Interpretation' of the French Revolution," *English Historical Review*, 93 (1978).

6. R. R. Palmer, *The Age of the Democratic Revolution*, vol. 1 (Princeton, N.J.: Princeton University Press, 1959); J. Godechot, *France and the Atlantic Revolution of the Eighteenth Century, 1770–1799* (New York: Free Press, 1965).

7. G. Lefebvre, *The Coming of the French Revolution* (Princeton, N.J.: Princeton University Press, 1947), pp. 1–3. In vol. 13 of the *Peuples et Civilisations* series, Lefebvre took the classic Marxist position that 1789 was a "bourgeois revolution" of the same sort that had occurred in England in the seventeenth century. His comment on England reads like a paraphrase of Marx's dictum in the *Eighteenth Brumaire*: "The rise of the British bourgeoisie, favoured by economic progress in which the nobility played a role, had provoked the first two modern revolutions in the guise of a struggle between Anglicans and Calvinists and against Catholicism." *The French Revolution from Its Origins to 1793* (New York: Columbia University Press, 1962), p. 79. In December 1848 Marx expounded his view of the bourgeois revolutions in England and France in "The Bourgeoisie and the Counter-Revolution," Karl Marx and Frederick Engels, *Selected Works* (London: Lawrence and Wishart, 1950), 1:62–65. Georges Lefebvre, however, like other Marxist historians of the first rank, transcended the limitations of the theoretical framework inherited from Marx. The bourgeoisie that is described in *The Coming of the French Revolu-*

tion, pp. 41–50, is not the capitalist bourgeoisie that Marx depicted as the agent of the "bourgeois revolution" or as the prospective victim of proletarian grave diggers. Moreover, Lefebvre's account of the intellectual origins of the Declaration of the Rights of Man, pp. 214–215, can readily be transposed into an analysis of the origins of the Revolution. Among the best discussions of the problem of the Enlightenment and the French Revolution are his "L'Encyclopédie et la Révolution française," *Annales de l'Université de Paris* (1948), and "La Révolution française et le rationalisme," *Annales Historiques de la Révolution française* (1946).

8. Doyle, *Origins*, pp. 7–24; G. Taylor, "Noncapitalist Wealth and the Origins of the French Revolution," *American Historical Review* (1967), 72:469–496; D. Johnson, ed., *French Society and the Revolution;* G. Chaussinand-Nogaret, *La Noblesse au XVIIIᵉ Siècle. De la féodalite aux lumières* (Paris: Hachette, 1976).

9. C. Lucas, "Nobles, Bourgeois, and the Origins of the French Revolution," *Past and Present* (August 1973), No. 60.

10. G. Taylor, "Revolutionary and Nonrevolutionary Content in the *Cahiers* of 1789: An Interim Report," *French Historical Studies* (1972), vol. 7.

11. A. Cobban, "The Enlightenment and the French Revolution," in A. Cobban, *Aspects of the French Revolution* (New York: Braziller, 1968), pp. 22–27. The essay includes a valuable account of the tension between enlightenment liberalism and the idea of popular sovereignty.

12. P. Gay, *The Party of Humanity* (New York: Knopf, 1964), pp. 162–181.

13. F. Furet, *Interpreting the French Revolution*, pp. 46, 23.

14. *Ibid.*, pp. 22–24.

15. *Ibid.*, pp. 25, 29, 13.

16. *Ibid.*, p. 79. See also pp. 24, 26, 204.

17. Palmer, *Age of the Democratic Revolution*, vol. 1.

18. Furet, pp. 22–23. See also reviews of Furet by L. Hunt, *History and Theory*, 20 (1981), and by K. Baker, *Journal of Modern History* (1981).

19. In addition to Baker's article on Mably cited above, see his "French Political Thought at the Accession of Louis XVI," *Journal of Modern History* (1978); "On the Problem of the Ideological Origins of the French Revolution," in D. LaCapra and S. L. Kaplan, eds., *Modern European Intellectual History: Reappraisals and New Perspectives* (Ithaca, N.Y.: Cornell University Press, 1982); "Enlightenment and Revolution in France: Old Problems, Renewed Approaches," *Journal of Modern History* (1981).

20. "Ideological Origins," pp. 206–212; "Enlightenment and Revolution," p. 80. For a rather different interpretation, which breaks new ground within a more traditional framework, see Higonnet *Class, Ideology, and the Rights of Nobles.* Higonnet takes as his theme the impact of capitalism on the inherited values and beliefs of civic humanism: "The new vigor of individualism and of capitalism placed intolerable strain on the ethic of civic humanism and com-

munity. By shattering the vision of a virtuous society, the development of individualistic capitalism forced a drastic rethinking of the central problem of eighteenth century social thought, that is, of the balance between individual and community." He characterizes "bourgeois universalism" as an unstable solution that attempted "to reconcile recent capitalism with the ancient tradition of civic humanism. It claimed that individualism, now become capitalist and more demanding, might none the less be fitted into the framework of a classically virtuous society." Higonnet locates Rousseau in this context: "What Rousseau understood in moral terms can, of course, be interpreted economically and socially as the effect of the rise of capitalism" (p. 17).

21. On the social and institutional foundations of the idea of popular sovereignty in the last third of the eighteenth century, see Palmer, *Democratic Revolution*, vol. 1, chs. 5, 8, and 9. On republicanism, civic humanism, and other political ideas received from the past, see F. Venturi, *Utopia and Revolution in the Enlightenment* (Cambridge: Cambridge University Press, 1971); J. G. A. Pocock, ed., *Three British Revolutions, 1641, 1688, 1776* (Princeton: Princeton University Press, 1980) and *The Machiavellian Moment: Florentine Political Thought and the Atlantic Republican Tradition* (Princeton, N.J.: Princeton University Press, 1975); N. O. Keohane, *Philosophy and the State in France: The Renaissance to the Enlightenment* (Princeton, N.J.: Princeton University Press, 1980); Q. Skinner, *The Foundations of Modern Political Thought*, 2 vols. (Cambridge: Cambridge University Press, 1978).

22. E. Burke, *Reflections on the Revolution in France* (London: Dent, 1910), pp. 55–56. In this vein, see also M. Oakeshott, *Rationalism in Politics* (London: Methuen, 1962).

23. K. Marx and F. Engels, *The Holy Family, or Critique of Critical Criticism: Against Bruno Bauer and Company* (Moscow: Progress Publishers, 1975), pp. 153–154.

24. F. Venturi, *Italy and the Enlightenment* (London: Longman, 1972), p. 18.

25. This emphasis on the persistence of the natural law tradition in the Enlightenment follows E. Cassirer, *The Philosophy of the Enlightenment* (Princeton, N.J.: Princeton University Press, 1951), pp. 234–253, rather than P. Gay, *The Party of Humanity*, pp. 114–132, 188–210, and *The Enlightenment: An Interpretation*, 2 vols. (New York: Knopf, 1966, 1969).

26. Lefebvre, "La Révolution française et le rationalisme."

27. R. Darnton, "In Search of the Enlightenment," *Journal of Modern History* (1972).

28. I. Knight, *The Geometric Spirit: The Abbé de Condillac and the French Enlightenment* (New Haven: Yale University Press, 1968), p. 277. After a subtle analysis of Condillac's social and political thought, Knight concludes, p. 294: "The commonplace thesis that the French Enlightenment was a period of radical and abstract political theories based on a naive faith in the goodness

and perfectibility of man and in the inevitability of infinite progress cannot be supported by Condillac's views. Condillac has all the pessimistic realism of the political conservative." It may also be said, however, that the latent radicalism of the Enlightenment assumes a particularly interesting form in a conservative like Condillac, whose "role in the struggle for an enlightened society was less than heroic." Knight's account of "the moral power of the Enlightenment" is very much to the point: "The collective mission of the philosophes was the destruction of the tangible and intangible obstacles to happiness, which, as they saw it, the evil intent of a few had engendered and the inertia and ignorance of the many had allowed to persist and to grow until they pressed upon society with all the weight of centuries of acquiescence" (*ibid.*, p. 265).

29. Cassirer, *Philosophy of the Enlightenment*, p. 244.

30. *Ibid.*, p. 245; for a different interpretation of Voltaire's relationship to the natural law tradition, see P. Gay, *Voltaire's Politics* (New York: Vintage Books, 1965), Appendix, "Voltaire and Natural Law."

31. John Passmore, *The Perfectibility of Man* (London: Duckworth, 1970), p. 67.

32. K. Löwith, *Meaning in History* (Chicago: University of Chicago Press, 1949) pp. 212, 2.

33. I. Berlin, "Introduction" to F. Venturi, *Roots of Revolution: A History of the Populist and Socialist Movements in Nineteenth-Century Russia* (New York: Grosset and Dunlap, 1960), pp. xiii–xiv.

34. See P. Ricoeur, "The Image of God and the Epic of Man," *History and Truth* (Evanston, Ill.: Northwestern University Press, 1960), pp. 110–128.

35. Frank E. Manuel and Fritzie P. Manuel, *Utopian Thought in the Western World* (Cambridge: Harvard University Press, 1979), pp. 1–4, 15, 112–114.

36. *Ibid.*, p. 3.

37. C. Rihs, "Les Utopistes contre les Lumières," *Studies on Voltaire and the Eighteenth Century*, (1967) 57:1321–1355.

38. B. Baczko, "Lumières et Utopie," *Annales* (1971), p. 358.

39. I. Hartig and A. Soboul, *Pour une histoire de l'utopie en France au XVIIIe siècle* (Paris: Société des études robespierristes 1977), pp. 20–23.

40. Manuel and Manuel, p. 559.

41. F. Venturi, *Utopia and Reform*, p. 97.

42. Manuel and Manuel, pp. 560–561; K. Martin, *The Rise of French Liberal Thought* (New York: New York University Press, 1956), pp. 241–242.

43. Manuel and Manuel, p. 561.

44. Martin, p. 249.

45. *Ibid.;* see also Baker, "Scenario."

46. Venturi, p. 97; Martin, p. 243; F. E. and F. P. Manuel, *French Utopias: An Anthology of Ideal Societies* (New York: Schocken Books, 1971), pp. 100–116.

47. Baczko, pp. 382–384. See also his review of Venturi, *Annales* (1973), pp. 1515–1519, and of the Manuels' *Utopian Thought, Journal of Modern History* (1981), pp. 468–476, "The Shifting Frontiers of Utopia."

48. Baczko, "Shifting Frontiers," p. 473. "L'utopie, comme forme du discours, permet de donner libre cours aux sentiments et aux attitudes de refus et de contestation même quand ils sont politiquement et sociologiquement vagues, imprécis." "Lumières et Utopie," p. 382.

49. E. Cassirer, *The Question of Jean-Jacques Rousseau* (Bloomington: Indiana University Press, 1963), p. 66.

50. A. Wilson, "The Development and Scope of Diderot's Political Thought," *Studies on Voltaire and the Eighteenth Century* (1962), 27:1874.

51. J. Lough, ed. *The Encyclopédie of Diderot and D'Alembert: Selected Articles* (Cambridge: Cambridge University Press, 1954), p. 6.

52. D. Diderot, *Rameau's Nephew and Other Works* (New York: Bobbs-Merrill, 1956), p. 200; Wilson, "Development and Scope of Diderot's Political Thought."

53. Cassirer, *Rousseau*, pp. 65–69.

54. J. J. Rousseau, *Discourse on the Origin and Foundations of Inequality*, in R. D. Masters, ed. and tr., *The First and Second Discourses* (New York: St. Martin's Press, 1964), pp. 114–115, 103.

55. *Ibid.*, pp. 101–102.

56. J. J. Rousseau, *Social Contract*, book I, chs. 1, 3, 4, in *Social Contract: Essays by Locke, Hume, and Rousseau* (New York and London: Oxford University Press, 1948), pp. 169, 177, 173. Rousseau, of course, was acutely aware of the limits of reason and in the first *Discourse* he had mounted a ferocious attack: "L'homme qui médite est un animal dépravé." By 1762, however, both in the *Social Contract* and *Emile*, he had arrived at a position that combined "the most resolute belief in reason" with a profound appreciation of the role of sentiments in the conscience and the moral life. Cassirer, *Rousseau*, pp. 56–57, 82; Gay, *Party of Humanity*, p. 232.

57. *Discourse on Inequality*, pp. 141–142, 156–157.

58. *Ibid.*, pp. 159–160, 181.

59. A. Cobban, *Rousseau and the Modern State* (London: Allen & Unwin, 1934).

60. *Social Contract*, book 1, ch. 8, M. Cranston, trans. (Penguin Books, Harmondsworth, Middlesex, 1968).

61. *Social Contract*, book 2, ch. 7 (New York, 1948).

62. Cassirer, *Rousseau*, pp. 51–82. For another good account of Rousseau's radicalism, contrasted with the more moderate liberalism of Montesquieu, see N. Hampson, *Will & Circumstance: Montesquieu, Rousseau, and the French Revolution* (Norman: University of Oklahoma Press, 1983), pp. 26–64. Hampson is especially useful in establishing lines of influence and affiliation between Rousseau and the writers and revolutionaries of the next generation.

63. For a rather different view of the political thought of the Enlighten-

ment, which stresses its reformist and empiricist character, see P. Gay, *The Party of Humanity*, pp. 162–181, 278–282, and F. Furet and D. Richet, *La Révolution française*, 2 vols. (Paris, 1965), 1:138, who argue that a *réformisme éclairé* of a rather moderate sort underlay the events of 1789, whereas a *dérapage* occurred in 1792–94.

64. See Hampson's discussion of the divergent aspects of Enlightenment thought represented by Montesquieu and Rousseau, *Will & Circumstance*, pp. 3–64.

65. K. Baker, "French Political Thought."

66. Furet and Richet, 1:78. This passage does not appear in the abridged English edition (London, 1970).

67. A. Cobban, "The *Parlements* of France in the Eighteenth Century," *Aspects of the French Revolution*, p. 77; G. Rudé, *Revolutionary Europe 1783–1815* (New York: Harper Torchbooks, 1966), p. 75.

68. Doyle, *French Revolution*, p. 153. The revisionist view of the nobility is expressed in G. Chaussinand-Nogaret, *La Noblesse au XVIIIe siècle*. For a somewhat different interpretation, see Higonnet, pp. 42–56.

69. Doyle, p. 20.

70. Doyle, p. 172; Lefebvre, *Coming*, pp. 78–87.

71. J. J. Mounier in P. Beik, ed. *The French Revolution* (New York: Harper & Row, 1970), pp. 37–44.

72. *Ibid.*

73. E. J. Sieyès in Beik, ed. p. 33. For another translation see E. J. Sieyès, *What Is the Third Estate?* (New York: Praeger, 1964), p. 152.

74. Beik, ed. p. 36; Sieyès, p. 166.

75. J. Godechot, *The Taking of the Bastille July 14th, 1789* (New York: Scribner, 1970), p. 273.

76. *Ibid.*, p. 261.

77. J. Egret, "The Origins of the Revolution in Brittany (1788–1789)," in J. Kaplow, ed., *New Perspectives on the French Revolution*, (New York: Wiley, 1965), pp. 151, 143.

78. Doyle, p. 185.

79. M. Robespierre, *Oeuvres Complètes*, (Paris, 1926), 3:42, letter to Buissot, July 23, 1789.

80. Godechot, *Bastille*, pp. 261–262.

81. Beik, ed., *French Revolution*, pp. 147–151.

82. Furet, *Interpreting the French Revolution*, p. 22.

83. G. Rudé, "Popular Protest and Ideology on the Eve of the French Revolution," in E. Hinrichs, ed., *Vom Ancien Regime zur Französischen Revolution*, (Göttingen: Vandenhoeck and Ruprecht, 1978), pp. 420–435. See also Rudé, *Ideology and Popular Protest* (New York: Pantheon Books, 1980).

84. R. Darnton, "The World of the Underground Booksellers in the Old Regime," in Hinrichs, ed., *Vom Ancien Regime*, pp. 439–478; "The High Enlightenment and the Low-life of Literature in Pre-Revolutionary France," *Past*

and Present (1971), 51:81–115; "Reading, Writing, and Publishing in Eighteenth-Century France: A Case Study in the Sociology of Literature," in Gilbert and Graubard, eds., *Historical Studies Today*.

85. The uprising of the peasants, so important in radicalizing the Revolution of 1789, had virtually no connection with the Enlightenment. The peasants were taking action of a traditional sort, but in a changed historical context. See Furet, *Interpreting the French Revolution*, p. 8; G. Lefebvre, *The Great Fear of 1789: Rural Panic in Revolutionary France* (New York: Vintage Books, 1973), pp. 34–46, 100–121.

86. Keith Baker has aptly characterized the problem of conceptualizing the role of the common people in the Revolution of 1789: "The 'masses' did indeed play a dramatic part in the events of 1789. But did they make the Revolution? On the contrary, the power of their actions depended upon a set of symbolic representations and cultural meanings that constituted the significance of their behavior and gave it explosive force." "Enlightenment and Revolution," p. 303. The nature of the dependent relationship between the masses and "the structure of discourse defining the political arena in which they intervened," is extremely difficult to specify. Baker has also pointed out that "the action of a rioter in picking up a stone can no more be understood apart from the symbolic field that gives it meaning than the action of a priest in picking up a sacramental vessel." Hence it is not necessary to establish that "everyone in the crowd attacking the Bastille in July 1789 was motivated to overthrow despotism" ("The Problem of Ideology," pp. 198, 206). The analogy to the priest is an apt one although the nature and origins of the "symbolic representations and cultural meanings" involved in 1789 pose more difficult problems of analysis, embracing the interplay between socio-political groupings in a changing context of events constituted, in part, by competing and changing discourses. Whereas Baker's formulation keeps open multiple lines of inquiry, W. G. Runciman's treatment of the problem of explaining the storming of the Bastille is confined within the limits imposed by logical empiricist epistemology. *A Treatise on Social Theory*, vol. 1: *The Methodology of Social Theory* (Cambridge: Cambridge University Press, 1983), pp. 183–186. (See also the second section of chapter 6.)

87. P. Beik, ed., *The French Revolution*, pp. 36–37; E. J. Sieyès, *What Is the Third Estate?* pp. 141, 170–72, 209; J. L. Talmon, *Totalitarian Democracy*, p. 71; N. Hampson, *Will & Circumstance*, p. 58, and "Friend Robespierre"; Doyle, pp. 28, 167, 169.

88. P. Beik, ed., *The French Revolution*, pp. 143–155.

89. *Ibid.*, p. 148.

90. R. R. Palmer, *Twelve Who Ruled: The Year of the Terror in the French Revolution* (New York: Atheneum, 1965), pp. 275–276.

91. A. Soboul, "Jean-Jacques Rousseau et le Jacobinisme," *Studi Storici* (1963), p. 21. See also "Classes populaires et Rousseauisme sous la Révolu-

tion," *Annales Historiques de la Révolution* (1962), 34:421–438; "Robespierre and the Popular Movement of 1793–94," *Past and Present* (1955).

3. MARXISM AND REVOLUTION

1. K. Marx and F. Engels, *The Holy Family, or Critique of Critical Criticism: Against Bruno Bauer and Company* (Moscow: Progress Publishers, 1975), pp. 44–45.

2. D. McLellan, ed., *Karl Marx: Selected Writings* (Oxford: Oxford University Press, 1977), p. 69.

3. G. Lichtheim, *Marxism: An Historical and Critical Study* (New York: Praeger, 1961), pp. 3–62.

4. J. A. Schumpeter, *Capitalism, Socialism, and Democracy* (London: Allen & Unwin, 1943), p. 143.

5. J. L. Talmon, "The Age of Revolution," *Encounter* (September 1963).

6. See G. Lichtheim, *The Origins of Socialism* (London: Weidenfeld & Nicolson, 1969), pp. 3–160, and *A Short History of Socialism* (New York: Praeger, 1970), pp. 1–64; G. D. H. Cole, *A History of Socialist Thought*, vol. 1 (London: Macmillan, 1953).

7. P. Singer, "Dictator Marx?" *New York Review of Books*, September 28, 1980.

8. G. Lichtheim, *A Short History of Socialism* (New York: Praeger, 1970), p. 72.

9. Lichtheim, *Marxism*, pp. 122–129.

10. S. Avineri, *The Social and Political Thought of Karl Marx* (Cambridge: Cambridge University Press, 1968), pp. 202–220.

11. Lichtheim, *Marxism*, pp. 33–62; L. Kolakowski, *Main Currents of Marxism*, 1: *The Founders* (Oxford: Oxford University Press, 1978); D. McLellan, *Marx Before Marxism* (New York: Harper & Row, 1970) and *Karl Marx: His Life and Thought* (New York: Harper & Row, 1974). See also J. Seigel, *Marx's Fate: The Shape of a Life* (Princeton, N.J.: Princeton University Press, 1978).

12. E. Wilson, *To the Finland Station* (New York: Anchor Books, 1953), pp. 122, 115; L. D. Easton and K. H. Guddat, eds., *Writings of the Young Marx on Philosophy and Society* (New York: Anchor Books, 1967), pp. 61–63; McLellan, ed. *Marx*, pp. 14–15.

13. McLellan, pp. 63–64, 72–73.

14. *Ibid.*, pp. 72–73.

15. *Ibid.*, pp. 73–89.

16. R. Tucker, *Philosophy and Myth in Karl Marx* (Cambridge: Cambridge University Press, 1961).

17. McLellan, p. 89.

18. T. Bottomore, ed. *Karl Marx: Early Writings* (New York: McGraw Hill, 1964), p. 202; Lichtheim, *Marxism*, p. 42.

19. McLellan, pp. 170–171, 190.

20. *Ibid.*, p. 178.

21. *Ibid.*, pp. 222–231.

22. *Ibid.*, p. 237.

23. Lichtheim, *Marxism*, pp. 3–62.

24. McLellan, pp. 237–238.

25. *Ibid.*, pp. 246, 233.

26. *Ibid.*, p. 234.

27. *Ibid.*, p. 569.

28. Bottomore, *Early Writings*, pp. 22–25.

29. P. Gay, *The Dilemma of Democratic Socialism* (New York: Columbia University Press, 1952); C. Schorske, *German Social Democracy, 1905–1917* (New York: Wiley, 1965), pp. 1–27.

30. E. Bernstein, *Evolutionary Socialism*, p. 163.

31. *Protokoll über die Verhandlungen des Parteitages der Sozialdemokratischen Partei Deutschlands. Abgehalten zu Hannover . . . 1899*, pp. 67–68, 243–244, 122–125.

32. *Protokoll . . . Dresden . . . 1903*, p. 418.

33. K. Kautsky, *The Social Revolution* (Chicago: C. H. Kerr, 1916), pp. 20, 8–9, 81–82.

34. Schorske, *Social Democracy*, pp. 28–284.

35. A. J. Ryder, *The German Revolution of 1918* (Cambridge: 1967), pp. 177–183.

36. L. Schapiro, *The Communist Party of the Soviet Union* (New York: Vintage Books, 1964), pp. 36–177; L. H. Haimson, *The Russian Marxists and the Origins of Bolshevism* (Boston: Beacon Press, 1966), pp. 75–91, 165–219.

37. R. C. Tucker, ed., *The Lenin Anthology* (New York: Norton, 1975), p. 313.

38. V. I. Lenin, *Selected Works* (Moscow: Foreign Languages Publishing House, 1952) 1(1):232, 244.

39. Tucker, pp. 313–350.

40. Tucker, pp. 326–328, 344–345.

41. Tucker, pp. 418–419.

42. Tucker, pp. 423–437.

43. Tucker, p. 423.

44. S. F. Cohen, "Bolshevism and Stalinism: New Reflections on an Old Problem," *Dissent* (Spring 1977), pp. 190–205. See also Cohen's "Bolshevism and Stalinism," in R. C. Tucker ed., *Stalinism: Essays in Historical Interpretation* (New York: Norton, 1977), pp. 3–29.

45. Tucker, *Lenin Anthology*, p. 313.

46. *Ibid.*, pp. xxviii–xxix.

47. L. Kolakowski, "Marxist Roots of Stalinism," in R. C. Tucker ed., *Stalinism*, pp. 283–298.

48. M. Markovic, "Stalinism and Marxism," *ibid.*, pp. 299–319.

49. *Ibid.*, pp. 320–324.

50. A. Rabinowitch, *The Bolsheviks Come to Power: The Revolution of 1917 in Petrograd* (New York: Norton, 1976), pp. xv–xxi, 310–314.

4. THE GENESIS OF FASCISM

1. *New York Times*, January 16, 1966, review of E. Nolte, *Three Faces of Fascism* (New York: Holt, Rinehart and Winston, 1966). There are serious flaws in Nolte's book, notably a rather formalistic definition of fascism in part one, and the use of the metaphysical concept of "transcendence" in the interpretation of fascism in part five. While the three detailed parts in between are not definitive, they remain invaluable. The conceptual issue raised by Laqueur's categories has been commented on by J. G. A. Pocock, who has noted "the practice of referring to the extra-intellectual or extra-linguistic as 'reality', and to the intellectual or linguistic equipment, at least by implication, as non-reality." *Politics, Language, and Time* (New York: Atheneum, 1971), p. 38.

2. R. Paxton, *Times Literary Supplement*, October 7, 1983, review of Z. Sternhell, *Ni Droite ni gauche: L'Idéologie fasciste en France* (Paris: Seuil, 1983). Since I have not read the book under review, the discussion in the text is confined to conceptual and analytical issues. It should be noted that Paxton's review also raises important questions about the substance of Sternhell's interpretation.

3. E. Weber, "Revolution? Counterrevolution? What Revolution?" in W. Laqueur, ed., *Fascism: A Reader's Guide* (Berkeley: University of California Press, 1976). See also Weber's review article, "Fascism(s) and Some Harbingers," *Journal of Modern History* (1982), pp. 746–65.

4. S. G. Payne, *Fascism: Comparison and Definition* (Madison: University of Wisconsin Press, 1980), pp. 10, 204, 39–41.

5. G. Barraclough, *New York Review of Books*, November 2 and 16, 1972; A. J. Gregor, *Young Mussolini and the Intellectual Origins of Fascism* (Berkeley: University of California Press, 1979); Z. Sternhell, *La droite révolutionnaire: 1885–1914: les origines françaises du fascisme* (Paris: Editions du Seuil, 1978); see also his "Fascist Ideology" in Laqueur, ed., *Fascism* and "Strands of French Fascism," in S. Larsen, ed., *Who Were the Fascists? Social Roots of European Fascism* (Bergen: Universitetsforlaget, 1980); D. D. Roberts, *The Syndicalist Tradition and Italian Fascism* (Chapel Hill: University of North Carolina Press, 1979).

6. A. J. Mayer, "The Lower Middle Class as Historical Problem," *Journal of Modern History* (1975), p. 411.

7. F. L. Carsten, "Interpretations of Fascism," in Laqueur, ed., pp. 431, 445.

8. A. J. Mayer, *The Dynamics of Counterrevolution in Europe* (New York: Harper & Row, 1971), pp. 62–63.

9. Carsten, "Interpretations of Fascism," in Laqueur, ed., p. 428.

10. Weber, "Revolution," pp. 453, 448.

11. F. L. Carsten, *The Rise of Fascism* (Berkeley: University of California Press, 1967), pp. 9–10.

12. R. de Felice, *Fascism: An Informal Introduction to Its Theory and Practice: An Interview with Michael A. Ledeen* (New Brunswick, N.J.: Transaction Books, 1976), pp. 44–49.

13. *Ibid.*, pp. 44–46.

14. Sternhell, *La droite*, pp. 22–23.

15. C. E. Schorske, *Fin-de-Siècle Vienna: Politics and Culture* (New York: Vintage Books, 1981), p. xxii.

16. A. Lyttelton, ed., *Italian Fascisms: From Pareto to Gentile* (New York: Harper Torchbooks, 1973), p. 74.

17. *Ibid.*, p. 79.

18. *Ibid.*, pp. 79, 81; E. Nolte, *Three Faces of Fascism* (New York: Holt, Rinehart, 1966), p. 183.

19. R. Aron, *Main Currents in Sociological Thought* (New York: Anchor Books, 1970), 2:215.

20. Aron, pp. 196–197.

21. Nolte, *Fascism*, p. 280.

22. Sternhell, *La droite*, p. 25.

23. W. Kaufmann, ed., *The Portable Nietzsche* (New York: Viking Press, 1954), p. 444.

24. F. Nietzsche, *The Use and Abuse of History* (New York: Bobbs-Merrill, 1957), p. 20.

25. K. Jaspers, *Nietzsche and Christianity* (Chicago: Henry Regnery, 1961); W. Kaufmann, *Nietzsche: Philosopher, Psychologist, Antichrist* (New York: Meridian Books, 1956).

26. F. Nietzsche, *Beyond Good and Evil* (Chicago: Henry Regnery, 1955), section 44.

27. Kaufmann, ed., *Nietzsche*, p. 211.

28. *Ibid.*, pp. 192, 647, 619.

29. *Ibid.*, p. 649.

30. H. G. Zmarlik, "Social Darwinism in Germany Seen as a Historical Problem," in H. Holborn, ed., *Republic to Reich* (New York: Pantheon, 1972).

31. M. Howard, "Empire, Race, and War in pre-1914 Britain," in H. Lloyd-Jones, ed., *History and Imagination: Essays in Honour of H. R. Trevor-Roper*, pp. 340–355 (London: Duckworth, 1981): "Among all the fiends in the liberal demonology today, Imperialism, Racism and Militarism reign supreme; an evil trinity at whose collective door most of the wrong-doing in the world

can conveniently be laid. Yet a little more than three generations ago, within the memory of people still alive, these words and the ideas associated with them evoked even among professed Liberal thinkers, a very different response."

32. K. Pearson, *National Life from the Standpoint of Science* (London: Adam and Charles Black, 1901), pp. 21–24, 41.

33. R. Hofstadter, *The American Political Tradition and the Men Who Made It* (New York: Knopf, 1951), pp. 209–210.

34. Sternhell, *La droite*, pp. 15–26.

35. Nolte, *Fascism*, pp. 58–68; Weber, *Action Française* (Stanford: Stanford University Press, 1962).

36. Nolte, *Fascism*, pp. 111–113.

37. *Ibid.*, pp. 108–109, 125, 133–134, 103.

38. I. Berlin, *Against the Current*, (New York: Viking Press, 1980), p. 299; L. Kolakowski, *Main Currents of Marxism*, 2:164.

39. L. Kolakowski, *Main Currents of Marxism* (Oxford: Oxford University Press, 1978), 2:169; G. Sorel, *The Illusions of Progress* (Berkeley: University of California Press, 1969), p. 71: "It is the syndicalist movement that can accomplish the intellectual liberation that would rid the working classes of all respect for bourgeois nonsense."

40. Berlin, *Against the Current*, pp. 309, 312.

41. G. Sorel, *Reflections on Violence* (London: Allen and Unwin, 1915), p. 295.

42. Sternhell, *La droite*, pp. 391–407; Nolte, *Fascism*, pp. 115–116, 71; P. Mazgaj, *The Action Française and Revolutionary Syndicalism* (Chapel Hill: University of North Carolina Press, 1979).

43. Sternhell, "Fascist Ideology," in Laqueur, ed., *Fascism*, p. 333.

44. Sternhell, *La droite*, pp. 391–393.

45. Nolte, *Fascism*, pp. 25–26.

46. D. Bracher, *The German Dictatorship: The Origins, Structure, and Effects of National Socialism* (New York: Praeger, 1970); F. Meinecke, *The German Catastrophe* (Cambridge: Harvard University Press, 1950).

47. Sternhell, "Fascist Ideology," p. 317.

48. Roberts, *Italian Fascism;* Nolte, *Fascism*, pp. 145–271; R. Wohl, *The Generation of 1914* (Cambridge: Harvard University Press, 1979), pp. 160–202.

49. A. Lyttelton, ed., *Italian Fascisms: From Pareto to Gentile*, pp. 137–138, 151–153.

50. Nolte, p. 184; Lyttelton, ed., pp. 138–139, 155.

51. Lyttelton, ed., pp. 147, 140.

52. *Ibid.*, p. 147; E. Santarelli, "Le socialisme national en Italie: Précédents et origines," *Le Mouvement Social* (January–March 1965), 50:52–53.

53. Lyttelton, pp. 103–105.

54. Lyttelton, ed., p. 212. See also Wohl, pp. 164–170.

55. Lyttelton, ed., p. 214.

56. *Ibid.*, p. 211.
57. *Ibid.*, p. 104. See also Wohl, *1914*, pp. 160–168.
58. See Roberts, ch. 1 and passim.
59. Roberts, pp. 55–82; Sternhell, "Fascist Ideology," p. 330.
60. Roberts, pp. 59–61; Kolakowski, 2:169.
61. Roberts, pp. 59–66.
62. Roberts, pp. 67, 162.
63. A. J. Gregor, *Italian Fascism and Developmental Dictatorship* (Princeton, N.J.: Princeton University Press, 1979), pp. 110–111.
64. Roberts, pp. 93–94, 102.
65. *Ibid.*, pp. 103–104.
66. *Ibid.*, p. 123.
67. *Ibid.*, pp. 107–111; Lyttelton, ed., pp. 200–201.
68. Lyttelton, ed., pp. 202–203.
69. *Ibid.*, p. 199.
70. *Ibid.*, p. 198.
71. Roberts, pp. 156–166.
72. *Ibid.*, pp. 170–175.
73. *Ibid.*
74. *Ibid.*, pp. 201–202.
75. *Ibid.*, p. 240; Lyttelton, ed., p. 229.
76. Lyttelton, ed., pp. 227–231.
77. Nolte, pp. 153–159.
78. S. W. Halperin, *Mussolini and Italian Fascism* (New York: Van Nostrand, Reinhold, 1964), pp. 91–93.
79. Carsten, *Fascism*, p. 80.

5. HEURISTIC ASSUMPTIONS

1. C. Geertz, *The Interpretation of Cultures* (New York: Basic Books, 1973), p. 145.
2. *Ibid.*, pp. 250, 144, 361.
3. See R. Bernstein, *The Restructuring of Social and Political Theory* (Oxford: Blackwell, 1976), pp. 57–114; A. Giddens, *New Rules of Sociological Method* (New York: Basic Books, 1976), pp. 7–92, and *Studies in Social and Political Theory* (New York: Basic Books, 1977), pp. 135–182; F. A. Olafson, *The Dialectic of Action* (Chicago: University of Chicago Press, 1979), pp. 1–37; M. Sahlins, *Culture and Practical Reason* (Chicago: University of Chicago Press, 1976); M. Roche, *Phenomenology, Language, and the Social Sciences* (London: Routledge & Kegan Paul, 1973); P. Ricoeur, *Freud and Philosophy* (New Haven: Yale University Press, 1970), pp. 3–6; Z. Bauman, *Hermeneutics and Social Science* (London: Hutchinson, 1978).
4. P. Winch, *The Idea of a Social Science* (London: Routledge & Kegan

Paul, 1958), p. 24. For a survey of the development of an analytic philosophy of action in the mode of the later Wittgenstein, see G. H. von Wright, *Explanation and Understanding* (Ithaca, N.Y.: Cornell University Press, 1971), pp. 22–33. See also Alan Ryan, *The Philosophy of the Social Sciences* (London: Macmillan, 1970), pp. 125–171; Olafson, *Dialectic*, pp. 133–188; William Outhwaite, *Understanding Social Life: The Method Called Verstehen* (London: Allen & Unwin, 1975), pp. 82–102.

5. Winch, *Social Science*, pp. 45, 121–123, 23, 128, 125.

6. C. Taylor, "Interpretation and the Sciences of Man," *Review of Metaphysics* (1971), pp. 24–25. See also J. G. A. Pocock, *Politics, Language, and Time* (New York: Atheneum, 1971), pp. 10–13, 36–41, 104–107. For a discussion of the analytical and methodological issues that arise in writing the history of utopias, see M. Goldie, "Obligations, Utopias, and Their Historical Context," *The Historical Journal* (1983), pp. 727–746.

7. Taylor, "Interpretation," pp. 24–26.

8. P. Ricoeur, *History and Truth* (Evanston, Ill.: Northwestern University Press, 1965), p. 202.

9. Taylor, "Interpretation," p. 24.

10. Outhwaite, *Understanding*, p. 107; Giddens, *Rules*, p. 53.

11. J. Habermas, *Zur Logik der Sozialwissenschaften* (Frankfurt: Suhrkamp Verlag, 1970), p. 289. The translation is from Outhwaite, *Understanding*, p. 99. For another translation see Dallmayr and McCarthy, *Understanding and Social Inquiry*, p. 361.

12. D. Hume, *An Enquiry Concerning Human Understanding*, section 4, part 1.

13. M. Mandelbaum, *The Anatomy of Historical Knowledge* (Baltimore, Md.: Johns Hopkins University Press, 1977), pp. 49–50. See also A. Ryan, *Social Sciences*, p. 111; Atkinson, *Knowledge*, p. 144.

14. Hume, *Enquiry*, section 4, part 1.

15. C. Taylor, "Explaining Action," *Inquiry* (1970), 13:81.

16. Von Wright, *Explanation*, pp. 67–74, 83–96, 135–145. "Conceptual clarity is seldom promoted by linguistic reform and it seems to me pointless and vain to protest, to warn against the causal terminology commonly employed in history and social science" (*ibid.*, pp. 200–201). See also Olafson, *Dialectic*, pp. 175–188; W. Dray, review of Olafson, *History and Theory* (1982), 20:84; J. Searle, *Intentionality*, pp. 107–108; Q. Skinner, "Meaning and Understanding in the History of Ideas," *History and Theory* (1969), pp. 42–45.

17. Von Wright, *Explanation*, pp. 97, 147. Olafson, *Dialectic*, pp. 12–15.

18. W. Dilthey, *Gesammelte Schriften* (Stuttgart: B. G. Teubner, 1958), 7:197, 153; H. P. Rickman, ed., *W. Dilthey: Selected Writings* (Cambridge: Cambridge University Press, 1976), pp. 196–199; M. Ermarth, *Wilhelm Dilthey: The Critique of Historical Reason* (Chicago: University of Chicago Press, 1979), pp. 308, 266.

19. Giddens, *Rules*, p. 43.

20. On the difference between Dilthey's view of historicity and that of "pure historicism," see M. Ermarth, *Wilhelm Dilthey*, pp. 354–357.

21. Dilthey, *Gesammelte Schriften*, 7:192, 232.

22. K. Rahner, "Man as an Historical Spirit," in G. A. McCool, ed., *A Rahner Reader* (New York: Seabury Press, 1975), pp. 54–55.

23. Ermarth, *Dilthey*, pp. 356–357, 259–261, 265–267, 251. For a suggestive use of Heidegger's conception of historicity, see Olafson, *Dialectic*, ch. 3.

24. Sahlins, *Culture*, p. 57.

25. See von Wright, *Explanation*, pp. 25–33.

26. Taylor, "Interpretation," pp. 10–17.

27. Von Wright, *Explanation*, p. 132.

28. P. Ricoeur, in *The Philosophy of Paul Ricoeur*, pp. 149–150.

29. Ermarth, *Dilthey*, pp. 245–267, 303–310; Outhwaite, *Understanding*, pp. 24–37.

30. Von Wright, *Explanation*, p. 147.

31. See L. Mink, "Philosophical Analysis and Historical Understanding," *Review of Metaphysics* (1967–68), 21:692–693; C. Taylor, "Interpretation," and "Explaining."

32. Giddens, *Rules*, p. 58.

33. Habermas, *Logik*, p. 178, quoted in Giddens, *Studies*, p. 153. See also A. MacIntyre, "The Idea of a Social Science," in A. Ryan, ed., *The Philosophy of Social Explanation* (London: Oxford University Press, 1973), pp. 22–24, who argues that it is necessary to take account of "causal regularities exhibited in the correlation of statuses and forms of behavior" and of cases in which "the relation of social structure to individuals may be correctly characterized in terms of control or constraint."

34. Von Wright, *Explanation*, p. 144.

35. L. Mink, "Historical Understanding," p. 693.

36. Taylor, "Interpretation," pp. 49–50.

37. M. Weber, *The Methodology of the Social Sciences*, (Glencoe, Ill.: Free Press, 1949) pp. 72–78.

38. M. Weber, *The Protestant Ethic and the Spirit of Capitalism*, pp. 47–48. (New York: Scribner, 1930).

39. Weber, *Methodology*, pp. 90, 96.

40. Weber, *Protestant Ethic*, pp. 47–48.

41. H. G. Gadamer, "Kausalität in der Geschichte?" in *Kleine Schriften* I (Tübingen: J. C. B. Mohr, 1967): "Es ist ein anderer Sinn von 'Ursache,' nicht der der Kausalität, was den Zusammenhang der Geschichte determiniert." Quoted in von Wright, *Explanation*, p. 201.

42. Weber, *Methodology*, pp. 92–102. At the same time, however, Weber also argued that the historian who assigns a causal role to "individual configurations" must bring to bear a body of nomological knowledge in his explanation. He emphasized that "the knowledge of *universal* propositions, the con-

struction of abstract concepts, the knowledge of regularities, and the attempt to formulate *'laws'* " are of considerable importance in the cultural sciences. Their function, however, is not as the end of the inquiry but to provide a necessary basis for the establishment of causal links between individual phenomena: "If the causal knowledge of the historian consists of the imputation of concrete effects to concrete causes," such an imputation would be impossible "without the application of *'nomological'* knowledge, i.e., the knowledge of recurrent causal sequences." While historical causes are unique, their causal efficacy has to be assessed by reference to nomological knowledge that tells us what, in all probability would have occurred if that unique causal factor had not been present.

Thus, nomological knowledge entered into Weber's account of the causal influence of Protestantism—and of other such "individual configurations"— by vindicating the counterfactual argument underlying the imputation of causal efficacy to a particular factor. In order to argue that in the absence of Protestantism the capitalist spirit would have developed in a significantly different way, the historian has to show, partly on the basis of general knowledge, that the other factors at work in early modern Europe would have produced a different result. *Ibid.*, pp. 174–188.

43. *Ibid.*, pp. 95–96.

44. *Protestant Ethic*, pp. 90, 277–278, 113.

45. For an excellent analysis of the theoretical and historical aspects of Weber's study of the Protestant ethic, see G. Marshall, *In Search of the Spirit of Capitalism: An Essay on Max Weber's Protestant Ethic Thesis* (New York: Columbia University Press, 1982).

46. P. Ricoeur, *The Conflict of Interpretations: Essays in Hermeneutics* (Evanston, Ill.: Northwestern University Press, 1974), "Structure and Hermeneutics," pp. 44–50.

47. For two solid studies of Weber's historical sociology, see G. Roth and W. Schluchter, *Max Weber's Vision of History: Ethics and Methods* (Berkeley: University of California Press, 1979), and W. Schluchter, *The Rise of Western Rationalism: Max Weber's Developmental History* (Berkeley: University of California Press, 1981).

6. SOCIAL SCIENCE PARADIGMS

1. T. Skocpol, *States and Revolutions: A Comparative Analysis of France, Russia, and China* (Cambridge: Cambridge University Press, 1979), pp. 36–37.

2. *Revue Philosophique* (1897), 44:645–651.

3. S. Lukes, *Emile Durkheim: His Life and Work* (Harmondsworth: Penguin Books, 1973), p. 231. Durkheim added: "Cette proposition nous paraît l'évidence même. Seulement, nous ne voyons aucune raison pour la rattacher, comme le fait l'auteur, au movement socialiste, dont elle est totalement indé-

pendante. Quant à nous, nous y sommes arrivés avant d'avoir connu Marx, dont nous n'avons aucunement subi l'influence. . . . Depuis longtemps, les historiens se sont aperçus que l'évolution sociale a des causes que les auteurs des événements historiques ne connaissent pas." *Revue Philosophique*, pp. 648–649.

4. Lukes, *Durkheim*, p. 231.

5. *Ibid.*, p. 232, quoting *Revue Philosophique*, p. 649.

6. M. Sahlins, *Culture and Practical Reason*. (Chicago: University of Chicago Press, 1976), p. 117.

7. M. Douglas, *Implicit Meanings* (London: Routledge, 1975), pp. 117–121.

8. M. Douglas, *Times Literary Supplement*, August 8, 1975.

9. Sahlins, *Culture and Practical Reason*, p. 117.

10. T. Parsons, *Societies: Evolutionary and Comparative Perspectives* (Englewood Cliffs, N.J.: Prentice Hall, 1966), pp. 10, 113.

11. T. Parsons, *The Social System* (Glencoe, Ill.: Free Press, 1951), pp. 5–6, 46, 539.

12. N. Smelser, *Social Change in the Industrial Revolution* (Chicago: University of Chicago Press, 1959), p. 11.

13. R. Bernstein, *The Restructuring of Social and Political Theory*, (Oxford: Blackwell, 1976), pp. 1–54.

14. G. H. von Wright, *Explanation and Understanding* (Ithaca, N.Y.: Cornell University Press, 1971), p. 10.

15. C. Hempel, "The Function of General Laws in History," *Journal of Philosophy* (1942), reprinted in P. Gardiner, ed., *Theories of History* (New York: Free Press, 1959), pp. 344–347; for a more flexible version of this position, see E. Nagel, *The Structure of Science* (New York: Harcourt, Brace, and World, 1961), ch. 15. Similar assumptions are set forth in W. G. Runciman, *A Treatise on Social Theory*, vol. 1, *The Methodology of Social Theory* (Cambridge: Cambridge University Press, 1983), p. 149: "I shall accordingly assume without further argument that one of the objectives of social-scientific research is, among others, the formulation of theories which will help to explain different categories of events, processes or states of affairs."

16. R. Vann, "The Rhetoric of Social History," *Journal of Social History*, 10:223–224.

17. Olafson, *Dialectic*, pp. 3–4.

18. K. Popper, *The Poverty of Historicism* (New York: Harper Torchbook, 1964), p. 145.

19. W. G. Runciman, *A Critique of Max Weber's Philosophy of Social Science* (Cambridge: Cambridge University Press, 1972), pp. 61–78. For a fuller statement of Runciman's position, see *A Treatise on Social Theory*, vol. 1, especially ch. 3, "Explanation in Social Theory."

20. P. Winch, *The Idea of a Social Science* (London: Routledge & Kegan Paul, 1958), pp. 133, 92; M. White, *The Philosophy of the American Revolution* (New York: Oxford University Press, 1978). White argues that "the philoso-

phy of the rebellious colonists was one causal factor in a conjunction that led to the Revolution and that we shall not be able to explain the Revolution unless we understand that philosophy in more than a superficial way" (p. 6). But the assumption that the Enlightenment was one of a number of substantially equivalent causes, each equally necessary, forecloses consideration of the more complicated problem of the relationship between ideas and the American Revolution, which Bernard Bailyn has grappled with. Moreover, White's tart dismissal of Bailyn's suggestion that "the American Revolution was above all else an ideological, constitutional, political struggle and not primarily a controversy between social groups undertaken to force changes in the organization of the society or the economy" indicates the presence of disparate paradigms, embodying divergent methodological and substantive assumptions. For a systematic exposition of White's theory of explanation and causation, see his *Foundations of Historical Knowledge* (New York: Harper & Row, 1965). White develops a version of "what is sometimes called the covering law, or regularity, theory of historical explanation" (p. 15).

21. C. Johnson, *Revolutionary Change* (Boston: Little Brown, 1966), pp. 90–91.

22. N. Smelser, *Theory of Collective Behavior* (New York: Free Press, 1962), pp. 316–317.

23. Winch, *Social Science*, p. 105.

24. Lukes, *Durkheim*, p. 231.

25. W. H. Walsh, "The Causation of Ideas," *History and Theory* (1975), pp. 191–196.

26. *Ibid.*, p. 193. For a good statement of the contrary position, see Runciman, *Social Theory*, 1:145–164, 183–186.

27. Runciman, *Weber*, pp. 86–90, 97.

28. Taylor, "Interpretation," p. 21.

29. *Ibid.*, p. 22.

30. S. Wolin, "The Politics of the Study of Revolution," *Comparative Politics* (April 1973), pp. 343–358.

31. Parsons, *Social System*, p. 520.

32. Wolin, p. 348.

33. Smelser, *Theory*, pp. 12–13, 21.

34. *Ibid.*, pp. 313–317.

35. Popper, *Poverty*, pp. 10, 146–147.

36. *Ibid.*, pp. 147, 144. Popper's position may be contrasted to that of Louis Mink, who points out that history "grasps events as stages of development rather than as states of a system, and aims at discovering the features of the process of development rather than the 'causal relations' of discrete events." Rejecting theories of historical knowledge that presuppose behavior that is "unvariant over time" and an ontology of time based on "the principle that the past and the future are not categorically different from each other," Mink notes that "of course the point of history is that it is the study of change, not

of invariance." Any account of historical knowledge must recognize the centrality of "the concepts of novelty, development and growth." "Philosophical Analysis and Historical Understanding," *Review of Metaphysics* (1967–68), 21:681–682, 193. From the perspective of a critique of psychohistory, D. E. Stannard, *Shrinking History* (New York: Oxford University Press, 1980), presents another good statement of the characteristics of the historical approach; see his discussion of objections to the assumption of psychic uniformity or immutability, pp. 119–144. For an account of antihistorical tendencies in twentieth-century thought as a whole, see H. V. White, "The Burden of History," *History and Theory* (1966), pp. 111–134.

37. Runciman, *Weber*, pp. 71, 93.

38. *Ibid.*, pp. 71–72.

39. Lukes, *Durkheim*, p. 235.

40. J. Culler, *Saussure* (London: Fontana/Collins, 1976), pp. 33–45.

41. C. Lévi-Strauss, *The Scope of Anthropology* (London: Jonathan Cape, 1967), p. 11. For a subtle critique of structural analysis see P. Ricoeur, *The Conflict of Interpretations* (Evanston, Ill.: Northwestern University Press, 1974), "Structure and Hermeneutics," pp. 27–61, and "Structure, Word, Event," pp. 79–96. Ricoeur points out that history involves a good deal more than the "diachrony" of structuralist theory. History embraces "not simply the change from one state of system to another but the production of culture and of man in the production of his language. What Humboldt called production and what he opposed to the finished work is not solely diachrony, that is, the change and passage from one state of system to another, but rather the generation, in its profound dynamism, of the work of speech in each and every case" (p. 84). Moreover, Ricoeur is careful not to attribute to structuralism "a pure and simple opposition between diachrony and synchrony." What he takes exception to is the subordination of diachrony to synchrony (pp. 32–33).

42. C. Lévi-Strauss, "History and Dialectic," in R. and F. de George, eds., *The Structuralists* (New York: Anchor Books, 1972), p. 211; the passage is from ch. 9 of *The Savage Mind; Structural Anthropology* (New York: Anchor Books, 1967), p. 22.

43. Lévi-Strauss, *Structural Anthropology*, p. 279.

44. *Ibid.*, p. 23.

45. *Ibid.*, pp. 21–22.

46. *Ibid.*, p. 23.

47. Lévi-Strauss, in de Georges, ed., pp. 225–228.

48. *Ibid.*, p. 229.

49. Geertz, *Interpretation*, pp. 362, 5, 43, 362–363.

50. K. Thomas, "The Ferment of Fashion," *Times Literary Supplement*, April 30, 1982. Clifford Geertz has been described as "virtually the patron saint" of the conference that yielded the essays collected in Higham and Conkin, eds., *New Directions in American Intellectual History* (Baltimore, Md.: Johns Hopkins University Press, 1979). John Higham has noted the increasing affinity

that intellectual historians have recently felt for anthropology, "the social science that shares most fully their own engagement with community and with culture—a science, moreover, that has in recent years notably enriched our grasp of the meanings expressed in symbol, ritual, and language" (*ibid.*, p. xvii).

7. MARXIST THEORIES

1. See W. L. Adamson, "Marx's Four Histories: An Approach to His Intellectual Development," *History and Theory*, vol. 20, no. 4, Beiheft 20 (1981), Studies in Marxist Historical Theory.

2. See P. Singer, "On Your Marx," *New York Review of Books*, December 20, 1979. W. Adamson, *History and Theory* (1980), 19:186–204, distinguishes between a "fundamentalist" or "technological" interpretation of Marx's theory of history and a "dialectical" interpretation.

3. K. Marx and F. Engels, *The German Ideology* (New York: International Publishers, 1947), pp. 1, 28.

4. K. Marx and F. Engels, *Selected Works* (London: Lawrence and Wishart, 1950), 1:328–329.

5. E. J. Hobsbawm, "Karl Marx's Contribution to Historiography," in R. Blackburn, ed., *Ideology in Social Science* (London: Fontana, 1972), p. 273.

6. Marx and Engels, *Selected Works*, 1:329.

7. R. C. Tucker, ed., *The Marx-Engels Reader*, 2d ed. (New York: Norton, 1978), p. 143.

8. T. B. Bottomore, ed., *Karl Marx: Early Writings* (New York: McGraw Hill, 1964), p. 127.

9. Tucker, *Marx-Engels Reader*, p. 144.

10. M. Rader, *Marx's Interpretation of History* (New York: Oxford University Press, 1979), pp. 59–60.

11. *Ibid.*, pp. 59–60, 75, 232.

12. A. Giddens, "Marx, Weber, and the Development of Capitalism," *Studies in Social and Political Theory* (New York: Basic Books, 1977), p. 201. The quoted phrase is from Georg Lukacs, *Histoire et conscience de classe* (Paris: 1920), p. 20.

13. Giddens, *Capitalism*, pp. 41–43, 209.

14. *Ibid.*, pp. 209–212.

15. Marx and Engels, *Selected Works*, 1:226.

16. G. Lichtheim, *From Marx to Hegel* (New York: Seabury Press, 1971), p. 204.

17. A. Schmidt, *The Concept of Nature in Marx* (London: New Left Books, 1971), p. 121: "Marx adopted an intermediate position between Kant and Hegel, which can only be fixed with difficulty. His materialist critique of Hegel's identity of Subject and Object led him back to Kant, although again this did not mean that being, in its non-identity with thought, appeared as an un-

knowable 'thing-in-itself.' " See also J. Habermas, *Knowledge and Human Interests* (Boston: Beacon Press, 1971), pp. 35, 324.

18. See K. Popper, *The Open Society and Its Enemies* (London: Routledge and Kegan Paul, 1952), 2:107–109, 118–119, and notes.

19. K. Marx and F. Engels, *Selected Correspondence* (Moscow: Foreign Languages Publishing House, n.d.), p. 500. See also L. Krieger's introduction to his edition of F. Engels, *The German Revolutions* (Chicago: University of Chicago Press, 1967).

20. Marx and Engels, *Correspondence*, pp. 498, 505.

21. E. P. Thompson, *The Poverty of Theory* (London: Merlin Press, 1978), p. 201. See also P. Anderson, *Considerations on Western Marxism* (London: New Left Books, 1976).

22. R. Williams, "Base and Superstructure in Marxist Cultural Theory," *New Left Review* (1973), pp. 3–10; see also his *Marxism and Literature* (Oxford: Oxford University Press, 1977).

23. G. Lukacs, *History and Class Consciousness* (Cambridge: MIT Press, 1971), p. 27.

24. G. Lukacs, *The Ontology of Social Being*, vol. 2: *Marx* (London: Merlin Press, 1978), pp. 31–32, 66–68. "This text forms the fourth chapter of Part One of Lukacs' work *Toward the Ontology of Social Being*." Translator's note.

25. K. Korsch, *Marxism and Philosophy* (London: New Left Books, 1970), pp. 70–72, 83.

26. M. Jay, *The Dialectical Imagination*, (Boston: Little Brown, 1973), pp. 53–55.

27. Thompson, *Theory*, p. 363. For a close analysis of Thompson's theory, see P. Anderson, *Arguments within English Marxism* (London: Verso, 1980), pp. 5–99. See also G. McLennan, *Marxism and the Methodologies of History* (London: Verso, 1981); R. Johnson, "Edward Thompson, Eugene Genovese, and Socialist-Humanist History," *History Workshop* (Autumn 1978); K. Nield, "A Symptomatic Dispute? Notes on the Relation between Marxian Theory and Historical Practice in Britain," *Social Research* (1980), pp. 479–506.

28. E. P. Thompson, *Whigs and Hunters* (New York: Pantheon Books, 1975), p. 265; E. J. Hobsbawm, *Labouring Men* (Garden City, N.Y.: Anchor Books, 1967), p. 444.

29. J. Jaurès, *Histoire socialiste de la Révolution française*, A. Mathiez, ed., (Paris: Libraire de l'Humanité, 1927), 1:49.

30. E. J. Hobsbawm, *The Age of Revolution, 1789–1848* (New York: New American Library, 1964), pp. 17–20.

31. V. I. Lenin, *Selected Works*, vol. 1, part 1 (Moscow, Foreign Languages Publishing House, 1950).

32. *Ibid.*, pp. 229, 243–244.

33. M. Seliger, *The Marxist Conception of Ideology: A Critical Essay* (Cambridge: Cambridge University Press, 1977), p. 91.

34. Lenin's fullest account of the "privileged upper stratum of the prole-

tariat" is in "Imperialism and the Split in Socialism," of October 1916, *Collected Works*, vol. 23 (New York: International Publishers, 1927), pp. 105–120; the most familiar passages occur in *Imperialism the Highest Stage of Capitalism* (New York: International Publishers, 1939), ch. 8, and the preface to the French and German editions of 1920, pp. 9–14. See also E. J. Hobsbawm, *Revolutionaries: Contemporary Essays* (New York: Pantheon Books, 1973), ch. 12, "Lenin and the Aristocracy of Labour."

35. E. J. Hobsbawm, *Labouring Men*, ch. 15, "The Labour Aristocracy in Nineteenth-Century Britain."

36. R. Q. Gray, *The Labour Aristocracy in Victorian Edinburgh* (Oxford: Clarendon Press, 1976), pp. 1, 114.

37. G. Crossick, *An Artisan Elite in Victorian Society* (London: Croom Helm, 1978), pp. 18, 241.

38. P. Joyce, *Work, Society, and Politics: The Culture of the Factory in Later Victorian England* (New Brunswick, N.J.: Rutgers University Press, 1980), pp. xv, 50, 80.

39. *Ibid.*, pp. 62, 81.

40. E. P. Thompson, *The Making of the English Working Class* (New York: Vintage Books, 1966), pp. 12, 830, 712, 9–10.

41. G. Stedman Jones, "The Language of Chartism," in J. Epstein and D. Thompson, eds., *The Chartist Experience: Studies in Working-Class Radicalism and Culture, 1830–1860* (Atlantic Highlands, N.J.: Humanities Press, 1982), p. 6.

42. *Ibid.*, pp. 6–7, 11–12. For another supple and sophisticated version of the Marxist theory of history, see E. D. Genovese, *In Red and Black: Marxian Explorations in Southern and Afro-American History* (New York: Pantheon Books, 1971).

EPILOGUE

1. G. Lefebvre, *The Coming of the French Revolution* (Princeton, N.J.: Princeton University Press, 1947), p. 215.

Index